THE WITNESS WORE RED

THE WITNESS WORE RED

The 19th WIFE Who Brought POLYGAMOUS CULT LEADERS to Justice

REBECCA MUSSER WITH M. BRIDGET COOK

GRAND CENTRAL
PUBLISHING

NEW YORK   BOSTON

Copyright © 2013 by Rebecca Musser

Unless otherwise noted, all photos courtesy of Rebecca Musser.

Grand Central Publishing
Hachette Book Group
237 Park Avenue
New York, NY 10017

www.HachetteBookGroup.com

Printed in the United States of America

RRD-C

First Edition: September 2013
10 9 8 7 6 5 4 3 2 1

Grand Central Publishing is a division of Hachette Book Group, Inc.
The Grand Central Publishing name and logo is a trademark of Hachette Book Group, Inc.

The Hachette Speakers Bureau provides a wide range of authors for speaking events. To find out more, go to www.hachettespeakersbureau.com or call (866) 376-6591.

The publisher is not responsible for websites (or their content) that are not owned by the publisher.

Library of Congress Control Number: 2013939296

ISBN 978-1-4555-2785-4

This book is dedicated to Kyle and Natalia... may you forever know how you have inspired me and taught me the greatest lessons of my life. Every day I love you more and rejoice in your ability to make your own choices. I also dedicate this book to Ben Musser, whom I've watched become a most incredible and loving father. And to my family, inside and outside the FLDS, who remain forever in my heart.
—Rebecca

To BreeAnna, McKenzie, Brent, Baily, and Jessica; each of you are a gift in your unique and very special ways. I kiss your eyes, and I hold you in my heart. Doug, your love makes my soul sing and my heart flutter and gives me wings to fly. And to my mother, I cherish your wisdom and example, and most especially your friendship.
—Bridget

Contents

THE WITNESS WORE RED

CHAPTER I

Feathers on the Wind

It was an unusually temperate day for early spring, and the delicious scent of new beginnings wafted through the open window, filling my body with pure joy. Instead of peering longingly out at the grass and budding crocuses, we were actually going to be allowed outside past our backyard.

While I waited impatiently for my seven siblings to gather to leave, I looked around the shadowy walkout basement we called home. The teak parquet flooring and matching wood paneling made it seem even smaller than it was. My mother had her own room, but the rest of us were stacked in bunk beds in every corner like sardines and forced to play musical beds every time another baby joined our family. My mother's swollen belly made it clear that we'd be moving beds again in just a few months. Drawers were built into the undersides of the bunk beds, and we each had one to fill with underwear, socks, and hand-me-down clothing.

Someone passing by our simple two-level redbrick home would likely never guess how many children lived in the basement alone. He would likely be shocked to learn that another large family lived upstairs; the only common denominator between the two families was one man who spent half his nights upstairs with his first wife and children, the other half downstairs with our mother—wife number two—and her children. This man was my father.

My bones always felt cold in this house, though the thermostat was set at a normal temperature. The eerie green fluorescent lights strained to brighten the darkest recesses of our rooms, tinting our skin and clothing with strange, shadowy hues. Light didn't seem able to fully penetrate the walls, as hope did not dwell long here.

Today, however, Mom promised time in the sun for all of us. Though she said we were headed for an "adventure," she kept the destination a secret. In my excitement, I danced in spinning circles around the room, nearly tripping over my worn, shin-length blue skirt. Mom asked me to quiet down before slipping outside with my siblings, and we furtively piled into Old Blue, our ancient station wagon.

As one of the younger children, I sat on the lap of my oldest sister, Christine. The seven of us watched the blocks roll past, as Mom drove us from our home on Cascade Way, in the Salt Lake City neighborhood of Mount Olympus, straight up into the green foothills of the awe-inspiring Wasatch Mountains.

Soon we all realized our adventure would take place on the grassy knolls behind my school, Eastwood Elementary. It was the same route we used when walking to school, but normally the trek would have been far too risky for all of us—and not because of the cars speeding by. We couldn't afford to draw too much attention to ourselves as a family. It wasn't just the honking, the stares, or the derogatory "Plygs!" bellowed out of windows. We were used to all of that. The danger lay in what the authorities would do if they discovered us. It was why I was a "Wilson" and not a "Wall" at my school, and why I could only rarely play with the sweet little girl across the street. If she learned the truth about me—about my brothers and sisters and our family living secretly in the walkout basement—we would risk being discovered.

The little girl was curious about us, though. Everyone was. It wasn't that it was unusual in this region to see large families. Salt Lake City was populated with a majority of prolific Mormons, and the small number of Catholic families often had many kids as well. Still, only a few thousand people in Salt Lake dressed even remotely like us. With the exception of July 24 every year, when the annual parade celebrated our state's Mormon pioneer history, we were highly conspicuous in our long-sleeved shirts, girls' long prairie dresses and skirts, and exceptionally long braids. Mom said we were *special*, but it wasn't until I went to kindergarten that I understood we represented a tiny fraction of the population around us. Mainstream Mormonism had given up polygamy in the late 1890s in order to secure statehood for Utah, so we were now the odd ones who hadn't fallen in line.

I hated how kids gawked at us, whispering loudly and pointing us out as if we were a tourist attraction. Sometimes the comments were innocent and simply curious. More often, though, they were intentionally demeaning, and it was frightening to wonder whom they would tell—and who might put my father in jail and split up our family. So we hid away from the prying eyes of the world.

That was also why our mother chose this place, on the edge of the mountain, where few would see us behind the empty school. We spilled out of the car and onto the grassy knoll, lush and vibrant from the melting snow. Our mother gathered us up on the top hill, where we could look down upon the Salt Lake Valley. Despite the warmth of the sun, I shivered as I looked in the direction of our home below, hidden amid the many houses of the Gentiles—the wicked people who did not believe in Joseph Smith or Jesus Christ. My mother's lap was full with her toddlers and her ever-expanding belly, but I squeezed in as close as I could. It was a rare treat to have her relaxing with us instead of cooking or cleaning or doing incessant laundry after a long day at work at HydraPak Seals, my father's manufacturing business. I scanned the city; to the north I picked out the capitol, towering on the hill above the downtown buildings that obscured the temple of the Church of Jesus Christ of Latter-day Saints—the Mormons who had *fallen away* from the Work. It was no longer our temple. A deep, unexplainable sadness filled me. We worshipped diligently at church, but our people did not have a temple of our own. Someday in the future, it was foretold, we would build one. But for now, we simply had to *endure* life. We had to suffer pain and sacrifice, because eternity was what mattered.

Dad so often said, "It's not *if*, but *when*, the Gentiles will hurt us. It will serve you to remember that always." I put my knees up protectively to my chin as I let my gaze drift across the valley. To my left, the southern part of the city was growing fast. Clumps of business developments and houses spanned nearly where the Salt Lake Valley met the Provo

Valley. Our Prophet, whom our people affectionately called Uncle Roy, had dreamed about the destructions. He said they would arrive when the construction of dwellings extended past that area known as the Point of the Mountain. It was a definite sign that the last days were imminent. I wondered how we would ever survive.

"Okay, children, we're going to play a game!" My mother's voice brought me back to the present. My fears melted away as I looked up at her beautiful face and warm smile. Her toffee-colored eyes gleamed with excitement as her lengthy brown hair, gathered up in a tidy French twist, fought the spring breeze. She was hiding something behind her back—a surprise brought from the car when we weren't paying attention. I held my breath in anticipation while my younger siblings fidgeted.

Mom brought out a very old feather pillow she had once sewn herself, and I noticed that she had unpicked the hem on one side. She scooted my siblings off of her lap and stood up. Suddenly she began throwing handfuls of feathers high into the wind. We were astonished—this was nothing like my mom, who was always fixing things, not tearing them apart.

"Help me scatter the feathers!" she cried, laughing. Stunned for a moment by her contagious giggles, we joined in enthusiastically, reaching into the bag and grasping handfuls of feathers to toss into the wind. Feathers began floating all around us like snow. The older kids— Christine, Savannah, Brittany, and Cole—and I threw them up into the air, watching them take flight as if they were wings themselves. Even my little brother Trevor joined in. Amelia toddled around in her long skirt, her giggles covering the hillside like the feathers now scattered across the grass, trees, and shrubs.

Suddenly, Mom became quiet. We stopped, too. The only sound around us was the wind whistling in the trees. We looked around in guilty pleasure at the mess we had made.

"Now," she cried, "run and gather them up!"

We looked at her in bewilderment. *Was she serious?* It was then we realized this must be part of the game.

"Gather them up now. Hurry! Hurry!"

Driven by her prompting, we ran fast, clutching as much down as we could, scraping our knuckles along the ground, trying to grasp the feathers before they blew away. Within a few minutes it was obvious our endeavor was fruitless. The sack of gathered feathers, mixed with old leaves and grass, was not even a third full. I looked around in awe. *How could the feathers have flown away so quickly?* Exhausted, I dropped at my mother's feet.

I never forgot what she said next.

"Words are like feathers...can you see that? It is so easy for them to come out, and they scatter on the wind before you know it. But like feathers, our words are not easy to gather back up again. Once out of your mouth, you simply *cannot* take them all back."

I looked at her. I knew what she was talking about. In my mind's eye I could see Aunt Irene, Dad's first wife, spouting words of anger and hatred at us, her mouth twisted in venomous disapproval. "Bastards! Little shits!" she would yell. She *hated* us, and we all knew it. All nine of her children knew it, too, and several of them used her hatred against us as well. Despite what our Prophet had told us about living together in harmony, existing together in the same house was nearly unbearable.

"Words make up glorious stories," Mom went on. "They make up our education, and even our prayers to our Heavenly Father. Using words the right way can build things—even great big things like bridges and buildings! But if we don't choose our words carefully, the effect of them can be a lifetime of pain and suffering."

I hung my head in shame. Here I was pointing fingers at Aunt Irene, when I had sassed her back plenty of times! I didn't like the names she called my mother, and how she treated all of us, especially when Dad wasn't present, but I showed my displeasure, unlike a good Priesthood girl. My words scattered like those feathers. How could I make it through the destructions if I used my words like Aunt Irene used hers? My mother never stooped that low. Even when Aunt Irene barraged her with bitter, caustic words, she would "keep sweet, no matter what," as we had been admonished by our Prophet. She refused to let her sister-wife's anger rob her of her own dignity.

That night as I lay in the small bed I shared with my sister Brittany, her feet near my pillow, I couldn't help but think of the feathers. I decided that like my mother, I would use my words carefully. Many times I had heard my dad boast about my mom proudly, "Sharon has never once defied me!" He was very gratified that she acquiesced to all of his demands and wishes like a good wife.

I thought about how my mother *did* use her words. She was kind and encouraging and prayed with us every night and morning, calling each of us by name before the Lord. My biggest delight, however, was when Mom would tell us stories. Since we did not have a television, stories were our primary form of entertainment. Our imaginations painted vivid pictures as she wove bright, elaborate tapestries of characters and lessons. Every story had a moral, one that entwined its way into my consciousness, coloring and shaping my perspective of the world and what I believed in.

Sometimes Mom's stories haunted me. If we skimped on a task or lied, she would tell a sobering story of life growing up on her father Newel Steed's remote farm and cattle ranch. It was vital during those hard times that all of his seven wives and nearly sixty children pitched in. Mom described piling sacks of potatoes into their rusty red wagon to pull for miles upon miles through and around Cedar City, just to sell them door-to-door for pennies apiece.

Each time her older brother Neil sold potatoes, he would pilfer a bit of money to buy forbidden sodas in town, and bully his younger siblings into silence.

"Little things you do now...grow into big things," Mom recounted sadly. "Later in life, he left the Priesthood," she went on, her eyes welling with tears. The first time I heard this I was shocked. *You couldn't know the truth and leave the Priesthood!* That was worse than being a Gentile. One who knew the truth and rejected it was an *apostate*. I shuddered every time I heard that word. Apostates were doomed to Outer Darkness in the eternities—a fate of never-ending agony! Samuel had died a horrific death. Some thought it was suicide, but Mom believed it had more to do with the local Mafia.

"He wouldn't give up all the money when he was little, and I don't think he would give it later, either. Remember the Golden Windows, my children. Remember..."

"The Golden Windows" was one of Mom's favorite stories, and it was about a poor, hardworking farm boy. He dreamed of a life in the distant city, its windows blazing with gold, which he could see from his hilltop home. Finally, after spending considerable time and energy to journey there, he wept to discover the golden windows were just a reflection of the sunset. Worse still, the tattered people of the town often dreamed of living a grand life on a faraway hilltop and pointed to the windows of his boyhood home, blazing with gold in the sunrise.

"He returned home," my mother would say, looking into each of our eyes, "realizing that what he had admired was a lie. He had become disillusioned, ugly, and broken from the pursuit of a lie. Don't let that happen to you. Nothing on the outside is as glorious as it looks. It may seem pretty, glittery stuff, but it is not real."

That story was used to squelch all of our questions, whenever one of us wished to engage in any worldly thing. Getting a haircut. Wearing lip gloss or nail polish. Anything that led us astray from the sacred duties of a polygamous family was morally wrong and shameful.

My father, Donald Wall, was just as adamant in upholding our religion, even though he had not grown up in the Work. He was proud of his conversion to the FLDS, one that was quite unusual, as our people didn't proselytize. Most were born into the faith, with parents who practiced polygamy. His did not. In fact, Dad had come from a broken home and a mother who had abandoned him physically and emotionally.

He first married Irene, who was not part of the Work, either. She and my dad had both grown up in the mainstream Mormon faith. Not long after their marriage, Irene's parents had become convinced of the truth of plural marriage. Horrified, she and my father set out to prove them wrong, but after diligent study, their hearts came to believe that the rest of the Mormons had discarded the truth. Both my dad and Irene converted to the "true gospel" under Uncle Roy, our Prophet.

Following their conversion, my father saw a beautiful and talented young woman singing at a church service. He believed she was meant for him. He came home and told Irene about her. Irene said she'd had a dream about my mother, and she gave her blessing for my father to take another wife. Dad spoke with Uncle Roy, and after a time she was "given" to him. Not long after Dad brought home his young and beautiful new wife, however, his first wife became unable to live the Principle without tremendous pain. Poisoned by jealousy, Irene made sure we all suffered right alongside her, especially when Dad was away.

By the time I was born, in 1976, I had three older full sisters and a full brother born less than nine months before me. My mother would ultimately give birth to fourteen of Dad's children. There were also plenty of half siblings—nine, in fact. Dad would eventually sire twenty-four children from three wives. Three was the "lucky" number among Priesthood men, as this was the number of wives Abraham had taken. It was believed that by having this number he and his family would achieve eternal salvation in the Celestial Kingdom, the highest kingdom of glory in Heaven. Otherwise, a man was doomed to a lower kingdom, and his wives to be servants or concubines in their husband's eternal household—another fate worse than death. The Terrestrial and Telestial Kingdoms were still a part of Heaven—the eternities—but it was only in the Celestial Kingdom that a man and his wives would attain the presence of God and become joint heirs of God with Jesus Christ, being able to rule and reign in their own worlds as gods and goddesses.

I couldn't understand why Mom would want to live in the eternities with Dad *and* Aunt Irene. What if the eternities mirrored life here? Irene had a television set and the most luxurious bedroom in the house, the nicer car, control over the family budget, and the seat next to my father in church. My mother had what was left over.

My father lived two vastly different lives. His public life was full of business success and renown. He was a brilliant civil engineer in the aerospace industry, as well as a noted geologist, having worked for such acclaimed companies as Thiokol Chemical Company, later known as Morton Thiokol, and on projects such as the Trans-Alaska Pipeline. Later he created other prominent businesses, of which HydraPak was by far the most successful. It manufactured O-rings, as well as mechanical and hydraulic seals and pistons, for NASA's space shuttle. His public and private lives did intersect—his ability to pay hundreds of thousands of dollars in tithing donations to the FLDS church made him popular with the Prophet. My father obeyed Uncle Roy without question—even at great financial cost—because he would be rewarded here *and* in the hereafter, and because he was being primed for FLDS leadership, which promised enormous power.

There were other times Dad's public life came up against his private one, like when he brought clients to our home to wine and dine them. Upstairs, Irene and her children would be decked out in their finest for a delectable meal. His worldly clients never knew that downstairs, his *other* family was huddled in the murky shadows, munching crackers.

Mom used those times in the dark to whisper to us her most dramatic childhood memories as we hung on to every word. On one of these nights, she recounted how Governor John Howard Pyle of Arizona instigated a raid in 1953 on our forebears in Short Creek (which later became the twin towns of Hildale, Utah, and Colorado City, Arizona).

"Since our family was well-known among the people for our musical talent," she murmured, "we all came into town to provide entertainment for the 24th of July celebration of 1953. We spent a few days in our Short Creek home, and had so much fun! My father let us relax before going back to the ranch—a rare luxury for us. We were happy we were going to share the Sabbath with our friends and family.

"I was only three years old... but I remember being woken up in the wee hours of that Sunday morning. My father had received a tip-off that authorities were closing in, and we quietly slipped out of town in our nightclothes, minutes before the authorities raided!" I imagined myself having to flee from police in my long nightgown. Every time a chair creaked upstairs, I jumped.

"That day, just before dawn on July 26, 1953, over one hundred Arizona state police officers and soldiers from the Arizona National Guard came into the tiny town. They took every man, woman, and child into custody. They literally ripped children away from weeping mothers and fathers." I gasped.

"We were so lucky Daddy had made us hightail it back to our ranch, more than two and a half hours away. At first, they didn't try to come after us, though we were watching for them. Heartbreaking stories poured in of young believers who were forced into foster homes in Phoenix—far from anything and anyone they had ever known. Then we got word that the raid was broadening to surrounding communities.

"Daddy and all of my mothers told us it was 1944 all over again, with raids to stop the Work from progressing and to scare the families into submission to the law. Nineteen forty-four was the year your grandpa was excommunicated from the Mormon Church for believing in the Principle and marrying Mama Olive, Mama Vilate, and Mama Kloe. That's when he became a target for the smaller raids, all the way up until 1953. But my father promised he wouldn't let us get taken by a lawman.

"My brothers were like sentinels. They watched main roads and fields like hawks. One early-warning signal was dust rising from the roads, which gave us plenty of time to hide! We had practiced drills, so we knew what to do. It was our duty to take cover in the rafters of our attic, to be quiet and still so that our father wouldn't get caught, and no one would know how many children he had." Suddenly my mother's voice became small, as if she was three again. I swore I could feel her body trembling.

"When our mothers sent us up there, we were compelled to be as still as death. I was terrified my little foot would break through the ceiling or, worse, that lawmen would arrest my father on bigamy, and take every one of us sixty children to Gentile foster homes far away."

"Mama?" inquired little Trevor, his whisper filled with fear. "Why did the 'thorities want to take you away?" He began to howl. "Why do they want to take us away?"

Mom shushed him quickly and held him in her arms for a long moment, until Amelia whined and pushed her way back into place. The lines in my mother's face etched a little deeper.

"The people upstairs are not the authorities; they are Gentiles," she whispered gently. "We can't take the chance that they wouldn't tell if they knew. Just as it was important for me to be so quiet in our attic, you must be as quiet as a mouse down here. Daddy is counting on us, just as my father counted on us back then. The Work has a lot of enemies, Trevor. As God's people we must face persecution. It's our test, to see if we can remain faithful." She looked around at each of us. "We have the truth, and the devil will inspire the Gentiles and the government to try to destroy us. But Heavenly Father won't let that happen if we stay the course. As long as we remain true to the Work, God has promised we will survive the destructions, and all the bad people out there will be destroyed."

We sat huddled in somber silence. Uncle Roy talked about the destructions in church nearly every Sunday. People would whisper about the things Gentiles would do to us if they caught us. That was why it was safest to play in the backyard, surrounded by the camouflage of trees. That was also why we had to put up with Aunt Irene, and the ugliness that pervaded our home. The destructions were upon us, and we had to hold together so we wouldn't be destroyed.

After Dad had quit working for Morton Thiokol under Uncle Roy's orders, his new business began to thrive. He often had to travel far from home, which made us daily victims of Irene's demonic rages. Some of her children refused to participate in the abuse, but others realized what they could get away with during Dad's absences.

Uncle Roy taught the women straight from the pulpit to put away their jealousies and criticisms. He admonished wives to "treat each other's children as if they were your own." Irene took that to a whole new level, and she would come down and snatch any one of us she wanted for a beating, especially when Mom was at work. The older children devised an ingenious way to prevent entrance, by wedging our small jogging trampoline against the door. Diligently we kept an ear out for that first telltale screech or slammed door. Christine would send scouts to grab those playing in the backyard. When they rushed in, we locked the door and hunkered down together. Our only safety was in numbers, but even then, we each experienced times when we were just not that lucky.

How I wanted to forget the stormy day I had been playing with my tattered dolls on the hard wooden floor. I was dressed in my favorite blue gingham dress. The skirt had ruffles on the bottom, and the yoke on the top had beautiful white eyelet lace with black ribbon woven through it. I pretended I was a beautiful mommy, and my dolls were my babies.

That day, Irene had gone food shopping, which meant there was a more easygoing feeling throughout the house. Two of her children, Victoria and Timothy, came downstairs to play, but the others were outside. Christine and Savannah were busy taking care of the youngest ones. My half brother Sterling sauntered down the carpeted steps and into the area where I sat with my dolls.

Sterling, a heavyset blond with greasy hair who had never paid me much attention, was one of Irene's favorite children. He could do no wrong in her eyes. More than once, however, I had seen Irene beat another son, Samuel, to a pulp, almost as if he were one of *us*. Similarly, she gushed over her daughter Janet but would beat Cindy nearly senseless if one of my full siblings wasn't within reach.

"Becky," Sterling said quietly, as if letting me in on a secret, "how would you like to play with Lillian's new doll?" My eyes lit up. Lillian was younger than me, but she had beautiful dolls that she played with in front of me on purpose. Sterling smiled and held his hand out to me. I reached for it, a bit puzzled, and he led me up the stairs. Fearfully, I peeked around the door at the top. Except as a baby, I had only ever been allowed to go upstairs during family Sunday School. I glanced out the window to see that Irene's car was still gone, and finally exhaled.

Sterling led me past the Formica kitchen table and chairs down the hall, and into what I suddenly realized must be his bedroom. Why did Sterling have Lillian's doll in *his* room? I turned in time to watch Sterling close and lock his door, his eyes glazed over. He grabbed my wrists roughly, binding them easily with one of his hands, leaving the other to travel beneath my dress and tug on my underpants. I squirmed and twisted for what felt like an eternity, but I could not escape his clutches. I couldn't understand why he was doing this to me. All I knew was that it *hurt*. Tears streamed down my cheeks, but he paid no attention. At one point he finally released my wrists to free up both of his hands, and I rushed past him and fled to the door, barely unlocking it before he could get to me. Racing down the hall, I ran straight into something solid.

I looked up into Irene's face.

My stepmother looked down at me in surprise, her dyed black hair perfectly coiffed as usual, with a French twist in the back. She took in the terrified expression on my face and then glanced up to see Sterling slowly closing the door to his room. When she peered back down at me, she glared with a hatred she usually reserved for my mother.

"You little *whore!*" she snarled. With one hand she picked me up by the neck of my dress and dragged me into her room. Seeing another door locked behind me, I began to panic, but I didn't dare move. She stood me up brutally against the bed and tugged my underwear again, but this time up into its rightful place. Then she grabbed my braids with vicious cruelty, to hold me while she slapped me over and over.

"It's your fault!" she shrieked. "It's all your fault that Sterling did this to you...*you* did this to Sterling. You *made* Sterling do this. You're such a little flirt! You're just a whore like your mother, you piece of shit!"

I don't know how many times the flat of her rigid palm lay into me, but I didn't dare look up. I noticed blood splatter against the white, lace-yoked collar of my dress, but even then she did not stop. Rage had overcome her. A torrent of blood poured from my nose and mouth onto the collar and down to the ruffle of my skirt, which was now no longer white. I felt numb and could not cry.

Then unexpectedly, as if a switch had been flipped, Irene collected herself and looked at me, as if for the first time. With dead calm she gripped me again by one of my long braids and dragged me into her bathroom. There she began to scrub my dress roughly with icy cold water. She scrubbed my swollen face and cleaned the blood from it, and finally scoured the collar and ruffle of my dress with a bar of soap until they were white again. Then she bent down to meet my eyes with that same calibrated look of hatred.

"This is all your fault, you whore, you hear me?" she threatened. "If you ever tell anyone, *I will kill your mother.*"

Drenched and trembling with buried sobs, I could barely breathe as Irene thrust me down to the stairwell. I opened the door and Christine's tender eyes and warm smile greeted me from across the room.

"There you are!" she said in surprise. "We've been looking for you!" She looked at me a little more carefully. "Are you all right?" I wanted to run to her, to be enfolded in her arms, to tell her everything that had just happened.

Rooted at the spot, I wondered how I could answer that question. I glanced over my shoulder, into the gloom of the stairwell, where the door was opened four or five inches. Irene's eyes stared back at me. I couldn't unburden myself. Not now. Not ever.

"I'm...okay," I lied, and walked toward Christine, letting her lead me away from Irene's sight line. I heard the door shut quietly behind me. I took off my dress and never wore it again, complaining it was too tight in the arms. In a way, it was. I never said a word, not wanting to put my mother at risk. But I did promise myself that I would never be that vulnerable again. I learned to run fast—faster than any of my classmates. I could outrun any of my brothers, and especially any of my half brothers. By the time I was in first grade, I made sure I was so fast that no one could ever catch me again.

CHAPTER 2

The Devil You Know

In her last trimester with the twins, Mom's belly seemed gigantic, and exhaustion was etched into her beautiful face. Aunt Lydia, the midwife in Hildale, told Mom to take it easy so that she wouldn't deliver prematurely. Mom felt it necessary to continue at HydraPak as long as she could—to please my father and support our growing family.

Everyone seemed eager for the twins to arrive, except Irene. Their birth would mean that Mom and Irene would have an equal number of children, so Irene could no longer hold that over my mother's head. In addition, Irene had stopped bearing children, while our mother, who was much younger, wasn't slowing down. I did not know how my father treated Irene behind closed doors, but he continued to stay with her on her allotted nights. Nevertheless, jealousy seemed to well within her like a deadly sickness.

Mom didn't work every day after Amelia was born, but on the days she left for HydraPak, the preventions we put into place just weren't enough. One day, Irene caught Cole alone. I found out much later she had almost beat him to death, rupturing one kidney and causing massive internal bleeding. He had gone to school the next day but began urinating blood. Mom and Dad rushed him to the emergency room, and that night, Irene invited the rest of my siblings upstairs for dinner.

We slowly emerged from the basement stairwell, anxious and disoriented by our stepmother's unfamiliar sweetness. Once we were seated, she told us that Cole had gotten very sick and had to be hospitalized from drinking too much water.

I pushed my glass away as if it were poison. Our people rarely went to doctors. We distrusted the medical industry—their meticulous, damning records and connections to the government. Once I had to get stitches in my forehead, and I was more afraid of the Gentile doctor than of the stitches themselves. I was relieved to have my father remove them ten days later. Not long after that, I had been playing on the porch on a hand-me-down bicycle. It had no seat and a rusted-out frame and was way too tall for me. When I went over a step and lost control, I gouged myself in my privates and felt the most painful burning sensation before passing out. Mom and Grandma Wall found me and carried me into the house. When I awoke, despite the severe bleeding, my mother doctored me up at home, using a baby medicine dropper to remove blood, and cutting some loose membrane with scissors. We knew that if our parents had taken Cole to see a doctor—especially to the *hospital*, it could only be for something exceptionally serious. As I glanced around the table I noticed not one of us touched our water.

Irene's behavior remained sickly sweet for several days, but it didn't last. Less than a month after Cole's hospitalization, rumors made their way to our father that Uncle Roy was attending church that Sunday. The Prophet had been in poor health, and we hadn't seen much of him lately. Dad decided it was important to make a showing—and that our mother should finally accompany him. Christine and Savannah were old enough to stay home to watch Trevor and Amelia, so the rest of us kids could go. Our family piled into the backseat of Dad's brown Buick, while Mom sat next to him in the passenger seat, radiant with appreciation for her husband. Irene was conspicuously absent, having thrown a loud tantrum all morning.

Just as he took his foot off the brake, Irene dashed out of the house brandishing a heavy iron frying pan. Her voice shattered the air as she shrieked, *"I will kill those little shits!"* The ugly snarl on her face suddenly contorted in surprise as Dad stared at her and, with great deliberation, put the car in reverse. He backed slowly out of the short driveway and whipped the car forward up Cascade Way, where we could still hear her threats. He did not slow until he got to the corner, where I noticed him hesitate, checking his rearview mirror. I glanced back to see Irene on the edge of the drive, still brandishing her weapon.

Would the victim be Trevor, who needed constant attention for illnesses, or tiny, towheaded Amelia, still a toddler? Neither of them was a match for a lunatic with a frying pan. Still, I was most afraid for tender, nurturing Savannah. Six years older than me, Savannah was almost ethereally beautiful, and she seemed to incite Irene's foulest abuse—more so than Samuel and Cole combined. Dad turned on the blinker, ready to round the corner. He hesitated again and glanced at my mother.

"I'm afraid she'll really do it this time, Sharon." He breathed in defeat, as he turned the car around. I felt a great sense of relief until I looked at my mom's crestfallen face. Once again, my father caved in to his first wife's manipulations.

As Mom got nearer to her term, my siblings and I prepared to visit Short Creek, where we would go whenever she was ready to deliver a new baby or when there was a special celebration taking place among our people. Short Creek, or the Creek (pronounced "Crick") as it was known by locals, was nestled among the stunning, crimson-faced cliffs and vistas of southern Utah. Short Creek's dusty, red-dirt streets in the twin cities of Hildale and Colorado City allowed us to walk freely among hundreds of our own kind without hiding. Our family was shown great deference by the locals. Even though Steed blood was relatively "fresh" among the people, Grandfather's very large family meant we were related to almost every single person in the town and outlying areas, if not by blood, then by marriage. Grandfather Steed was a well-respected polygamist who had survived the raids with both his family and his pride intact.

Most often we stayed at Grandpa Steed's Short Creek residence, a unique building that had been added onto a bit at a time as the family flourished and grew. While the rusty, dirt-stained stucco home wasn't even remotely dazzling by worldly standards, it was beautiful to me. I loved all of Grandfather Steed's wives, and most of them treated us with great affection. I hadn't always known that Mama Alice was my mother's mother—they all treated her as one of their own. There was always a loving lap to sit on and a delicious smell coming from the large kitchen.

The twins, Joshua Roy Wall and Jordan Roy Wall, were born on the Prophet's birthday, June 12, 1982. With the naming, Uncle Roy was being *doubly* honored on his birthday. Their birth was an occasion for a glorious celebration among the whole community. Aunt Lydia, the midwife, happened to be a wife of Hildale's bishop, Fred Jessop. While she had never gone to medical school or had babies of her own, Aunt Lydia had a special gift for delivering them. She had exceptional skills that local doctors and nurses respected—and we could keep the births hidden from the government.

Joshua and Jordan were beautiful baby boys, and I felt such sweet tenderness anytime I looked at them. When one of them cried, a fiercely protective, mothering instinct overcame me. Their lives deserved to be absolutely perfect, and we were all a little distraught at leaving the security of Hildale for our Salt Lake home.

"Mom," Christine said, courageously raising the question that was on all of our minds. "How are we going to protect the babies?"

My mother threw up her hands in frustration. "I *never* had to face anything like this when I was growing up!" she said. "There was always peace in our home." Christine and I looked at each other, our eyes wide. This was the first time we'd ever heard Mom speak openly about our situation.

I thought about my grandmothers. Eliza and Vilate had already passed, but I dearly loved Mama Olive, Mama Kloe, Mama Alice, Mama Cynthia, and Mama Ida, all of whom were here to support their daughter. Mom's siblings were her dearest friends, especially her sister Martha Steed Allred, who lived in Salt Lake. Aunt Martha and her sister-wife treated each other kindly, and their relationship showed me a genuine closeness and respect that was missing within my father's family. Uncle Jim Allred was a patient man with a great sense of humor. Through them I glimpsed that plurality might be not only endured but even enjoyed.

Our last night at Grandfather's, I went to bed exhausted from playing. Dad had come to take us all home. I usually slept soundly, but that night I tossed and turned. When I heard quiet voices in the kitchen, I snuck upstairs to cajole a snack from an indulgent grandmother.

Suddenly I stopped still, recognizing Grandfather Steed's voice. I loved him, but he was no-nonsense. He would send me straight back to bed. I had almost turned to go back downstairs when I heard my mother's trembling voice. Curiosity piqued, I snuck around the other way to the kitchen and slipped silently under the table.

"Daddy, you don't understand how hard it is!" my mother cried. "If I leave the house for any reason, to go to work or go out with my husband, I have no idea if my children will even be *alive* when I get home. How can I take these two new precious souls back to that?"

"She's telling the truth!" I wanted to shout. A wellspring of hope rose inside of me. Grandfather Steed could surely help us! He was powerful in the family and in our community—as revered as any FLDS leader besides the Prophet. He could do *anything*, couldn't he?

When Grandfather's voice thundered, I almost jumped and hit my head in fright.

"You *stop* that crying right now, Sharon!" he bellowed. *"Go home, and obey your husband!"*

After we arrived back in Salt Lake with two little ones in tow, our chore list grew ever longer. My favorite tasks involved anything having to do with the twins, though I wasn't yet allowed to pick them up or carry them. How I longed to be as big as Christine and Savannah!

That fall I received the most glorious news. My beloved Mrs. Garrett, my kindergarten teacher at Eastwood Elementary, would be teaching my first-grade class! She didn't mind my incessant questions or voracious appetite for knowledge. She put my bubbly energy to good use by letting me explore, experiment, and read. Her gentle nurturing made facing the bullies who pulled my braids and made fun of our long clothing bearable.

That year our class studied dinosaurs and the ecosystems of early earth life. I was fascinated, but that wonder was about to be superseded by a visit from an astronaut, now a Utah politician, who told us about his flight into space. He showed us his space suit and let us taste the dehydrated ice cream the astronauts ate.

Mrs. Garrett took advantage of our enthusiasm over our guest to teach us the solar system. Each day I would soak in as much as my six-year-old brain could handle, then run home as fast as I could.

Completing my chores and homework in record time, I'd anxiously await the arrival of my father. He had to divide his time among a lot of children, but given his background in the space industry, I loved being able to discuss what I was learning with him.

When the school year ended, I said good-bye to Mrs. Garrett. The promise of summer thrilled me, though no one in our family sat idle—especially the girls. At nearly twelve, Christine was in charge of all eight of us younger siblings, and there was never-ending laundry, cleaning, and enormous meals to prepare.

That summer began a series of extraordinary events that would forever alter our lives. Mom stayed home full-time and even became pregnant again after the twins turned one. The promise of another baby meant a longer refuge from Irene. It was glorious to feel Mom's warmth, cheerfully singing as she went about her duties.

Music had always been a part of the Steed legacy. Grandfather's family was still often requested to provide musical entertainment in the community on every possible occasion. The early Mormons had been great purveyors, contributors, and patrons of the arts. Among our own people, we had carried on that tradition with operettas, plays, parades, and musicals. With Mom at home full-time, music made a grand entrance into our lives. There I discovered a place of exquisite peace and rest; it awakened my creativity and was a safe haven from a harsh world.

Christine began playing the viola and later switched to the violin. When I heard the stringed music, I was in Heaven! I hung on every note and hovered around her as she played. I could tell when she was on note or not—something had awakened within me, probably due to my mother's sweet singing voice. I had a natural ear for pitch, tone, and tempo. When Christine practiced, I played on wooden spoons beside her.

The next summer, I turned eight and was presented with a miniature violin for my birthday. It was the loveliest thing I had ever seen, and I cradled it, watched over it, and protected it like my baby brothers. It was unusual for one among my siblings to receive such an expensive possession, especially with Mom no longer working. The birth of baby Zach marked my mom's tenth child and my father's nineteenth. I did not take it for granted.

The day of my birthday celebration, which I shared with my brother Trevor, we were each presented with a beautiful homemade cake of our own. I was wearing a pretty, hand-me-down, gunnysack-style dress, and when Trevor and I posed for our picture, my sleeve caught fire on the birthday candles. Someone snuffed it out quickly, but the plastic from the material melted into my skin. I showed up to my first violin lesson dressed in bandages with huge, painful blisters down my arm, but I didn't care. No one could pry the violin away from me, and I played it night and day, even sneaking it into the bed I shared with Brittany— until she put a stop to it.

I became proficient quickly, with the help of Mrs. Guertler, a Mormon woman who taught violin to students of different backgrounds. Even though she didn't practice plurality, Dad allowed us to go to her lessons. He began to call me a virtuoso and loved to show me off whenever a guest from the FLDS came over.

"Play something, Sis!" he would say, grinning broadly. I would pick a hard piece I had practiced well, and it usually stunned the listener to hear intricate music from such a tiny person. I loved to shine for Dad, and I drank in the praise he gave me. Sometimes my siblings called me a show-off.

Months later Mom got a sleek new Yamaha piano, and she would occasionally sneak a few precious moments to play with me. My love affair expanded to the piano, and I practiced that for hours, too. Irene would inevitably scream down the stairs, "Can you make Becky *stop?*" I'm sure my siblings felt the same way. But the magic of the music seemed to fill my life with light. It also opened unexpected doors.

Anxiously awaiting my turn at Mrs. Guertler's rock house on Millcreek Way, I consumed her *Reader's Digest* and other magazines. Reading *Guideposts* (a Christian publication) and the *Ensign* (published by the LDS church) shocked me. Each issue showcased at least one story where a life was spared and hope provided. How could God's hand extend to Gentile Christians who knew not the truth, and apostate Mormons who had turned away from it?

I pondered these questions and many others, though I learned very early never to ask them aloud. My parents had made a momentous decision as to our FLDS education, one whose ramifications would affect our entire household. The previous fall, my siblings and I had been "blessed" with the opportunity to attend Alta Academy, an elite educational facility for children of families who strictly observed all of the principles of the FLDS. Housed inside Uncle Rulon Jeffs's enormous white mansion within his large estate at the mouth of Little Cottonwood Canyon, it was considered the "Yale" of the FLDS, even though it originally went only to eighth grade, later expanding to the twelfth grade. I was eager to enroll, as Uncle Rulon's estate was a place where we didn't have to worry about what the outside world thought. As part of the throngs of children in prairie dresses and long sleeves playing in the courtyard, we could be ourselves without ridicule. And for the first time, all of Dad's children could be the "Walls," instead of some of us having to carry the seemingly shameful name of "Wilson."

We had attended church on the property for our entire lives, as it was the only FLDS building in Salt Lake that could hold our large congregation for Sunday services. My father had designed the home and said it was the largest single-family dwelling in the state of Utah when it was built. Before now, I had been familiar only with the vast meeting hall areas and a couple of nearby bathrooms on the first floor. As a student, I got to explore the rest of the building, including the third floor, which housed the principal's office and eventually the home economics rooms and tool shops. The house also had forty-four bedrooms, twenty baths, two full kitchens, two half kitchens, and two laundry rooms. Upstairs, the Jeffses did their best to maintain a household and raise their families, despite the hundreds of children below. There was also an area reserved for birthing rooms. Women from the Jeffs families, especially second and third wives and so on, were often instructed to deliver their babies here, so as not to arouse the suspicions of outsiders. It was not uncommon to be headed to class and hear the eerie reverberations of a mother in labor, or the cry of a newborn.

As good Priesthood children, we had to make a lot of changes in order to live up to the standards being set at Alta Academy for the rest of our community. We also now had to wear long underwear, once reserved for adults, which I helped Mom and my aunts to sew. It was vital that we follow each and every rule to the letter.

These standards were strictly enforced by our principal, Warren Jeffs, known to us as "Mr. Jeffs." The son of Rulon Jeffs, who was in the First Presidency with our Prophet, Uncle Roy, Warren had become

Alta's principal within a few years of graduating from Jordan High in 1973, despite having no college education. Mr. Jeffs was strange, but his position demanded respect. He had a gangly, lean frame and wore glasses that made his dark brown eyes look beady. Around his father he was obliging, seeming to hang on his every word. In the halls of Alta Academy, however, he was in charge. While he often had a goofy smile plastered to his face, everyone knew when he was serious. His expression would grow somber while his soft, almost hypnotic voice would get a sudden, deadly edge.

Every morning in the great meeting hall, an expansive area with a low, flat ceiling, we had devotionals or Morning Class. There we gathered together as a student body to hear Mr. Jeffs, joined on rare occasions by another FLDS leader or the Prophet, to speak on church doctrine. Then we would go to our classes for age-appropriate Priesthood subjects. Finally upon our return home, we had large amounts of homework on the same—usually accompanied by sets of tapes of Mr. Jeffs speaking on each subject. We were quizzed each day on that content, and we had to get the answers right or listen to the tape again until we did. A low-grade test score meant you had a low-grade testimony of God.

I was at the school for only two days when I first heard Mr. Jeffs soberly address appropriate behavior between boys and girls. He seemed obsessed with ensuring we were keeping ourselves pure.

"To warn you," he said, "your boy-girl relationships here, young people, are being closely watched, as you are quite aware. As our Prophet, President Leroy Johnson, has taught the young people, the boys particularly, 'Treat the girls in your acquaintance as though they were snakes. Hands off!' And the girls should treat the boys the same way until they are placed by the Prophet." I was determined to be a good Priesthood girl and please Uncle Roy, my Prophet, as were my sisters and friends, so we started treating males as if they were, indeed, foreign, scaly, and reptilian in nature. We avoided even our brothers and cousins. We ran from them, refused to sit by them, and were careful not to converse with them, especially near our principal.

Mr. Jeffs paid strict attention to the styles of women and girls. I was learning to sew, which was hard work! I carefully considered acceptable styles, looking for attractive fashions that were still considered "pure."

One friend's mother made her a princess dress, an elegant style with a modest bodice designed to make the waistline look slim. My friend was delighted until Mr. Jeffs sent her home in tears, after raving that the V-waistline pointed down "there—that place of a girl's body where the mind should not go" and was therefore a wicked, evil design. Her own mother, in her innocence, could not explain to her daughter why Mr. Jeffs considered it evil. Still, she was never allowed to wear it again.

Every child at Alta tried to stay on his or her best behavior. With nearly everyone related, any misstep was bound to get back to our families and cause them considerable shame. My siblings and I avoided being called into Mr. Jeffs's office as if our lives depended on it. We dreaded hearing any of our own called in over the PA system that was present in every one of the seventy rooms on the property. We also quickly learned to keep our mouths shut in the classroom, as Mr. Jeffs seemed to enjoy making an example of a student in front of his or her own classmates.

Unfortunately, the Walls, especially my mother's children, seemed to be a little more curious and stubborn. I focused on my studies and my homework and did my best to keep out of trouble. But once in a while, my Wall traits emerged, especially when I knew I was right about something.

I crossed swords with Mr. Jeffs several times during my first two years at Alta. On the first occasion, even though I had seen dinosaur bones and been able to touch and study them, Mr. Jeffs forced me to say that dinosaurs did not exist, had never existed, and were a lie made up by my worldly teacher! Deep down, I *knew* Mrs. Garrett would not have taught me anything that was a lie. But, greatly humiliated, I mumbled the words and sat down, with a red face and hot tears of defiance leaking from the corners of my eyes.

The second time, Mr. Jeffs was called to our classroom by my teacher to reiterate that astronauts had never landed on the moon.

"But, Mr. Jeffs," I exclaimed, "*I met an astronaut in real life!* I touched his space suit! He even signed his autograph!" I went on, ignoring his contorted expression. "He flew in space, and he told us about it! He told us all about Russian astronauts going up into space first, but U.S. astronauts raced ahead to be the first ones to land on the moon!"

"The government is crafty, Miss Wall," he snarled, and I jumped, recognizing that edge in his voice. Mr. Jeffs cocked his head condescendingly, as if I had been totally led astray. "They have made films and erected lies to make the public *think* they have landed on the moon."

"But—"

"Your teacher was a *Gentile.*" He spat the word as if it was poison. "Never speak of these things again!" He stared hard at me, and I returned his gaze for a moment before putting my head down on my desk in defeat. *Mrs. Garrett was not evil. My dad was selling stuff to Morton Thiokol for their solid rocket boosters for the space shuttle! There was such a thing as men landing on the moon!* But I was too smart to say another word. A boy I knew had been forced to drop his trousers to his knees and was whipped by Mr. Jeffs with a yardstick in front of the entire class until it broke. It had been horrifying to all of us to hear the boy's cries of pain echoing down the hallway. I didn't want to be the next example.

When I finally dared to lift my head, Mr. Jeffs was gone. I was sad now for my cousins and friends who would never know about dinosaurs or men on the moon. I felt a burning defiance, but just like at home, my survival meant knowing when to keep my mouth shut.

At Alta, we studied Priesthood History, Priesthood Math, and Priesthood English and Science—just enough for the girls to read recipes and work safely in kitchens, factories, or businesses run by Priesthood men, and the boys to become excellent carpenters and builders. In Home Economics, Mr. Jeffs seemed particularly obsessed with imparting certain principles to us young ladies. It seemed very important to him that our age group of girls have "proper teachings"—more than boys and adults combined. He would often bring up subjects that made me feel uncomfortable, with daily reminders of morality and purity. Each time he said the word "body," I felt sick to my stomach.

Alta Academy did have some benefits, like the small library in the basement. Books were a sweeter treat for me than candy. Between chores and homework, I had little time to read but was allowed *Encyclopedia Brown*. In the series, author Donald J. Sobol presented the most incredible thing: choice! I could choose where the story would take me, and I could choose the ending. Since my choices in everyday life were strictly limited, I relished being able to select a variety of outcomes. The best part? No matter what I chose, it wasn't *wrong*.

One day I walked into the musty library planning to exchange my stack. I politely greeted Mrs. Dutson, the librarian, as I set my stack down and walked over to select some more volumes. Mrs. Dutson glared at me.

"Don't you even *think* of checking out those books!" Tears stung my eyes, and I hung my head and walked away.

Later that day, word got around that they were removing most of the books from the library for the good of the students. Going to see for myself, I went down to the basement and turned the corner, dismayed to find the shelves empty. The only items remaining included Priesthood-approved materials—similar in content to our homework. *Encyclopedia Brown* was gone, and I grieved as if I had lost a best friend.

The library was just the first level of cleansing. Mr. Jeffs and the teachers began to closely monitor and eliminate any information we received from the outside world. The teachers removed any cartoons, caricatures of animals or people different from us, from our textbooks, warning that the outside world had planted "alligator eggs," things that were seemingly innocuous but that would grow to kill us. Every textbook became riddled with large, gaping holes. Eventually, texts were replaced by materials written just for us. In the classes and hallways, decorations were ripped from the walls. The only pictures in any classroom were pictures of the Prophets, from Joseph Smith down to Uncle Roy.

At home, fortunately, Mom allowed us to read some outside books and stories as long as she had read them first and considered them "faith-promoting." *Little House on the Prairie* and *Anne of Green Gables* were on the short list of titles that were acceptable—or at least not publicly unacceptable.

One book popular in our community was *The Hiding Place* by Corrie ten Boom, about a family of Christians living before, during, and after the Nazi occupation of Holland. Gathering us together before bedtime, Mom read to us about how Corrie's family hid several Jews in her room behind a secret wall before being discovered by authorities and taken to the federal prison of Scheveningen and then Vught. She tied in the ten Booms' experience with stories of the '53 raid, reinforcing our faithfulness to the Priesthood and our terror of government. It struck a fearful and familiar chord within us: armies were dangerous, government control was evil, and families could be torn apart by them.

The book raised deep philosophical and religious questions for me. I was astounded that Corrie's sister considered being eaten by fleas as a miracle, since they kept the guards away so the prisoners would not be killed for studying the Bible. Could there be miracles in even the hardest of situations? My mother's stories seemed to validate that idea. But I couldn't wrap my head around the contradiction that the Jews didn't practice plurality, and therefore couldn't be God's chosen people. Worse than that, they had killed Jesus Christ! So why would God show up miraculously in the midst of the Holocaust? Or, if he was a merciful God, as Corrie's sister suggested, then why would he allow such achingly horrific suffering in the first place? My mind roiled with these questions.

I also drew personal connections between the experiences of the women in the book and my own life. The women in the camp shared one bottle of vitamin drops, which miraculously never ran out. The Mormon pioneers had hundreds of similar stories, ones I'd been told all my life. But I had to ask myself, *Would I have shared my vitamins under those circumstances?* I hoped I would, but I wasn't sure. I made up my mind to grow to be the kind of person who would consider others' needs even when the consequences were life-and-death. Otherwise, what was the point of life?

When Irene got a new color television set, Dad gave Mom her fuzzy black-and-white one. Most often the TV had a towel or laundry draped over it, but occasionally we would watch an "appropriate" program after school. Uncle Roy had admonished families in church many times:

> Shame on you parents, for allowing these evils of immorality to be in the lives of your children right in your own homes! One of the tools parents have allowed into the home that creates this immorality is the television. . . . If you just flood them with evil, and let them see all the nakedness and corruption, and they're not prepared to resist it, they will naturally lean toward it.

Little House on the Prairie and *Disney Sunday Movie* were safe. *Mister Rogers' Neighborhood* and *Sesame Street* were on the list, too, until the Prophet deemed them worldly and idolatrous because puppets, like cartoons, were an imitation of God's creation.

The television helped my mother control her restless natives, especially with the baby getting into things, the twins' never-ending energy, and her eleventh child on the way. Aunt Irene created a lending library that included *Seven Brides for Seven Brothers, Heidi, Anchors Away,* and *Brigadoon*—generally older films, and always G-rated. A few full-length Disney features snuck by for a while, even though they were cartoons. I loved *Cinderella, Sleeping Beauty,* and *Snow White and the Seven Dwarfs* with all the passion my young heart could muster. Of course, these stories affected my psyche, like any other young girl's.

In the hidden recesses of my mind, I dreamed that a handsome prince would sweep me off my feet, rescue me from Irene's clutches, and carry me away to live happily ever after! However, our teachings stated clearly that the Prophet would be inspired with the knowledge of which man would be my perfect husband, the one to whom I would always defer and keep sweet. It was everything an FLDS girl was supposed to dream of.

I knew that I wasn't likely to marry a young man whose kiss would make me swoon, like in the movies—no matter how much I longed for it. The most romantic thing an FLDS girl could secretly hope for was to be a first wife and enjoy a few precious moments of one-on-one time before additional wives and myriad children arrived. We never dared speak of that hope. As with the vitamin drops in Corrie ten Boom's story, it would be morally wrong not to share.

CHAPTER 3

Up in Flames

Just before I entered the fourth grade in August 1985, we moved into a large new house on Claybourne Avenue in Salt Lake City, just a few months before our newest baby girl, Elissa, was due. There we would live without separation, even breaking bread together on the main floor.

That year, our frail Prophet, suffering from the debilitating effects of shingles, had admonished FLDS families to live more openly for the first time since Brigham Young and John Taylor settled Utah. The country had been through the roaring '50s, the free-love '60s, the civil rights '70s, and the alternative-lifestyle '80s, so surely it was not only our right but our duty to show the world how the true people of God lived.

He spoke with great fervor, glowing with love for his people, as he prophesied that the Lord wanted our families to put away our petty differences to stand together in the coming destructions. He could see signs all around us and believed he would soon be meeting Jesus Christ to return to him the keys of the kingdom. Although we heard this kind of thing every Sunday, I thought he really might, because Uncle Roy was the most ancient man I had ever seen. His tall forehead, accentuated by his bald scalp and scarce side hair, made everything below his brows look extra wide, and his expansive smile was as warm as summertime.

After so many decades in hiding, the thought of living openly unnerved many people who had survived the '53 raid, including my mother. Since Dad hadn't grown up in plurality and hadn't experienced the raid, he was more inclined to prove his obedience to Uncle Roy and make the move. I liked the Claybourne house's flat and spacious layout much better than that of our old home. Its orange-and-yellow décor, which would have been groovy in the '60s, didn't look quite modern, but I didn't care—we had a dishwasher! For us girls, who had spent years hand-washing mountains of dishes every day, it was a wonder. I dreamed of all the things I would do with my newfound time.

Sterling and Samuel moved out, and Janet and Cindy were married off to young men that the Prophet had chosen for them, but that still left nineteen kids and the mountains of laundry, cooking, and cleaning we required. Irene decided that because she was done raising babies, she should not have to do any cooking or cleaning, so the burden was left to my mom, my sisters, and me. It felt bitterly unjust, but my mother didn't breathe a word against her sister-wife, so I dismally resigned myself to being a servant in Irene's household.

One day, one of my gorgeous brunette half sisters, Victoria, who was about three years older than me, walked over and put her name on the family chore chart! We all looked at her in surprise. Victoria didn't exactly enjoy household duties, though she would at least do them, grumbling, when the others refused. None of Irene's other children signed up, but Victoria provided an example of decency. Over the next several months, Victoria stood up to her mother and had the guts to treat ours with genuine kindness in many ways. I adored her for it.

At first my siblings and I found it quite unnerving to live side by side with Irene and her children. Without the buffer of separate floors, we were easier targets. However, we discovered an unexpected boon: there were many more escape routes in this house! Our little ragtag team of siblings became adept at battle tactics and survival strategies. If a smaller sibling was being picked on, an older one would create a distraction while a third swept in and shuttled the younger child to safety. Working together, we minimized most physical damage. Emotionally, however, it was worse, in that my mother was subject to Irene's nasty criticism, rules, and budget all the time. Her sister-wife retained her position as the alpha wife.

Irene and Dad had both begun teaching at Alta Academy, and getting the entire brood promptly to Morning Class was a daily adventure. Breakfasts had to be gobbled and lunches packed, and a dozen schoolchildren sharing three bathrooms was a nightmare, especially as some of the older girls like Christine and Savannah wanted to carefully style their hair in the trendiest fashion acceptable in the church. They'd also do the younger kids' hair, and I quickly learned which of my sisters was most patient and gentle as they tugged my hair into tight braids. Hairstyles were rigidly monitored by Mr. Jeffs and our teachers, and makeup was banned. The slightest infringement carried severe consequences, like a temporary expulsion and being used as a public example to others.

Wisely, Dad would have already left the house in his brown Buick Century. His place at Morning Class was up front with the Priesthood brethren, and he had to be on time. The rest of us would cram into "Big Blue," Irene's Chevy Suburban, and wait for the older girls, who were inevitably running late.

It was a catastrophe to be tardy for Morning Class. Most mornings, I pled with Heavenly Father to let us arrive at least during the opening song, so we would not have to creep in, humiliated, with all eyes on us.

One very cold November morning, when I was ten, we arrived late, with Irene screaming hatefully at us as she parked the Suburban. As we approached the enormous white building of the Academy, I noticed the parking lot was devoid of any stragglers.

By the time we reached to the door, shushing one another as we entered, the opening song was obviously over, and there was no way to slip in unnoticed. We tiptoed into the colossal hall as Dad and Mr. Jeffs, seated in the front of the presiding Priesthood, glared at us with stern disapproval. I made my way quietly across the green-carpeted floor to where my fifth-grade classmates were seated, determined not to let anything ruin *this* day.

Today was glorious for two reasons. First, it was my beloved brother Cole's birthday. He was turning twelve—an enormously important milestone for a male in our church. He would be the first of my mother's boys to be ordained to the Aaronic Priesthood, an honor to be superseded only when he would receive the Melchizedek Priesthood at eighteen, and later when he was married for time and all eternity. I hoped for him that he would marry many wives so he could obtain his Celestial Glory. He deserved it more than anyone else, for the way he cared about others and took care of Mom in ways our father did not. It was often the case that when a father's life became packed full of the demands of multiple wives and many children, the sons took his place in labors of love and emotional support. After all, a man can have countless wives, but he will only ever have one blood mother.

Dad had a lot of responsibility between teaching at Alta and running HydraPak. His burden had greatly increased with Mom home full-time since the birth of our darling new baby sister, Elissa. Since two of Irene's daughters had recently married and left home, Dad still had sixteen children living at home in 1986. I was proud of him. I knew he paid a generous tithe to the church, and I had overheard his comments to Mom about Uncle Roy's plans for him in the Priesthood leadership. Any day now, he would be "called" to an important position in the church.

I shifted in my seat. Mr. Jeffs was giving another monotonous sermon. I was trying to sit attentively, but I noticed my classmates were as restless as I was. This was the other reason for my good mood: today we got to have a class party, something that happened only a few times a year, when mind-numbing amounts of lessons and homework were set aside for board games and treats. I glanced at the old ice cream bucket near my feet, the mouth-watering aroma of the brownies I had baked wafting up.

Suddenly there was a small commotion toward the front. Dad swiftly rose and followed someone outside while Mr. Jeffs was still speaking. Our principal looked annoyed, and I was worried. Dad cared too much about his standing just to walk out in the middle of class—something had to be going on! Someone passed a note to Mr. Jeffs, who nodded, and then Morning Class continued.

When it was finally over, my classmates and I waited for everyone to leave so we could section off our part of the great hall into our classroom. Forgetting the commotion, I dove into the activities, my reverie interrupted only when several high school boys were paged to the office. Later some of the eighth graders were called, too, but we were all focused on the rare chance to play games.

After lunch we played another fun game called Fruit Basket Upset, a modified version of musical chairs. It was total chaos and it felt so good to laugh! Mr. Jeffs often told us that laughter was "light-minded" and a road to hell. At one point during the games, I was surrounded by boys on both sides. For a brief moment, I wondered why it was so important to treat boys like snakes. Sometimes, I thought, they didn't seem *that* slimy. Guiltily, I glanced into the hallway, grateful Mr. Jeffs wasn't walking by.

All too soon, it was 1:40 p.m. and time for closing prayer. As we prepared to bow our heads and fold our arms, Mrs. Nielsen said, "Rebecca, come and see me after, please." There was no severity in her voice, but during the whole prayer I wracked my brain. *What had I done wrong? Had I sat with my legs apart at some point? Had I spoken to a boy? Had I pushed my sleeves up? That must be it!* The dress I was wearing that day had elastic at the wrists and pretty ruffles, but they often got paint or glue on them, and without thinking I would pull them up to my elbows throughout the day. More than once Mr. Jeffs had admonished me, "Becky Wall! Pull your sleeves down!" When the prayer finally ended, I hung my head and walked to Mrs. Nielsen's desk. She waited for the remainder of the kids to rush out before turning to me. Instead of anger or judgment in her eyes, there was compassion. She put her arm around my shoulder.

"Becky, your new home caught on fire." My hand flew to my mouth as I immediately thought of my mom and younger siblings.

"Everyone is okay; no one was hurt," she said comfortingly. "However, your house has been completely ruined. Uncle Woodruff Steed has graciously invited your entire family to stay with him while your family rebuilds your home."

It had been arranged that one of the teachers would drive Trevor, Lillian, Amelia, and me to our house. As we neared our block, which was packed with cars, I bolted from the vehicle before it stopped half a block away from our house. I ran toward it, shocked that it looked like a bomb had hit it. Only a burned-out shell remained, and an acrid smell of smoke hung in the air. The surrounding trees were blackened, and jagged glass covered the lawn.

The windowless house, seemingly devoid of furniture, was filled with people. Students, neighbors, and strangers with garbage bags and shovels peered out of the gaping holes from the living room. Muddy rubble covered the no-longer-recognizable hardwood floor, and every-where I looked, I saw evidence of destruction. The orange Formica was bubbled, cracked, and bowed. Huge ceiling beams now lay on the floor. I made my way carefully along the hallway to my mom's room and burst into tears as I flew into her arms.

"It's all right, Becky," she murmured into my hair. She smelled of smoke, but I didn't want to let her go. "Everything is going to be all right. Everyone is safe, and that's all that matters."

I hadn't believed this was true until I heard it from her lips. I looked at my mother's bandaged arms. She had gotten burned at one point during the fire in her zeal to save her children and home. She would heal, she promised me. Slowly, I climbed back through the debris and made my way into the room I shared with several sisters.

The moment I saw that my new pink seersucker plaid dress had been burned beyond salvation, I cried hard, though silent, tears. It was my only dress that wasn't a hand-me-down, and Mom had sewn it special for me, even adding pleats to the skirt. With so many babies, it had taken her a very long time to finish. Long gone was the time when Mom could work through the night so that my sisters and I would awaken to the luxurious surprise of brand-new matching dresses for the 24th of July or another special occasion. I determined that day that I would become a master seamstress. I would have to.

I helped Mom gather up what few possessions were salvageable, which we shoved into big black garbage sacks to wash later. As I started hauling the heavy bags outside, I was stunned to see that neighbors had brought stacks of blankets, clothing, and food for our family. I looked at the items with great suspicion. They were apostates and Gentiles! Had they poisoned the food? Or infected the blankets? We had kept hidden for so many years, trying not to let our old neighbors see who we really were. We had only recently made our lives more public, living among the evil people.

But what I witnessed on that day and the ones following was not the presence of evil. How could all of these people who brought clothes and bedding from their own closets, made food from their own kitchens, be evil? In wonder, I noticed our neighbors had the same expression as Mrs. Nielsen had had when she told me the news. It was compassion.

I begged to stay at the house to help, but I was told it was too dangerous. We were gathered up and carted over to Uncle Woodruff Steed's home, an immense structure several miles away in Sandy. It housed Uncle Woodruff's many wives and children and, in the upper rooms, the Salt Lake City wives of the Prophet. When we walked in, Uncle Woodruff's wives greeted us with great tenderness and sympathy. Aunt Daisy, her name aptly reflected in her blonde hair and sunny disposition, asked me to come and help her in the kitchen while we talked about my experience that day. Her attention and affection made me feel warm and safe for the first time since I'd heard the news. Uncle Woodruff joined us for the evening meal, and he, too, was extremely gracious. The meal was delicious and took a bit more of the sting out of the day.

After dinner, we settled into the enormous room Mom had been given for all of us. Between the bedding lent by the Steeds and donations from our neighbors, we made ourselves at home, and I was amazed to think that so many people had shifted their lives around to make room for nineteen more of us. I already loved the Steed family and, of course, the Prophet's wives, but my heart was filled with gratitude.

Several of us ran outside with the Steed children to play evening games. We'd been out for over an hour when one of Uncle Woodruff's wives came to the back porch.

"Children!" she called out urgently. "Come inside *now!*" Stricken, we looked at one another and rushed indoors, wondering what more could possibly have happened. We fell silent as we looked around the living room at our extended family members hunched together in shock, their faces filled with tears. I looked at my cousin Lisa, who was a dear friend at school, Uncle Woodruff's daughter, and one of Uncle Roy's granddaughters.

"Grandpa is dead," Lisa said simply.

"Don't say that!" I blurted. There had to be a mistake. The Prophet couldn't be dead.

I couldn't process it, and somehow I couldn't cry. I was overwhelmed by everything that had happened that day, and my body shut down. I loved my Prophet like a grandfather and revered him as our spiritual leader. He was the closest to Heavenly Father I would ever get, and now he was gone. A deep, black hole of fear opened inside of me.

The Prophet of all of our people was dead. He was our shepherd. How would God speak to us now? How would we know what to do?

"We'll wait for answers from Uncle Rulon," said Uncle Woodruff, as if reading my thoughts. Uncle Allen Steed echoed his words, and the adults around the room nodded. I hadn't realized I was holding my breath. I let it out.

All was not lost. Uncle Rulon would have answers from God.

It didn't take long to realize that things would be different at the Steed home for the Wall children. At our home the Steed name and legacy were stomped on, but here we were treated with the greatest of respect, because we were Steeds, too. When any of our half siblings tried to bully us, they'd be swiftly put in line by the older Steed boys. Despite my sadness over the loss of our house, I was feeling more at home here than I ever had anywhere. While Dad made us aware that he paid Uncle Woodruff handsomely from the insurance, as he wanted to instill in us the principle of self-reliance, we also recognized the many ways that the Steeds went out of their way to welcome and accommodate us.

Things were different with Irene, too. Here, she did not dare to raise a hand or her voice to us. She and her children were far away on the bottom floor, where she tended to hibernate. Though Irene was treated with equal respect, it was the first time she could not manipulate my father, which seemed to breed even greater resentment inside her. We didn't question it; we reveled in our newfound freedom and emotional stability.

While I knew my father had a lot on his plate trying to rebuild our house, he never said one word to acknowledge Cole's interrupted birthday. I couldn't help but be impressed by the Steed boys, who took up the mantle. In January, Roy Steed and his brothers said, "We gotta get that boy spruced up!" and over the next few days took him out and spent their own money to buy him a suit for his ordination, as well as a special combination of scriptures—the Holy Bible, the Book of Mormon, the Doctrine and Covenants, and the Pearl of Great Price—to call his own. They included Cole as one of their own, and I saw his face glow with gratitude and a new confidence.

On the third Sunday in January 1987, Cole was ordained to the Aaronic Priesthood of God. As a female, I wasn't allowed to attend, but I was very proud of him, and my older sisters were as well. The Steed boys congratulated him warmly, but my father was strangely distant. The older Cole grew, the more difficult it seemed for Dad to connect with him, especially when Cole excelled at church and school.

I did notice, however, that Dad seemed to have a new appreciation for Mom and her family ties, as well as for the peace we felt at the Steeds'. But something else seemed to be troubling Dad, too.

Overhearing snippets of conversations between him and my mother, I picked up on the fact that the change in Prophets held devastating consequences. Dad had been waiting for Uncle Roy to make a big announcement about his major advancement into the top rungs of leadership, but with Uncle Roy's death came the demise of his bid for Priesthood leadership. Everything he had built with Uncle Roy would no longer be honored. Dad threw himself into remodeling our burned-out house, but it was obvious that his morale was greatly lowered.

Five months later, in April 1987, we moved back into our newly renovated home. The quick rebuilding was a testament to FLDS workmanship and the teams of young builders. Even though my siblings and I had helped a great deal during the process, we were filled with a mixture of awe, joy, and a bit of trepidation as we entered the house. It looked and felt brand-new. Gone was the '60s Formica, tile, and carpeting, the dark brown paint, and the paneling. The kitchen boasted beautiful blonde oak cabinets, Corian countertops, and cream-colored walls. The doors all matched, and our furniture had been either refinished or scrubbed until not a hint of smoke was left and everything shone brightly.

Irene continued to spend much of her time in her room. Most of her kids would join her, watching VHS recordings, doing homework, or reading. There were several times we had the run of the house, which was new and frankly enjoyable. However, when Dad would take Mom on dates, Irene's jealous temper would rage like in the old days. In reaction, we hunkered down together, usually in Mom's room, which now had a lock on the door.

One night early that summer after Mom and Dad had left on one such date, my siblings and I were waiting for Irene's storm to pass, knowing it might be a while, as our parents were having a special overnighter. Christine often read us stories when we were holed up in

Mom's room, and we wanted her to read from the new library book we had started that week. However, it was down in the living room, and none of us dared pass Irene's room to retrieve it. The younger ones were restless and bored, and I knew they would soon be out of control. That was dangerous for all of us.

I motioned to Christine and listened at the door. Apparently, Irene had grown tired of her rage.

"I think I should go get that book," I whispered to Christine. A look of trepidation came into her eyes. Christine had finally graduated that year, but Irene still terrified her as much as she did me.

"Can you sneak past without getting caught?"

"Yes, I think so." I wasn't as sure as I sounded.

Silently, we opened the door to peek down the darkened hallway. Irene was crying, but it was a snuffling, defeated sound. A crack of light from her room spilled out into the hallway. *Why hadn't she shut her door?* Heart pounding, I slipped from Mom's room, tiptoed past Irene's, and made it down into the living room, where I seized the book.

I returned to the hallway, thinking that if I shot past Irene's room quickly enough, I would be safely ensconced in Mom's room before anyone knew what had happened. Christine beckoned furiously at me from Mom's doorway. I took a deep breath when suddenly Irene's door flew open.

"You little whore!" she screamed. "What do you think you're doing?"

I stood, frozen in fear, as memories of past beatings came over me.

"You illegitimate bastard!" She grabbed my shoulder, her fingers sinking into me like talons. "You are a little whore...*just like your mother.*"

I had heard it all before, but the moment Irene said that about my mother, something within me snapped. I hinged back with my right arm and punched her square in the eye!

In slow motion I witnessed my stepmother tumbling backward, as much from surprise as from the force of my little hand, and I fled before she or her kids could react. I reached Christine, who slammed and locked the door behind me. We sat in silence, holding our breath and one another as I shook uncontrollably. Strangely, nothing and no one emerged from Irene's room.

My rush of adrenaline did not subside, even after everyone else settled in to listen to Christine read. As I tried to concentrate on the story, I couldn't help but think of the coming destructions. I had just hit my mother! Though she was not my blood mother, I was supposed to treat her as such, and I would *never* have hit my own mother. Surely God would punish me.

Finally I started to calm down, and I realized that I was tired—tired of Irene's foul mouth and hurtful hands, of being on alert for a beating every second. Those thoughts ignited a familiar fire.

Let the destructions take me, then, I thought.

Though most of my siblings slept peacefully in Mom's room, I kept waiting for a vengeful *crash* of something against the door. I felt like a caged animal, and in the early hours of morning, I snuck out of the house the back way and into the yard. Quickly, I climbed twenty-five feet or so up the tree I had claimed as a nest of safety many times before, and I waited. And waited.

Three hours later, I was still in the tree when Dad's Buick came into view. Certain I was in for a beating, I didn't get down. My mother came outside.

"You can come down now, Becky," she said. Slowly I descended, prepared to meet Dad and his belt at the door. Though I babbled apologies to my parents, I was astonished not to receive any formal punishment. Irene was nowhere in sight.

A few days after the incident when she came into the main room, I tried not to gasp. She was sporting the most richly colorful black eye I had ever seen.

"Do you like your handiwork?" she snapped. While she gave me a horrible look, there were no consequences...at least not immediate ones.

We had spent only five months with the Steeds, and yet something else had been "remodeled" in our home, far more extensive than plush carpet and pretty new wood cabinets. Oliver Wendell Holmes once wrote, "Every now and then a man's mind is stretched by a new idea or sensation, and never shrinks back to its former dimensions." My siblings and I had learned that we were perfectly worthy of being treated decently and that we were not second-class citizens. On a deeper level, we gained something we'd never had before: self-respect.

*   *   *

That summer and the next, Mom sent Cole and me to spend most of our school vacation in Canada—something that the adults understood to be an exile, but an exciting trip for the two of us. Cole still seemed unable to please Dad, who would not listen to him or protect him from Irene. Though she never said a word, I sensed that Mom was sending us both away to keep us safe from Irene's increasing abuse, however much it broke her heart to do it.

For those in Utah, Canada was the most logical place to send "wayward" FLDS youth. Boys provided cheap labor, and work kept them away from the girls. While Cole slaved away at the logging camps, I stayed on my uncle Jason Blackmore's large property in Bountiful. Though I enjoyed all the breathtaking beauty that British Columbia offered, the material comforts there were few and far between. Jason's wives, including two of my mother's sisters, and his daughters were responsible for massive amounts of cooking, cleaning, sewing, and working the wild and rugged land.

While in Canada, I was introduced to Uncle Jason's brother Winston Blackmore, the bishop of our FLDS community there. He was a jovial yet callous man, a product of his environment and his beliefs. I laughed at some of his jokes but cringed at how harshly he treated his wives. Even at the pulpit, he would couch unkind remarks in humor. "Like Brigham Young, I don't like whiny women! Just like him, I tell 'em, 'Leave! I'll replace you in an instant with another wife, and she will serve me the way a woman should serve her Priesthood Head.'" On the walk home from church, I would glance around at the wilderness. *Where would a woman go to survive alone out here if she left the FLDS?* We didn't know that divorce was easy in the early church, because it certainly wasn't now. Leaving meant being cut off from all family and all support—physical, financial, emotional, and spiritual. With nowhere to go, women rarely left.

I enjoyed letters and an occasional call from home, learning that there was much excitement in our community about Alta Academy building a new high school. Our members were constantly fulfilling the commandment to reproduce, and there were far too many school-age children to fit comfortably in the lower level of the Jeffses' home.

Things had felt bleak since Uncle Roy's death, but the construction project poured renewed hope into our hearts. Surely our new Prophet wouldn't have us build a high school if the end of the world was coming so soon.

My father utilized his engineering skills to aid in the design of a new building that would safely hold a large number of students. Sometimes FLDS builders would cut corners regarding safety and compliance, but my dad was adamant about every detail, especially where children were involved.

When Dad filled me in on the phone, it seemed to me that he saw this as a way to prove to Uncle Rulon what a ready and loyal member he was, worthy of another wife and of the leadership so recently snatched from his fingertips at Uncle Roy's death. Dad had sold HydraPak at Uncle Roy's urging and Uncle Rulon's insistence and was now working as a geological consultant. He hoped that the new Prophet would be aware of him and all of his sacrifices for the church. Dad saw that the building would be a daily reminder of his prowess as an engineer—and something Warren could not do.

Although Dad didn't openly share details, my siblings and I were aware of tension between him and our principal. So while Dad was unable to do anything *inside* of the school to shine, the outside of the impressive building would be hard to ignore. He also had Mom bake a hundred loaves of bread each week for sandwiches needed for the swarms of FLDS craftsmen who had come up from Short Creek to work at the construction site.

One day, after the foundation was laid and the framing begun, Uncle Rulon came by to take a look at the progress. He glanced around appreciatively at the expansive and handsome new building.

"Maybe I'll just use this for *my* home," he said. There was a split second of shocked silence, and then everyone chimed in, "Oh yes, this *should* be your home!" and "Yes, a new home for the Prophet!" When I learned about this a little later, I was really disappointed, as were most of the students. If my father felt the same way, he didn't voice it, but set to work to redesign the interior as a residence.

That fall we returned to school in Uncle Rulon's old thirty-thousand-square-foot house, which Alta took over entirely. The building had been retrofitted to include the high school students now as well. We discovered that rules had become stricter, the schedule more extreme, and the homework more arduous.

In the beginning, Mr. Jeffs's homework tapes had been limited to the elite members of the church whose children attended Alta. Eventually he leveraged their air of exclusivity to create high demand in every FLDS home, to the point where any home without the tapes was somehow seen as suspect. It was almost as if listening to Mr. Jeffs's monotone sermons was the only way to ensure salvation and avoid destruction.

At Alta Academy, he was often heard speaking on behalf of the Prophet. "Father says we must..." was a phrase that would haunt not only the great hall but every classroom. Mr. Jeffs ended every sermon, talk, and class, and nearly every conversation, with "I'm just the humble servant of my father."

After another arduous year at Alta, the summer offered the relief of time to think—to hear my own voice in my head, and not just that of Mr. Jeffs. Tapes still played continuously in our home, but I could go outside and hear the sounds of nature. The summer of 1990, just before my eighth-grade year, I found myself in the awkward stage where I was no longer a child and not yet a teenager. My body was beginning to change, and where I had been chunky before, I was beginning to slim down and fill out. Becoming a woman was confusing, and I noticed that people, especially males, treated me differently. No one explained it to me; I was left alone with my chaotic feelings.

Dad had begun acting rather protective of his daughters. Ever since Uncle Rulon himself had married my mother's little sister Ora, over fifty years his junior, it seemed that our uncles and other older men in the FLDS were beginning to see possibilities for young brides among several of us who were no longer considered children but "options." So when Christine and I raised the question of going back up to Canada the next summer, Dad said, "Absolutely not!" He had always had some reservations about Uncle Jason, who had flirted with my mother even though he had already married her older sister.

I was disappointed by my father's refusal, but I determined to continue my study of music. I utilized that time well. In June, the local Suzuki Music Camp invited some of the greatest violinists in the world to instruct us. Brian Lewis was the first chair at Juilliard, the famous music conservatory in New York, and I had the privilege to be coached by him on one occasion.

That day, he asked me to play a technical passage several times. Although I did fairly well, my trained ear knew it sounded muddy. I had been a bit of a virtuoso as a child, but I had reached a wall that was keeping me from a higher level of proficiency. I was already nervous to begin with, so when he cried out, "Stop!" I nearly fell to my knees.

I looked up in shock to see the teddy bear of a man holding his violin out to me. We had just been told that Brian's precious Fisher Stradivarius had been insured at $1.8 million. He looked at me patiently, and although I was frightened, I held out my hands. I cradled the violin in my arms with the same mixture of wonder and awe with which I'd held my very first instrument. The Strad's proportions were perfect, and I found myself playing the passage impeccably, my fingers like dancers on the strings. After playing it through twice, I discovered I could replicate it on my own violin! I glanced up to see the rapture I was feeling mirrored on Brian's face. Not only was my barrier shattered, but something within me bloomed into being.

One of our world's greatest musical performers had passed away just the summer before. Grandfather Steed had been conducting a choir when he fell off his platform and hit the back of his head, resulting in a coma and his eventual death. We still grieved for him but took comfort in the fact that he had lived a full life and died doing something he cherished. Grandfather had not been afraid to shine in his music, but he was also a man. It was only at Suzuki camp that I felt like there was a place for a female musician in my world.

Mr. Jeffs had come to think of most music as being worldly and showy. Although he would call on me to play at nearly every school program, he constantly reminded me that all the glory must go to the Lord lest I become an instrument in the hands of the devil. I became quieter about my talents. Fortunately, around that time, another special artist entered my world. Peter Prier made and sold string instruments in his shop on 200 East and 200 South in Salt Lake City, which was a treat to visit. On these rare and special occasions, Peter would ask me to play various pieces of music on different violins. When I finished, he would clap and rejoice as if I were playing at Carnegie Hall! I learned to celebrate the musician within me, even if only privately. It was enough to keep going, and the validation kept me from seeking other sources.

Some girls my age had begun covertly wearing makeup or arranging clandestine meetings with boys. While the occasional thought of boys was secretly exciting, I had no desire to sneak around. I was influenced in part by a book called *Fascinating Womanhood*, which made the rounds among married and singles alike in the FLDS around that time. It included advice on how to stand out in a crowd; how to please a husband and awaken his deepest feelings of love; and how to make him think every good idea was his. "The role of a woman when played correctly," wrote the author, Helen Andelin, "is fulfilling, fascinating, and full of intrigue. There never need be a dull moment. The practice of this art of womanhood is an enjoyable one, filled with rich rewards, numerous surprises, and vast happiness."

Since FLDS women literally had to stand out in a crowd of their own sister-wives in order to be noticed, it was little wonder this book made waves, and the men loved it. For a girl like me whose only desire should be to fashion myself into that kind of bride, it held a certain amount of intrigue. I read it with great fervor, and I began to carry myself quite differently than before. Still, much of the book drove me crazy! We were supposed to slyly remind the man of how *weak* we were compared to him, but FLDS women were physically very strong. We had to be—it wasn't like there was always a man around to carry a fifty-pound bag of flour or crate of newly canned peaches. So now I was supposed to jump up on a chair and cry out, "Ohhh! Come and kill this spider!" whenever a man was present? I had killed plenty of spiders and hauled many heavy boxes.

Still, my mother and Mama Alice encouraged me to act more like a refined lady. I practiced to please them and found that sometimes these skills seemed to work. My brothers noticed I didn't climb my tree anymore or beat them in races. However, I began to feel different *inside* than I had before. I was realizing I could create the kind of woman I wanted to become. The question was, what kind of woman was that? Frail and weak? Or a woman of genuine grace and strength who could make a difference?

The concepts of obedience and self-worth filled my mind as I returned to Alta for my eighth-grade year that fall of 1990. Classwork and homework would again be demanding. Mr. Jeffs was bound to be just as hard on us, if not harder. I did my best to respect him, but sometimes his behaviors were downright creepy, though I would never say it aloud. For example, he had signed my yearbook fifteen times, all over his pictures. Not even my best friends did that! At times his body language was strange around me and other children. Rumors abounded throughout the school of his beatings whenever a child didn't toe the line. Although we faced abuse in our home from Irene, I knew plenty of families who didn't practice corporal punishment, so this was quite shocking. I noticed that children also left his office changed in a way that I couldn't put into words. I deliberately steered clear of there.

We had all grown up afraid of the secret rooms in Uncle Rulon's old home, which were now part of Alta Academy. There were secret panels that could be locked from the inside, but we noticed that others locked from the outside. They had supposedly been built to hide women and children in case of another raid. However, it was rumored that ill-behaved children learned what it was like to be locked up in the dark. If I simply remembered that Mr. Jeffs, my father, and the Prophet were always right, perhaps I could stay out of trouble entirely.

Once during Priesthood History, Mr. Jeffs asked us to raise our hands if we thought women should have the right to vote. Immediately I raised my hand—and realized I was the only one to have done so. My principal berated me. How could I possibly think that a woman could have the faintest idea of how to vote, or what the country would need more than her husband? "The only reason a woman should vote," he said, "is to give more power to her husband and the church."

It wasn't only in the classroom that Warren antagonized me. He seemed to notice that something had changed over the summer in the way I held myself. He went almost crazy pushing the girl/boy issue, incessantly asking, "Did someone pass you a note?" "Did he touch your body?" Every time, I answered with a firm no. His questions made me feel sick inside. I wasn't interested in boys, except as the perfect Priesthood bride for a man when I was older—or at least creating a life that would be pleasing to God, whether that entailed the affections of a man or not. I looked at my FLDS role models—my mothers, aunts, and cousins—and everything they had to endure. Like most of them, I felt that I could handle anything in this life if it meant my salvation in the next.

CHAPTER 4

Armageddon

During the next few years, my only refuge was my music. I was allowed to go to Suzuki camp again and continue my lessons. Although I had been classically trained in violin, I began to adore the energy and adventure of fiddling, as well as the unique sense of belonging when a group of us fiddled anything from Irish reels to "The Devil Went Down to Georgia," a song that would have been strictly forbidden at church or school. At home, everything except the monotony of homework seemed to change rapidly. In 1991, Savannah graduated from Alta Academy, followed the next year by Brittany. It seemed impossible to me that my babies Joshua and Jordan had now begun second grade, Zach was already in first, and Elissa was no longer toddling around. Sometimes I cried quietly at how quickly my siblings were growing. However, Mom had had another sweet baby girl, Sherrie, who had come on the heels of Levi, so there wasn't much time to miss diapers and bottles.

As we adjusted to an ever-changing household, it became apparent that something was dreadfully wrong with Christine. No one was able to pinpoint the cause of her mysterious suffering, but she had difficulty breathing, suffered from headaches and intense pain in her chest, and couldn't seem to rest. We didn't dare take her to a doctor, so she became the subject of many experimental treatments. Our mother, aunts, and concerned friends tried multiple homegrown and home-tested remedies—everything from fasting to colon cleanses to ice baths. She chopped raw onions and pressed them onto a paper towel, which she laid upon her chest and abdomen every night for a year.

Sometimes when I went to visit her room to brush the hair back from her dark and sunken eyes, I listened to the sounds of the house and wondered if she was suffering a physical manifestation of the hopeless-ness of her eventual fate. She was now twenty, hardly a spring chicken in the eyes of the FLDS.

When Rulon Jeffs had become our new Prophet, he had halted the practice of quickly marrying off women as soon as they turned eigh-teen, desiring "to get to know his people" first. Only recently had the aging Prophet begun performing marriages again, so there *was* hope of a marriage and family for Christine soon. But daily my sister saw the ugly reminders that while marriage could be a way out, it could also give entry into a graver situation than ours. Certainly there were healthier families, but we knew some who were much worse off. What would it mean to be shackled here and in the eternities to an undeserv-ing Priesthood holder? Or a sister-wife who beat our children?

Whatever the case, at school when the girls separated from the boys in Home Economics, we received constant training from Mr. Jeffs about exactly what kind of obedient wife we should turn out to be. Spouting the words of the Prophets, he said we must keep sweet, never complain, and always, always, defer to our husbands in every important decision. Women were *not* to try to lead their husbands.

Boys, on the other hand, were taught never to let a woman get the best of them, or be seen by the Lord as weak and undeserving of his Heavenly kingdom. Having to be manly in word and deed, they espe-cially studied building and craftsmanship.

Cole used those skills and went to work for Warren's brother Lyle, who owned a construction company. Occasionally I would go to visit him or bring him lunch on Lyle's construction sites. When lookouts warned of oncoming OSHA inspectors, boys as young as eight would hide out, lying on the floors of pickup trucks with tinted windows until the inspectors drove away. Then they went back to work in pits, up on scaffolding, framing, and rooftops. Lyle took advantage of his young labor crew, often refusing to pay by saying proceeds were going to support the Prophet and the church. Cole finally quit, but Lyle didn't care; he had an endless supply of young labor.

By 1992, my sophomore year at Alta Academy, doing my best at school kept me out of much trouble for a sixteen-year-old. Not all of my classmates were of the same mind-set. Some were secretly cutting a class or two, even hitting the slopes with members of the opposite sex—an unpardonable sin in our society—especially among the "illustrious" elite at Alta Academy!

Mr. Jeffs began catching wind of some of these clandestine meetings. "If you know of this happening, you are as guilty as they are!" he would say sternly. Those who were trying to toe the line were getting the short end of the salvation stick—none of the fun and *all* of the damnation!

My half brother Timothy often cut class, then came home to brag to me and Cole about his snowboarding adventures. One day in spring when the weather was exceptionally pleasant, several students were missing from Geometry, a class taught by Mr. Jeffs. It was painfully obvious they weren't all sick or at work, as the alibis usually went. When Mr. Jeffs couldn't get answers from anyone else, he turned to me.

"Rebecca Wall," Mr. Jeffs said sternly, "is Timothy home sick today?" I'm sure I looked like a deer in the headlights. I had *never* ratted anyone out! But I had warned Timothy that I would *not* lie for him.

"No," I answered, feeling equally relieved and terrified at the same time. Within a few minutes, several students were in serious trouble. By the following day, the fallout was unbearable for me. Most of my classmates were cold, and the ones who had gotten caught were mean and bitter. They began making snide comments whenever a teacher left the room. While I had been somewhat popular in my circle of friends, I now felt like a total outcast. Only my best friend Sandra Keate and a handful of others remained kind, but even then they were somewhat withdrawn, given the way I was being treated.

Toward the end of the school year, I waited in Big Blue one afternoon for my older sisters. I expected Irene to be cranky because they were late, but she seemed to be in an exceptionally good mood.

"Are you going to the baseball game tonight?" she asked. Among the Northern Utah FLDS, ball games were the only times we met for recreation.

"I don't think so," I said glumly. "Even though it's Friday, I have a lot of homework. I'm going to need the whole weekend to get it done!"

"Oh, but it's such a beautiful day! We'll find a way to get you there, if you want to go."

I stared at her, a bit dumbfounded. The games were held far south of town in Riverton, and she was never that generous to me. Irene then suggested I run in and grab the girls, which I did. We all jumped back into Big Blue and were making our way home when Timothy asked me to help him with some slivers in his hand he had gotten from wood-working. I rummaged through my large Home Ec sewing kit and found him a needle—but also discovered something else in the box.

It was a note: a typed note signed by Carl Keate, asking me to meet him during the ball game. Carl was Sandra's brother. He was a quiet, shy, "good" Priesthood boy; I had never known him to break the rules, but there it was in black and white! What on earth was so important that he would dare to write a note? This could get us both in *huge* trouble. No boy had tried to talk to me alone before, and certainly not Carl. A terrible knot rose in the pit of my stomach.

Nervously I arrived at the ball field that evening. I looked for Carl and saw him pacing the pavilion in the distance. Quietly, I made my way through the crowd toward him. He turned and looked at me.

"What the hell is this?" I asked, pulling his note from my pocket. I didn't normally speak this way, but I was furious. Carl's own face, which had been masked in anger, changed to a look of surprise.

"What do you mean? I got one just like that, except it's signed from you!" We looked at each other, realizing we had been set up. But by whom?

We looked over at the crowd but didn't see anyone watching us. Together we agreed we wouldn't fall for any more notes. "I'm sorry for the trouble," we both murmured, and quickly went in separate directions.

That night I confided in Christine, who suggested I tell Dad. My adrenaline still pumping, I decided she was right. Fortunately Dad believed me. He said not to worry about it. Still shaking, I went to bed, only to toss and turn. Who would do this, when our reputation was all we had?

The following Monday after school, I was in the computer room with several other students working on our papers. Carl Keate was in there, but to my relief he didn't acknowledge me. Several minutes later, Mr. Jeffs poked his head in the door.

"Carl Keate, go home right now!" We all looked at Carl in surprise. For the first time, he glanced in my direction, grabbed his stuff, and headed out the door. Our principal went back to his office, and the moment he left, I ran and called my mother.

"Mom, what's going on?" I asked breathlessly.

"Sis, Mr. Jeffs called us. Someone took a video of you and Carl Keate together."

Suddenly the principal's voice boomed over the intercom, calling me to 310—the dreaded office.

"I want you to see something," he said when I entered, and handed me a video. "Put this in."

Even though my mother had warned me, I still trembled as the screen clearly showed me walking out to meet Carl Keate at the pavilion at the ball field.

"Why don't you tell me what's going on here?"

"Exactly what you see," I blurted. "I found a note in my sewing box. I was so upset at him—thinking he was getting us into trouble. We found out we each had a typewritten note and someone else signed our names." Warren asked me several more questions regarding the video. I was grateful that we hadn't touched, not even elbows or fingertips. The video showed no signs of anything improper.

"Do you know who took the video?"

I shook my head.

"Well, let me tell you how I came to find out. Someone set this against the door to my office." He showed me a manila envelope, and a note in block writing:

To whom it may concern:

Rebecca Wall has been sneaking around, engaging in multiple encounters with Carl Keate. They're always making eyes at each other. We just happened to have a video camera handy to prove it because no one would believe it.

Signed,
A concerned individual.

"Do you recognize the handwriting?"

"Yes, sir. It looks like Devon Johnson's." Most of us knew each other's writing as we had been in small classes together since grade school.

"I was ready to expel you. Your saving grace was that you already talked to your father."

I trembled, knowing what the outcome would have been if Warren Jeffs had thought I had been lying. He pressed further anyway.

"Did he say or do anything inappropriate to you? Did he touch you? Are you having any boy problems with him?"

"No! I'm too busy to have boy problems! I have too much homework."

"Good," he said. "We'll get to the bottom of this. The one who points the finger is the one who is guilty of this themselves. Don't speak of this to anyone."

I took a small measure of comfort in his words, but my mind was spinning.

The very next morning, Mr. Jeffs had all the high school stay for a Morning Class test.

"Now I want to talk to each and every one and you. 'The words of the wicked lie in wait for blood, but the speech of the upright rescues them.' Last week, there was an attack on two of our student body. We have a good idea of who was involved. If you do not come forth and confess and apologize, you will be expelled for the rest of your years in school." The classes held their breath, but no one spoke. A few days later, Nancy Jeffs and Stefanie Fischer apologized to me. Nancy was the one who'd signed my name. She said the boys had come to them, and because of Devon's handwriting, I had sort of figured it had to be them. I realized my half brother Timothy must have been involved, but what she said next was shocking.

"Mrs. Wall helped them to write the note. Becky, it was her idea."

Irene? That hit me hard, at the pit of my stomach.

That night, I told my father. He became very upset and stayed away from his first wife for two or three nights, but she never apologized. While her plan had fortunately backfired, the dagger remained in my heart, made worse by the fact that Carl Keate was sent to Canada for the summer by his strict and angry father, and Sandra was told never to speak to me again. She was pulled out of Alta "to care for her grandmothers," and although she had never taken her education for granted, she was not allowed to return to graduate.

From that point on I lost my heart for school, a place where I had no friends and many tormentors. Devon Johnson and Gregory Jeffs were very cruel. Every time I walked into a room, they gagged and dry-heaved. When Devon corrected my paper, he scratched out my name and wrote "Rectal Wall." I didn't even know what that meant. With only twenty students in our class, I had to see them every day, and they made it a living hell. My one reprieve was when the girls had Home Economics and the boys had Woodworking.

Mr. Jeffs forced me to be in Math, where both Gregory and Daniel were my classmates, so I started staying home. I got all my classwork done, but I didn't have to put up with their hurtful behavior. I felt like Christine, with no hope for the future. I would not have returned to school had Mr. Jeffs not called my home and ordered me back.

That year our principal turned up the heat on our Priesthood lessons. He seemed obsessed with Armageddon, and he quoted the Prophet as saying it would happen at any moment. We had to be prepared. Our thoughts and actions had to be of the utmost purity so that we could inherit the earth.

We did not know our Priesthood History was vastly different from the world history and American history taught in other schools. Ours was dictated by lessons from the Bible, the Book of Mormon, and our modern-day Prophets. Beginning with Adam and Eve, then Aaron and Melchizedek, as they were both instrumental in the special Priesthoods of the church, we then skipped to the Romans and Jews in Christ's time. Touching somewhat on Christ's ministry, his crucifixion, and his resurrection, we studied the principle of plural marriage. Even Jesus Christ engaged in plurality, at least as far as the history taught by Mr. Jeffs. Not only had Jesus been married, but he first appeared to his *wives* when he rose from the dead, as explained in the Bible, even before his beloved disciples.

Following Christ's resurrection, the Great Apostasy covered the earth in ignorance and blackness, including the ensuing "Dark Ages." Mr. Jeffs's lessons included many terrible details of the Spanish Inquisition and the methods of torture contrived as well as the total corruption of churches and governments. Skipping several centuries deemed unimportant, we studied Columbus coming to America for the purpose of a New World where the gospel of Jesus Christ would finally be brought back in its fullness. We were taught that the United States was the Promised Land as foretold in the Book of Mormon, and that in 1820, God and Christ visited fourteen-year-old Joseph Smith in a sacred grove of trees, with a message of the truthfulness of the gospel. This visitation would begin the restoration of the gospel on the earth.

Later Joseph received a visitation from John the Baptist, who conferred upon him the authority to baptize; and one from Peter, James, and John, who conferred upon him the authority to organize the Church in 1830. In the early 1830s, Joseph quietly instituted the principle of polygamy, although it would not be publicly discussed and upheld until 1852. After Joseph and his brother were martyred in Carthage Jail in Carthage, Illinois, all authorities and keys were granted to Brigham Young, who was succeeded by John Taylor. In 1890, the document that denounced plural marriage precipitated our falling out with the mainstream Mormon Church.

Mr. Jeffs reiterated the words of our Prophets that the Mormons had sold out to the federal government by not adhering to God's commandment of plurality. That was when our people followed the true order of God and obeyed our own Prophets: after John Taylor, there were John W. Woolley, Lorin C. Woolley, John Y. Barlow, Leroy S. Johnson, and finally Rulon T. Jeffs.

In fact, said Mr. Jeffs, the *entire* history of the world had led to this one point—to Rulon T. Jeffs becoming the Prophet of the church! This was why, Mr. Jeffs explained, it was so vital to listen to the Prophet. Fathers and husbands must choose to obey him *and none else*. Wives must obey their husbands who were faithful to the Prophet *and none else*. This was the correct order of the family. In this way, we could not go wrong.

"You only get to Heaven through the living Prophet in your time. Because of this great power our living Prophet holds, he is *everything* to us."

While teaching this period of Priesthood History in the Americas, Mr. Jeffs focused primarily on the corruption of government. For example, during the United States Civil War, Mr. Jeffs emphasized how it had not only been improper but immoral for Lincoln to have fought for the rights of slaves. Mr. Jeffs had a particular dislike for blacks and considered them lower than whites. In his view, the result of the Civil War was a major loss for mankind.

Just as I observed in my classmates, there was some haughty, arrogant part of me that wanted to believe that we retained some kind of mental and spiritual superiority over others. But a deeper part of me cringed every time my principal ridiculed others. I couldn't help but think of *The Hiding Place*, and how the Nazis referred to the Jews as disposable.

That book was at the front of my mind as our class began to focus on the World Wars and the atrocities one people could commit upon another—even within their own ranks. As we reached World War II, Mr. Jeffs made us pay particular attention to Hitler and the Holocaust. With great fervor, he spoke in detail of the events surrounding this colossal period in history, and forced us to watch films portraying the thousands who died of malnutrition, starvation, and exhaustion. It served as a warning to us that governments regularly lied, terrorized, and exterminated people like us. Although I had always been fascinated by history and geography, Priesthood History quickly became my least favorite class.

It was about to become much worse.

On the twenty-eighth of February, 1993, the United States Bureau of Alcohol, Tobacco and Firearms waged a siege on the Branch Davidian ranch near Waco, Texas. Officials had attempted to serve a search warrant, but a ferocious gun battle erupted, resulting in the deaths of four ATF agents and six Branch Davidians. The people barricaded themselves inside the ranch, and a standoff between authorities and the Davidians began.

Rarely had I seen our principal as animated as he was by this siege. Mr. Jeffs brought a big-screen television into our eleventh-grade classroom, and every day we would watch news coverage of the fifty-one-day siege. Pacing back and forth in front of the television, pointing out teams of ATF agents in intimidating SWAT gear with long-range rifles, Mr. Jeffs made sure we understood the gravity of what was taking place. He said that this surely was the sign of Armageddon that our Prophets had been warning us of.

Every morning when we gathered for Morning Class during the siege, Mr. Jeffs waved the headlines in front of the whole student body, describing what was happening to the Davidians, blow by blow. One morning I remember him being particularly theatrical.

"See how the government seeks to destroy these people because of their beliefs?" he ranted, still pacing. Then he stopped and, with great dramatic flair, looked slowly over the students, holding up the paper. "Beware! Because *we* are next!"

I saw the frightened looks upon the faces of the tiniest children, and knew they were reflected in my own. Everyone looked afraid, even the teachers. Principal Jeffs made us stand repeatedly, and pledge to stand by Christ, the Work, and the Prophet, "even if our hearts are to be ripped from our bodies!"

It was my heart that felt so sick for those people. For nearly two months we watched in trepidation and fear, praying for a peaceful ending and deliverance. Mostly we prayed for ourselves, while we listened for the sounds of helicopters overhead and men with assault rifles climbing the fence onto Uncle Rulon's estate. The tension at the school kept us at a breaking point. After listening to so much news commentary and the taped sermons of their leader, David Koresh, I couldn't shake the feeling that there was something eerily familiar about their leader, whom I found creepy and terrifying.

Fifty-one days after the standoff began, a second assault was finally launched, during which a disastrous fire broke out and destroyed the compound. Seventy-five of the Branch Davidians died in the fire. Accompanying the announcement was footage of the charred and smoking bodies of twenty children and two pregnant women. I couldn't help it—I ran out into the hall and retched.

Though I tried to block it out, the voice of Warren Jeffs echoed in the room behind me.

"This is just a test case! What they will do to us will be much, much worse."

CHAPTER 5

Matchmaker, Matchmaker

Though I continued to struggle with Mr. Jeffs, my sister Christine got along incredibly well with him. We all *had* to, but she was always animatedly saying, "Mr. Jeffs said this" and "Mr. Jeffs said that." Christine's health had improved considerably, and she was preparing to go back to teaching at Alta Academy when she was strong enough. She had finally stopped the compresses, and her skin and eyes had some color back in them again. She was still frail and weak, but she had returned from the jaws of death.

One night when Mom and Dad went out and we barricaded ourselves once more in our mother's room, we were watching the video *Fiddler on the Roof.* We'd all seen it many times and most of us had it memorized. Watching Christine smiling and singing, I felt a chill. The words made sense to me like they never had before—and I didn't like it. The last few months, the practice of arranged marriages had exploded within the FLDS, taking place one after another. Gone were the days when young men and women had any say in whom they married. God was our matchmaker.

We were at the part where the Jewish sisters were singing "Matchmaker, Matchmaker," the two youngest ones scared to death about their future. In their marriages, they were "stuck for good," but in the FLDS, we were stuck for *all eternity*. The Prophet, upon hearing the word of God, told us who was to marry whom. As for women, we were told over and over that enduring life here on earth meant that we would be happy in the eternities. That raised all sorts of questions inside of me.

"What happens if I marry someone I don't like?" I asked Mr. Jeffs, who didn't seem to like the fact that I could often quote scripture and the Prophets as well as he did.

"You'll grow to love him."

"But if I *don't* like him, it won't matter to *him*, because he's promised to have hundreds, even thousands, of wives in the eternities. You have said that as his wives, we all must serve him, whether we like it or not."

"If you honor his Priesthood, you'll grow to love him, Becky," he growled, and then dismissed me.

For the last four years, I had worked hard to become a worthy woman of the Priesthood. I hoped that meant that when the time was right, I would be married to a righteous man whom I not only loved but respected. At that time I would have to accompany my father to turn myself in or "check in" regarding marriage. However, I did not have to worry about checking in with the Prophet for several years. After all, Christine was six years my senior and not yet married. Although some of the girls had started marrying a bit younger, like during earlier decades within the church, my father would not permit that for us. He made it clear he wanted us to experience a bit more of life before we married, and even though it was essentially up to the Prophet, a father could hold some sway, however minuscule, over his daughter's future.

One day Dad came home from a Priesthood luncheon with several leaders and said to Christine, "Uncle Rulon asked after your health." I was surprised, but my brothers all said, "Ooo-ooooh! He's getting ready to marry you off!" Christine blushed profusely, but the table was cheery.

Uncle Rulon had taken another young wife, and fireworks went off among the people. No one dared say it aloud, but fathers began to wonder, *What if my daughter marries the Prophet?* It was sure to affect their standing in society—something consistently on the minds of all FLDS members, especially fathers. Mine was no exception. He had made sacrifice after sacrifice for Uncle Roy, and then for Uncle Rulon, and it had all seemed in vain. Now with business going well again, Dad prepared to make another attempt at a political coup.

One day, he asked for my help on a project. I had studied calligraphy and was often asked to make use of my skill. Dad had recently paid off our home's mortgage, and he wanted me to prepare a beautiful document to sign the deed over to the Prophet and to the church. Joseph Smith had introduced the Law of Consecration in 1831, in which members were asked to voluntarily consecrate their property to the church. The church would then allow us stewardship over the property to provide for our needs, but it was a concrete way for Dad to show his dedication to the Prophet. As he still had only two wives, he had to prove that he was worthy of Celestial Glory.

I worked hard to produce the documents on parchment paper, and they were beautiful. Papers in hand, our family dressed in our best and headed off for a special appointment with our Prophet. I had never had much interaction with Uncle Rulon except to shake his hand on Sundays, so I was a little nervous as we entered the mansion. Several of the Prophet's local wives greeted us warmly and chatted with us until it was our turn. Because he was meeting with our entire family, Uncle Rulon came out to greet us, and we sat in the large living room together.

Our Prophet had a strong, angular jaw with a broad, high forehead and a surprisingly full head of hair, now nearly white. I noticed right away that he was very different from Uncle Roy. Despite his extreme age and the wrinkles around his eyes and his jowls, Uncle Rulon was an imposing presence and held himself with great authority. He reminded me so much of Grandfather Steed; he could be jolly or stern, and he was definitely used to commanding others.

Dad proudly produced the deed and we chatted for a while, before the two men went into Rulon's office alone. I waited uncomfortably with Mom, Irene, and my siblings until Dad was finished. When he finally walked out, I noticed that my father's face looked jubilant.

Soon after that Dad had another private meeting with Uncle Rulon. The next thing we knew, he was taking Christine to see the Prophet for an appointment. It was late April and Christine was wearing a cream lace dress, looking exceptionally pretty.

When they arrived home, Dad tried to gather the family together, but Christine stayed outside, walking around the yard. The floodlights were on, and I watched her through the window, singing to herself and dancing among the flowers. She looked like a maiden from a storybook, twirling in a meadow. Only one thing could make her that happy.

When Christine finally sashayed inside, I turned to see my father grinning from ear to ear.

"Our Christine's getting married!" Dad announced, beaming at her and then the rest of the family. Then he paused for dramatic effect as everyone clamored around him, dying to know whom Christine would belong to. Finally he couldn't wait and he burst out:

"She's marrying Uncle Rulon, the Prophet!"

There was a stunned silence, and then a burst of cheers. We all thought she would marry Mr. Jeffs. But Rulon? I could not help but cringe inwardly. Our Prophet was eighty-four years old! While it was not unusual for an FLDS young lady to marry a much older man, my stomach churned inside of me. Something didn't feel right.

Christine, however, didn't seem bothered one bit. In fact, she was beaming as brightly as Dad, and went about her evening chores humming and smiling, so very happy. I prayed she might remain so.

The following week, Christine married Rulon Jeffs. She had already made her wedding dress the year before during her time of illness, as it was a passive activity and had seemed to bring her hope. It was not unusual for a young girl to have a wedding dress in her dowry, as this was the biggest preparation of her life.

Christine's worries about our family seemed to be over, for what she was doing for us would raise our standing in the community. Beyond that, providing a marriageable daughter was another area in which Dad could outshine Mr. Jeffs. After all, Rulon could not marry his own granddaughters (although grandnieces and second cousins were not out of the question).

The following spring, I graduated Alta Academy with honors, having the highest number of credits earned by a student up until that time. I was to take the summer off, but I would be back in the fall, this time as an eighteen-year-old, to teach younger children. We went on our annual Wall camping trip deep in the heart of the Uinta Mountains, but when we arrived home, we were stunned by two visitors standing by the utility sink: Irene's daughter Sheila and her husband, Orrin Steed, Uncle Woodruff's son.

Orrin, who had a penchant for laziness and stirring up trouble, was not among the Steed boys I adored and respected. There he stood, with the stem of a red rose between his teeth, rubbing his hands together in triumph. He had come to claim Victoria as his wife. Beautiful, exquisite, sweet Victoria, who had always been so very nice to me growing up, had also been the butt of her sister's unkindness. Surely the Prophet would not allow this man to have her!

Later on, we found out that Orrin had gone to see the Prophet with an agenda.

"I had a dream that Victoria belongs to me," he had reported. The first time didn't work, but he went to see Uncle Rulon three or four more times. Finally the Prophet said he would "take it up with the Lord." A few days later, after more prodding from Orrin, he told him, "Okay, go get her."

I couldn't help the thoughts raging through my head. Victoria was a good Priesthood girl who had played by the rules—and for this?

I had to go outside. I couldn't handle it. I was walking in the yard when I overheard voices in Irene's bedroom.

"Aren't you happy?" Sheila asked Victoria.

"I'm just surprised; that's all." Victoria clearly didn't know how to express her feelings about the marriage. What could she say? I stuffed my own emotions inside, but Cole was bursting with anger. He and Victoria were very close in age, and she had always been kind to him, too. He was appalled that Orrin could just come in and get away with this. Our parents tried to soothe him, saying if the Prophet took it up with the Lord, then it must be right. The wedding was to take place just two days later. Orrin was granting her no time.

Still furious, Cole was refusing to attend the ceremony.

"Will you please come to my wedding?" Victoria begged. "It will not be the same without you." All Cole could do was to pound on the wall. "I know," she added. "It's hard for me, too."

He turned and looked at her. "Then don't do it."

"I have to."

Defeated, Cole showed up to the event but sat far in the back and refused to shake Orrin's hand. Within a short period of time, a sadly ironic pattern appeared. Sheila treated Victoria with great cruelty—exactly like Irene had always treated Mom. She and Orrin mocked Victoria, and Irene had to endure watching abuse being inflicted on her own darling daughter. I couldn't stand to watch what was happening, and in spite of my very strong faith, I began to question how the Prophet could have not only allowed but helped to create Victoria's situation.

I remembered a recording of Warren teaching a Home Economics class. He told the girls they didn't want a "sniveling" little boy who would let them rule over him like the Gentiles. Instead he preached:

> ...to lead you, to be the example to you, whom you can look up to. What an advantage you have over anything the world could ever offer! And the strength of your marriage will be that the Lord appointed it through His Prophet.

Had the Lord really appointed it? Or had Orrin's wheedling exasperated the Prophet into giving in to him? I prayed that, indeed, the Lord had directed the match and, because of that, Victoria would eventually be happy and be given the gifts needed to get into Heaven. If I were in her shoes, my thoughts of killing Orrin would surely keep me from getting there.

Very soon it was time for me to take up my job as a teacher at Alta Academy. I showed up for my first day a little nervous. There was no formal teacher training. The biggest prerequisite was having the recommendations of my father, Mr. Jeffs, and the Prophet. I was simply handed the teacher textbooks, along with a schedule of what subjects I needed to cover, and off I went to my classroom. Luckily I began as a team teacher, and after having helped so many younger siblings with their studies and homework, I found the skills actually came naturally to me.

At Alta, I kept up with my meticulous notes during Morning Classes and conferences. Mr. Jeffs had noticed those skills through my years of Home Economics, and he now asked me to bring in my many notebooks. My notes were copied and compiled in the spring of 1994. The result was the major foundation for the book of our Prophets, *In Light and Truth: Raising Children in the Family Order of Heaven*. It would come out four years later copyrighted in Rulon's name. I didn't receive any recognition for it, nor did I expect it. Women were not to stand out in any way, and I worked hard to blend in so I would have no reason to be singled out for any reprimands.

Every year in the spring we gathered in Short Creek for April Conference to listen to the Prophet and the rest of the patriarchal authorities of the church give counsel as to how to behave on an individual basis, as families, and as a church. My siblings and I loved gathering with all of our friends and relatives and other members. Just as we could at Alta Academy, here we could openly walk the red-dirt streets and gather in large crowds, unabashed in our prairie dresses and long sleeves. At April Conference the following spring, there was a huge change in how we were taught to address one another. Following in the footsteps of the strict Jeffs family, we were no longer allowed to call our parents "Mom" and "Dad" and were ordered to immediately begin addressing them formally as "Mother" and "Father." Aunt Irene now had to be strictly referred to as "Mother Irene." Other persons of respect, like FLDS Priesthood holders, teachers, and our principal, would be called "Uncle" or "Aunt." It was all very hard to get used to, but to not do what the Prophet had asked would be immoral, so we got into the habit quickly.

As the school year wound to a close, Mr. Jeffs—now "Uncle Warren"—kept an increasingly vigilant eye on me. He had an entourage of wives and teachers who were supposed to "check in" and wait for him for hours in the hall outside his office. Groups of women camped out in the corridor every day, just waiting for a sliver of his time. I thought it was absolutely ridiculous, and when it was supposed to be my turn, I spent time preparing for my class or teaching instead. This refusal to "check in" did not go unnoticed. One day Uncle Warren called me into his office to admonish me. While I nodded in agreement just to please him, he could tell I wasn't thrilled with the idea. Even at that moment I was anxious to get back to my classroom. He sat and stared at me with his piercing eyes.

"Speaking of checking in, Becky," he said, his voice deliberately slow, "I think you need to check in with Father." My mouth open in shock and horror, I looked at Warren as he picked up the phone and dialed my father. To "check in with Father" meant I had to check in with the Prophet for marriage! My father had been told to turn in his eligible daughters to be wed, but except for Christine, he had put it off several times. Warren was my principal and a Priesthood leader, and I was not to say no to him. It was a blatant show of force between Uncle Warren and my father—and once again Warren was winning. Fumbling, I mumbled some things into the phone to my father. He was not happy.

"Do you realize what you have done?" my father asked sharply when I arrived home later. Tears filled my eyes.

"Uncle Warren picked up the phone and dialed it. What was I to do? I'm only eighteen, Dad! I don't want to get married yet!" He hadn't noticed that I didn't use the term "Father" in my distress. He just stared at me, disgusted.

"Looks like you don't have any choice." I watched him walk away, my heart heavy with despair.

Two days later, on a Saturday morning, Savannah, Brittany, and I set off in silence with our father to see Uncle Rulon. All through the previous day and night, my head had been swimming. This was *supposed* to be a day that the girls in the church rejoiced over. To be turned in to the Prophet for marriage—all our work, our training, our habits, behaviors, and character sculpting all to become the very best bride we could be. I hadn't expected this for at least three or four more years, so now I struggled to remember the "right" things I was supposed to do. I could hear Uncle Warren's words as he repeatedly taught us in Home Economics about keeping our hearts open for his father's revelations.

"President Jeffs reads your heart when you present yourself to him," he would repeat. "For those who have been praying fervently that the Lord's will is done in their life, it's easy for the Prophet to receive the impression about whom that girl belongs to. It's your heart or the spirit you keep that is all important. Stay open and pure."

I was praying to keep that channel open, but all the way to Uncle Rulon's estate, I was near tears. I tried very hard to keep calm, even as we were greeted at the door by several of Uncle Rulon's wives, who seemed to be eagerly anticipating our arrival. It made me even more anxious.

One at a time, our father turned us over to the Prophet. My older sisters went first. When it was my turn, I was led down a hall and into a very large office with multiple chairs and cubicle dividers.

Uncle Rulon sat behind a large and ornate desk. I was struck again by his authoritative stance, although today he seemed to be making a greater effort to be kind, jovial, and friendly to set me at ease. After several preliminary questions, however, he got down to business.

"I need to ask you a very serious question. Do you have anyone in mind to marry?" He looked at me with his dark eyes, and my heart felt like it would leap out of my chest. We were not *ever* supposed to carry a thought of a man in our hearts, because that channel would become cloudy and the Prophet would not know who we were to marry.

"The only person…that ever crossed my mind…was you," I said, stammering. I saw his eyes sparkle, and that instant I realized he had taken that comment in precisely the *opposite* way I had intended! We were only *supposed* to think of the Prophet, as he was the mouthpiece of God. "I mean, I ummm, I haven't allowed myself think of anyone else." That wasn't right, either!

"Please," I said, pleading, "I just want to marry the man *Heavenly Father* feels I am to marry." I looked in his eyes, and I could tell he didn't understand. I hung my head in defeat. I had given my Prophet the wrong idea. Nothing I could say without being offensive was going to change his mind. I wanted to scream, *I don't want you!* But my mouth was sealed shut by all of the admonitions, sermons, and stories I had ever been told about honoring my elders, and especially the Prophet.

"I will take it up with the Lord," he said simply, and all I could do was bow my head and get out of there as quickly as I could.

I found out later that it wouldn't have mattered if I had mentioned another man or not. My fate had already been decided. Unbeknownst to me, the Prophet had been watching me throughout high school. Even if I had another man in my heart, I would never have been given to marry him. I belonged to the Prophet.

Over the course of the next few weeks, I discovered that my sister Savannah was being given to Uncle Warren's brother Seth Jeffs. My sister Brittany was being given to our uncle Jason Blackmore, and she would be moving up to British Columbia to live with him as his fourth wife. I shuddered a little at that one, even though it wasn't surprising. Uncle Jason was in his fifties and, like Uncle Winston, did not treat his wives with much respect.

"Who will you be marrying, Becky?" they both cried.

"I…I don't know," I stammered. Uncle Rulon had never actually said the words, only that he would take it up with the Lord, and I had prayed and prayed that the Lord would give me someone younger, worthy of the Priesthood, and a good and righteous man. If the Prophet was our connection to God, and God knew my heart, then surely he would have the last say.

Savannah, now twenty-three, married Seth Jeffs on June 6, 1995, in Uncle Rulon's living room. Just eleven days later, Brittany, aged twenty-two, married Jason Blackmore in the same house. Brittany had gotten into some trouble not long before for having kissed a boy, and she was quickly married off to an "appropriate Priesthood man" for it. I prayed for her to be happy. After the ceremony, Aunt Aubrey, Jason's wife from Canada, hugged me.

"We all thought you would marry Jason," she murmured. I had never loved Jason except as an uncle, but I would have given anything to be in Savannah's or Brittany's shoes instead of my own. They both seemed relatively happy.

After the ceremony, which Uncle Rulon officiated, the family stood in formation for the greeting line, which had been a tradition for over a century at every wedding. I stood behind Cole, who was very restless. "Can't this line move any faster?"

We finally made it up to the line to greet everyone—first my father and mother, then Brittany and Uncle Jason, whom we congratulated, and then Uncle Rulon. When I shook Uncle Rulon's hand, he seized mine and squeezed it three distinct times. My heart sank in fear and despair. Our Prophet had a tradition. If he squeezed your hand three times, each squeeze stood for a word in a message: "I-LOVE-YOU." It also meant that you had the honor and privilege of becoming his next bride. I knew those behind me were watching for my reaction, so I kept moving to hide my face, which had become inflamed with panic, fear, and embarrassment.

My mother had seen this interaction, and if my father hadn't, she would surely tell him. As the celebration wound down, Dad said I could go home with Cole and Timothy. My brothers had been ahead of me in line, so they didn't know what had transpired, and I didn't tell them, hoping against hope that it was just a figment of my imagination. We drove around for a while, and by the time we got home, everyone had gone to bed except Dad, who was sitting in the living room with just a small lamp on. His eyes lit up when he saw me.

"There you are, Sis," he chuckled. "Next in line for marriage, and next in line for the Prophet, no less!"

I burst into tears. "Please, Father—I'm not ready! I'm not ready!"

"Holding the hand of the Prophet, you will make it," he said, trying to sound reassuring.

"Dad—"

He wouldn't listen to anything I had to say. I turned away and rushed into my mother's room, not caring if she was awake or asleep.

"I can't marry the Prophet!" I cried. "I can't!" I paced back and forth, unable to calm down. She sat up in bed, her nightclothes and blankets wrapped around her.

"I choked, Mother! I didn't know what to tell him, and they say to keep that channel open, so I told the truth that he's the only man that ever crossed my mind, but that's because he played the role of Prophet in deciphering *who* I am to marry! I don't want to marry him, Mother! I'm sorry, but he's *old!*"

"Your sister is married to him, and she's not struggling with his age," she reminded me gently.

"But I'm not Christine!" I burst out. "Oooh! I am going to go do something *so bad* that I won't be good enough for him to marry me!"

"Becky!" my mother scolded. "Just what do you think you would do?"

"I don't know. But I will do something." In my mind, "so bad" meant wearing lipstick, or cutting my hair. Surely our Prophet wouldn't want a wife who cut her hair!

I woke up the next day wracked with pain. My head felt thick and my eyes were nearly swollen shut from crying. Everyone could tell I was unhappy, and within the hour, my father asked me to go for a ride. He took me out to McDonald's on 33rd South, a very rare treat. I could easily count on one hand the number of times I'd ever tasted fast food, so normally I would have relished the fries and the shake, but I saw my father's ulterior motives lurking.

"You notice how happy Christine is at the Prophet's home, Sis?" he said, his eyes overly merry. "It's because she is making the best of it. The same with Ora and Naomi. They're *blissfully* happy." I wasn't sure I would call it "blissful," but they did seem happy. Mom's sister Bonnie was now known as Ora. Rulon took the name everyone had always called her away from her because *Bonnie* meant "beautiful," and he wanted to humble her. He felt she should go by her real name "Ora Bernice." Was that bliss?

Naomi Jessop was a newer, younger bride like Christine, and the daughter of my uncle Merrill Jessop. She, too, seemed happy, I had to agree. But there were others…

My father seemed to read my thoughts. "Not everyone is so happy, though, are they? You don't want to turn out like Ellen, do you? She has a sour countenance, and you can see it on her face." He paused thoughtfully for a moment, and then burst forth with a new idea. "You know, you could make it your goal to cheer Ellen up!"

I started to protest when he interjected firmly. "Remember, your salvation is assured now, Sis! Your salvation is assured."

Upon my mother's urging, my father talked to Uncle Rulon the next day. Of course he would not think to refuse his Prophet's wishes. Desperate for his family's salvation and political standing, he merely asked for more time. I was allowed to go to Canada for the summer and work with my aunts on my wedding dress. By this time I was an accomplished seamstress and could have sewn a dress in a matter of days, but I was incredibly grateful for the few extra weeks.

I was just eighteen and would be married shortly after I turned nineteen ... to a man more than four times my age.

I traveled up to Canada with the newlyweds Jason and Brittany, and Amelia joined us later. My aunts could tell I was not very excited to get married, but I did my best to hide it. One day, though, my rebellious streak came out in full force.

Uncle Rulon made a special trip to British Columbia in July for his third-quarter visit and to check on his bride-to-be, ensuring my preparations to come back and marry him. Christine and I were requested to play for him like we had many times before, but this time I was looking for one last vestige of freedom before being forced to marry. My sister Amelia and I had made darling sailor outfits for Spring Conference. They were electric blue, a much more vibrant shade than we were generally allowed. And they were striped with sassy, striking, inch-wide panels of blue and white all over, including the ruffles. We dubbed them our jailbird dresses.

Donning our matching outfits, we defiantly made our way out into the celebration. Amelia was also showing some signs of rebellion, although hers was directed at Uncle Jason; he had just married our sister Brittany, and now he wanted to wed Amelia, too. She was being a little cheeky with the boys to make him mad, but I was crossing a definite line. Rulon Timpson Jeffs did not like stripes on women, and *everybody* knew it.

It irritated me that Uncle Rulon utilized his position to make his preferences suddenly seem like they were what *God* wanted from us. Though Uncle Roy, who had reinstituted prairie dresses as the appropriate style for women, had also done this, he had at least liked vibrant colors and fabrics. Uncle Rulon quickly intimated that such vibrancy bespoke a proud and arrogant woman. He also outlawed wearing the solid and bold color red. A little bit of pinstripe on a man's shirt or on a checkered long dress was acceptable. What started out as "the Prophet's preferences" eventually became "God's law." Nowhere was this more clearly marked than in the Prophet's household. Most of his wives dressed the same and even piled their hair up high, as a crown. I did not want to carry my very long, thick locks above my head and suffer from headaches like many of his wives. God's law or not, I would find a way to express my individuality.

With great defiance, I deliberately hung back to wait until the last possible moment to surprise him publicly with my dress. Uncle Rulon hadn't noticed me yet, but people nearby were starting to stare and whisper. Suddenly Christine saw me from across the large lawn where the celebration was being held. Within seconds, her face showed abject horror. She turned to Brittany and I could hear her high-pitched and frantic whisper as they practically galloped across the lawn toward us.

"We have got to get her to change before Father sees her!" Soon enough, they had reached me.

"Becky!" she whispered, tears gathering in her eyes. "You must change now! You mustn't let him see you like this! You know he won't approve!"

I looked at her insolently. "I am *not* his wife yet!" My head was hot, like it had felt in his office. I wanted to wear this dress to symbolize everything that I had not dared voice: I did not want to marry him. Except as my Prophet, I wasn't seeking a relationship with him.

I tried to turn away into the crowd, but both Brittany and Christine pulled at me, pleading now with full-blown tears streaming down their faces. The look in their eyes spoke the truth: my rebellion would reflect badly not only upon me but upon them and quite literally my entire family. I stood rigid and then sighed and went in to change, though not without several muttered, unladylike words under my breath. By the time I came out to play for the Prophet, I had changed into something he would find demure and pleasing. Still, I played "Orange Blossom Special" as defiantly as I could. Oblivious, our Prophet whistled merrily along.

A few days later, after Rulon and the rest of the visitors had left, I went for a long walk with my sister Brittany along the pond. We talked casually, but suddenly her tone became somber.

"Jason pressured me to consummate our marriage," she whispered.

"Consummate?"

"That means he and I had marital relations." I nodded, not wanting to appear stupid. I had overheard Warren use this term many times before, but I didn't fully understand what it meant. Because of the strict admonitions in school and church to never let our thoughts wander to those topics, I had always shied away from any conversation regarding this subject. I looked more closely at Brittany for clues and noticed the twinkle in her beautiful blue eyes hadn't returned, and she had the beginnings of dark circles. I wanted to kick myself. I had been so caught up in my own impending marriage that I hadn't seen through her outward guise of happiness.

"On our wedding night, I said I wasn't ready," she revealed. Her bottom lip began to quiver. "I *begged* him for more time. He said he would." Brittany paused, and looked away. "He gave me only one day... and then no more."

A tear slipped down Brittany's cheek, and she quickly wiped it away. My heart felt a stabbing pain, and I looked at her, horrified, with great compassion. Uncle Jason was the older brother of Winston, the bishop. The thought of him forcing anything on my sweet Brittany made me appalled.

Still, I was confused as to what exactly she meant. I had seen Dad peck my mom on the lips, or give her a hug. I knew he slept side by side in the same bed with his first wife on her allotted nights, and my mother on hers, but what did that mean? I had seen my uncle Jason around his wives. He seemed jovial and often swatted their bottoms mischievously. I began to suspect maybe there might be more going on in the bedroom than I had ever realized. Visions of farm animals I had seen worked their way into my mind, but I quickly brushed them aside.

We were *not* like animals. We were taught in our lessons that we were *higher* than animals. It was only when we were carnal that we became just like them. Was that what Uncle Jason was doing? Was that what my husband would expect?

The knot that had formed in my stomach the day Warren forced my dad's hand had swollen to enormous size. I didn't understand what it meant to have marital relations—whether for pleasure or procreation. I only associated anything remotely akin to it with guilt and shame because of how my half brother Sterling had touched me.

Then, in spite of my compassion for Brittany, I pulled in a deep breath of relief. My husband-to-be was much older than Uncle Jason! Just like women were "put out to pasture" once they were too old to bear children, surely men of a certain age didn't partake, either. Our Prophet was way past the age of fathering children—by decades! None of his younger wives had children.

I suddenly felt steadier. Uncle Rulon wouldn't think of touching me, not like *that*. Not if he could no longer have children. Surely that could not be Priesthood approved!

CHAPTER 6

Sudden Royalty

At the end of the summer, I was given no choice but to return to Salt Lake City to face my destiny. On September 17, 1995, wearing the dress I had sewn with my aunts and sisters, I became the nineteenth wife of Rulon Timpson Jeffs.

The wedding was a blur of activity. From the crowds of relatives, friends, and other FLDS members who came to celebrate, only a handful of faces remained in my memory. The first was that of my Prophet, clasping my hands and standing across from me, bent from extreme age. Dad, who had been temporarily given authority by the Prophet himself to perform the ceremony, repeated the words I'd heard so many times before:

"Do you, Brother Rulon Timpson Jeffs, take Sister Rebecca Wall by the right hand, and receive her unto yourself to be your lawful and wedded wife, and you to be her lawful and wedded husband, for time and all eternity, with a covenant and promise, on your part, that you will fulfill all the laws, rites, and ordinances pertaining to this holy bond of matrimony in the new and everlasting covenant, doing this in the presence of God, angels, and these witnesses, of your own free will and choice?"

"I do," said Uncle Rulon, his eyes twinkling at me from behind his glasses.

"And do you, Sister Rebecca Wall, take Brother Rulon Timpson Jeffs by the right hand, and give yourself to him to be his lawful and wedded wife, for time and all eternity…" I only half heard the rest of the oath, which mirrored Rulon's.

How could I say *I do*? I had asked that very question of my mother that morning. She had said I could do it because God and the Prophet were *always* right. And if I were to keep sweet and not complain, I would be blessed. I had heard that all my life, and yet here I was.

"I…I do," I answered finally, my voice faint. My father sealed our marriage by the authority of the Holy Priesthood in the name of the Father, the Son, and the Holy Ghost. I froze, and the crowd laughed at my wide eyes as Rulon pecked my lips matter-of-factly, and then grinned triumphantly. I put on my best smile for the people, but it didn't match my eyes, and somewhere in the crowd was a person who knew the truth. My brother Cole had graduated with honors from ITT Technical Institute as a drafting engineer in June. An exceptionally brilliant student, he had learned to ask critical questions to fully understand the object of his studies. Feeling like his sisters were each being auctioned off to the highest bidder at the whim of our Prophet, he left the reception early. I felt he was the last of those who truly cared about my destiny.

That night, after the wedding festivities were over and the crowds had departed, Rulon's wives were still enjoying the celebratory energy. They mistook my melancholy countenance as wedding-day jitters. We made our way down the hall slowly to his office, a few new sister-wives giggling at me, while others helped our elderly husband get there safely. We entered Rulon's office, and my sister-wives set Rulon and me down on the visitors' couch. I was grateful to see them perch around us, not yet ready to leave.

"Father, can we get you a glass of wine?" one of them asked. He nodded cheerfully and accepted the alcoholic beverage. I was not surprised. Although for well over a century Mormons had believed in the "Word of Wisdom" from the revelations written in the Doctrine and Covenants that strictly discouraged alcoholic drinks, tea, and coffee (as well as tobacco, narcotics, and overconsumption of meat), the FLDS had long argued that the Mormons had cowardly set aside the Celestial Law of polygamy for the lesser law of the Word of Wisdom. We believed the WOW was more of a suggestion, and these items were commonly imbibed among many of the FLDS. My father, who had been through the Mormon temple before partaking of plural marriage, still did not have alcohol in our cupboards at home, but the Prophet liked his wine, liquor, and coffee. Among the people it was felt that as he had the courage to live the *higher* law, his drinking was considered morally justified.

Rulon winked at me as he sipped carefully from his glass, and another wife unclipped his tie. When they handed me my own glass, I sat, blinking at it. I had never consumed alcohol before. The liquid was shockingly nasty and dry, though surprisingly warm in my throat. The heat from my sips seemed to creep all the way down into my stomach. In the company of all these women and in the spirit of the festivities, I almost let my guard down. Then one of my sister-wives spoke.

"She could stay with you tonight," Ora giggled.

"That's a great idea!" Rulon agreed, and my heart leaped back into my throat, all comfort and warmth forgotten. I tried not to panic as each sister-wife said good night. These women, who had played a variety of roles in my life—as teachers, mentors, cousins, aunt, and sister—hugged us before parading out of the room. Christine was the last to go, sashaying happily, her long skirt swinging and swaying. Just before she shut the heavy oak door, she turned to us with a playful smile upon her face, and then playfully waved her fingers good-bye. She was gone.

Under Uncle Warren's strict edicts, I had genuinely taken a lot of comfort from a society that told us men were snakes and prohibited girls from being alone with them. So now, alone with Rulon, I had no idea even what to say.

Does it matter? He can read my mind. He knows my heart. He's not a man. He's the Prophet.

Rulon motioned to me to help him up. I'd never imagined that my wedding night would involve a crash course in geriatric care, but my new husband was older than my grandpa Wall. Rulon was very tall, and it took all of my strength to get him up. He leaned on my arm and we shuffled to his bathroom, one small step at a time. I had never realized how unstable he was. I helped him into the small bathroom, where he placed his hands upon the guardrails.

"Now go upstairs and get your nightgown on," he commanded. I left him there, hanging on to the railing, and went to Ora's room, where I had left my purple duffel bag. My aunt wasn't there, and it was a relief to be alone with my thoughts as I stepped out of my wedding gown. It had been extremely stressful for me to be in the presence of the Prophet, since it meant I was in the presence of God—just me and him.

Come on, I told myself. *You can get through this.*

Mechanically, I slipped on my nightgown and looked at myself in Ora's bathroom mirror. The gown, which I had sewn myself, was beautiful. It was simple but soft and silky, even over my long underwear. My robe, though, was almost too elegant—a soft, pink georgette with one long, asymmetric ruffle, made from the same soft fabric as the gown. But all I could see were my frightened eyes, like those of a cornered rabbit on Grandfather Steed's farm. Taking a determined breath, I descended again to the Prophet's room. When I arrived, he was sitting at his desk, grinning at me.

"Well, hello, sweetheart!" He motioned to me and I pulled him up out of his chair again, using my whole body to steady him. He motioned to a wall partition that divided his office from his bedroom. We went around the right-hand side, where one lamp illuminated a sparsely furnished bedroom. There was a king-sized bed, a bedside table, a gold-and-tan Schwinn exercise bicycle, and an oxygen machine.

Carefully shuffling to the foot of the bed, where he faced me, he used my weight as leverage to lower himself onto the bed. With all my strength, I held him carefully until he set himself down. Abruptly he tapped the top button of his white dress shirt.

I scrambled to unbutton it, embarrassed that he had to ask me that way and nearly forgetting I was undressing a grown man. I had helped my younger siblings prepare for bed, but I had never imagined I would have to help the Prophet undress. Kneeling at his feet, I silently undid the rest of the buttons. My fingers trembled, but I refused to look at his face. He was unable to undo his own cuffs, so I did that, too, surprised at how smooth and superthin his skin felt.

He pointed to the bike, where I hung his shirt; then he began tapping again—only this time it was on his suit pants button. My mind was racing. As I unzipped his pants, the sound filled me with horrific panic. It took me a moment to realize the last time I had heard it was when I was locked in my half brother's room as a child, right before I escaped.

I choked back bile and rising fear, but Rulon didn't notice my watery eyes. He leaned back.

"Now pull," he demanded. I had to tug his pants down to his hips and then pull them off.

Wearing only his long undergarments, he stared at me for a long moment. It felt sacrilegious for me to be alone with him this way. I kept my head bowed until he was ready to move back onto the bed. Lifting his legs as he instructed, I pushed his body into a more comfortable position, and tucked a pillow beneath his knees. He didn't get under the covers. Instead, he had me pull up the crocheted sea-foam-and-cream tasseled blanket that lay folded on the bottom of his bed.

Suddenly he patted the bed beside him. I stared at him for a moment, and then carefully removed my robe and placed it beside his shirt and pants on the bike. I was about to get on the bed when he remembered his oxygen. I helped place the clear tubing precisely into his nostrils and behind his ears. The purr of the machine filled the room as Rulon got settled. Once again, he patted the spot next to him. Gingerly, I went around the other side and lay down, as far on the other side of the bed as I could. Again, he patted the spot right next to him, this time rather impatiently. I reluctantly pulled myself as near as I could without touching him. I couldn't breathe. He turned onto his elbow, and the strain of it holding him up caused the whole bed to shake.

With surprising strength, however, he roughly pulled me to him with his other arm and kissed me. It was over before I realized what had happened. Then he kissed me again, and my whole body shook from disgust. The slobber from his mouth was still on my lips, and though I flinched, I didn't dare wipe it off. He held on to me for a long moment before pushing himself away.

"Good night, sweetheart," he said. "A kiss is enough for tonight." He turned over, and I stared at the back of his head.

A kiss is enough? Enough of what?

Within moments Rulon's breath came even and deep, the hum of the oxygen machine the only other sound in the room. I inched myself away from him to the far edge of the bed. I usually never had trouble dozing off, but his words troubled me. I lay wide awake, not daring to move. I was alone in bed with a man. Not just any man—a man as close to God as any man on earth would ever be.

I had been groomed for this my entire life. Surely marriage to my Prophet was supposed to be divine. So why didn't it feel the least bit

Heavenly? I was related to plenty of women who had married under similar circumstances. Mama Ida married my grandfather Steed at twenty, when he was seventy-eight. Aunt Shirley had been just seventeen when she married Uncle Roy, age eighty. And my own aunt Bonnie—now Ora, my sister-wife—had married Rulon when she was twenty and he was eighty. My situation was normal, I tried to reassure myself.

Suddenly Rulon lurched in his sleep and our feet touched. I recoiled instinctively and gripped the covers in fear. My heart had just started to beat normally again when Rulon began making gasping noises like a big fish out of water. Once again I panicked, ready to jump out of bed and run for help.

Rulon began to breathe again—normal breaths—and went right back to sleep.

I just stared at him, adrenaline coursing through my veins. I longed to just sleep on the floor, though I was pretty sure that would be severely frowned upon. Just before dawn, I fell into a fitful sleep, only to have an endless loop of nightmares play, nightmares that involved Uncle Warren and my new husband leaning on my arms, crushing me with all of their weight.

The next morning Rulon crisply informed me that he had breakfast served to him every day at seven a.m. sharp. He sent me upstairs to get dressed, admonishing me to hurry. When I rushed back down, I learned from the next sister-wife companion for Rulon that my sister-wives and I would all take turns being on duty with him. That meant that we took care of his every need during our twenty-four-hour watch, including the overnight stretch. I had taken over the night portion of one wife's watch, so now it was another wife's turn. Rulon kept track of who he was staying with in the order in which they were married. I quickly calculated in my head. *Nineteen wives, eighteen of them still living . . . between his Salt Lake and Hildale wives' schedules, perhaps it would be nearly three weeks between shifts.* A sense of guilty relief rushed over me.

I entered the dining room to discover that my sister-wives had made a special place for me—to the Prophet's right on the foldout bench. Unconsciously, I think I had been waiting for the type of fallout my mother had faced from Irene. I had just spent the night with *their husband,* and yet I was met with kindness and sincere smiles. As I sat, I discovered another unspoken protocol in the Jeffs household: near silence during meals while the Prophet ate. After the meal was through, however, the wives resumed a lively conversation. Ora, who sat next to me, chatted animatedly.

"Becky's family from Canada is asking if she and I can go for a hike in the mountains today before they leave town, Father," Ora announced. My face went white, and I glanced sideways through my lashes at Rulon. What would he think?

"Up the canyon?" he asked.

"Yes, to Secret Lake."

He studied Ora carefully, and then turned to me.

"Do you want to go?" he asked.

"Yes!" The word leaped out of my throat before I could contain it. Some of my sister-wives looked at me in surprise.

"Look at that," he chuckled. "My new bride would rather go hiking with her cousins than spend the day with me." I flushed deeply. I had messed up again! Although the Prophet seemed good-natured about it, I didn't dare leave to get ready for the hike until long after breakfast was over.

My cousins picked me up, and as we made our way up the canyon, I was awed by the changing colors. We spent the day hiking, picking wildflowers, and laughing. When it was time to turn back around and hike down the mountain, I felt suddenly heavy and exhausted. There was such an element of expectation in being one of the Prophet's wives. My future seemed joyless, and I was afraid of letting everyone down— not just my family, but all of my people. After I said good-bye to my cousins, I watched their taillights disappear into the distance.

Upon entering the house, I discovered that the Prophet was flying out to Short Creek that Monday, and I was to go with him. It had been determined in my absence that I would move to Rulon's Hildale mansion because they had run out of room in his Salt Lake residence. Christine told me Rulon said he wanted to show off his new bride to the people.

I felt a strange glow, and while I was packing I got excited, in spite of myself. Even though this marriage wasn't what I had dreamed of, perhaps I was genuinely appreciated. I remembered my father's words and realized I had a choice—I could enjoy being married to Rulon or

I could be miserable. I pondered that for a while, and my gaze rested on some flowers on the dresser. For my wedding, I had amassed a very large number of long-stemmed red rose buds, every stem wrapped with a note from each one of Rulon Jeffs's children who were still at home, my students, and each of my seventeen living new sister-wives. The roses were beginning to bloom, and I realized it could represent a bouquet of love. I read several seemingly heartfelt messages from women I deeply admired and loved, including Christine and Ora. I was not used to people making such a fuss over me, but note by note, I began to feel accepted into the Jeffses' home.

Christine, who thankfully would be accompanying me, suggested I bring the bouquet with me, to enjoy the beauty of the roses while it lasted. I felt like royalty holding them as Warren's older brother from the same mother, LeRoy Jeffs, picked us up at the door in Rulon's Lincoln Town Car to take us to the airport. There we would board the Learjet the FLDS leased for the Prophet to fly back and forth between Salt Lake City and Colorado City.

The pilots and staff were very respectful, and Wendell Loy Nielsen, known as Uncle Wendell, watched over the whole process carefully. While I had been on a Cessna with my dad, who was a pilot, I had never before traveled on a large plane—much less a jet. This one was stocked with an array of sodas and sugary junk food that most FLDS members were discouraged from stocking their cupboards with, which somehow added to the thrill.

Uncle Wendell fixed Rulon a Bloody Mary, and we settled in for the short flight. As we landed, movement outside caught my eye. Security guards lined up to greet Rulon, and I was soberly reminded of my duties as the Prophet's wife. I decided I would do everything I could to be a caring Prophet's wife among the people. Holding my bouquet, I carefully descended the stairs into the hot stillness of the southern Utah sun, secretly praying I wouldn't trip.

We drove straight to the Jeffs property, where the Prophet's home was located, a sprawling mansion, which, over the next seven years, would eventually entail six massive wings built into the shape of a giant letter P. Several hundred thousand square feet, the mansion was surrounded by a lush green lawn and hundreds of trees—an oasis of sorts in the middle of the desert town, totally encircled by gates, tall hedges, privacy fences, and security cameras. Eventually Seth, Nephi, and War-ren would build houses on the property, creating a Jeffs family estate even more colossal than the Salt Lake City one. A prominent citizen of Hildale and member of the church had built much of the original man-sion with his own money and labor for his family. I came to understand that Rulon acquired the house much as he had acquired his new home in SLC. He saw it, he wanted it, and despite the fact the man had built it to house his own family, Rulon got what he wanted—another perfect reminder that no one said no to the Prophet.

At dinner that night, all of Uncle Rulon's "Hildale wives," the over-flow wives who did not fit in his Salt Lake City home, were just as kind and gracious as their city counterparts had been.

"Sit here by Father!" they cried, guiding me to the place of honor at his side. Again, the atmosphere during the meal was grimly quiet as we ate the fine food, but afterward there was plenty of chatter and revelry. I still didn't know quite what to say, so I remained silent.

Abruptly, Rulon pounded the table to get our attention.

"So, ladies," he drawled, patting his belly. "Are you ready for two more?" Marjorie and Christine, along with the other women, exchanged puzzled looks.

"What, Father?" someone asked. "Two more of what?"

"Two more wives!" he boasted, and beamed at us.

I felt astonishment ripple over me and through the room as I looked at the shocked faces around me.

"Yes, this Saturday," he continued, "we've got two more coming: Helen and Rebecca Steed, daughters of Lawrence Steed." He turned to me. "Three young 'uns! Isn't that great? I told them you were on deck, and that they had to wait."

I just sat there, mute. Christine stared, still horrified.

Marjorie glanced at us nervously. "How . . . *exciting*, Father!" she said, her enthusiasm sounding contrived. "I went to school with Helen." The rest of the wives murmured niceties and congratulations to Rulon, but they kept glancing my way. Christine's expression changed to one of pity and sorrow, but I couldn't look at her any longer. My head felt like it was about to explode.

I turned my anger inward, on myself. *You fool! You damn fool! And you thought you mattered? And what is this "on deck"? What the hell is that? Why had there been this great rush for me, then?* Just when I had begun to think that I could do this—that I could fulfill my role as the Prophet's wife—it'd been made clear that in my five-day-old marriage, I was simply another number. And there'd be another Rebecca? I wondered if I would be given a different name just like Ora had.

Staring down at my cup, my heart ached with a kind of pain I had never known. But I couldn't show it. I knew quite well what was expected of me. As the Prophets taught, there was no room for jealousy in an eternal, Celestial marriage. Doing all the right things meant an increase in blessings in the world to come. In fact, not only was my husband likely to obtain even more wives on this earth; that number would increase exponentially in the hereafter, as it would for every man faithful to the Work. As the Prophet, then, he would marry thousands, if not millions, more women in the Celestial Kingdom of God.

I looked at the examples these women had already set for me—their kindness and charity. I had been taught that envy was a manifestation of evil, and the last thing I wanted was to be an ungrateful sister-wife, or anything resembling Mother Irene. I tried to alleviate the crushing sadness inside of me. Christine reached underneath the table and gripped my hand. I held on to it for comfort.

A little later I numbly helped wash dishes, eager to be excused. I left the room with as much dignity as I could muster, but as soon as I was out of sight, I fled down the stairs to my room. Flinging myself on the bed, I sobbed into my pillow like a little child, tears soaking the fabric. Not long after, Christine quietly let herself in.

"I don't know why this happened, Becky," she said, her expression filled with compassion. "God never gives you something you can't get through." Though she meant well, her words felt empty. God seemed to be overestimating my abilities.

A few days later, the entire Jeffs family came down to Short Creek. I was happy to see Paula, Cecilia, and Naomi, three of my sister-wives from Salt Lake. They were kind and bright to my face, but Christine told me later they had quietly asked, "How is Becky?" Not one of them openly expressed sorrow or indignation, though. Decorum wouldn't allow that.

I was shocked by my own sadness. I certainly didn't love Rulon Jeffs as anything more than my Prophet, and I had never wanted to be married to him. But something in my heart died that day. I had to throw away the authentic Becky, keep sweet, and do what was expected.

When Saturday night arrived, I joined my sister-wives in singing to the Prophet and his new brides: "We Are Blessed of the Lord to Be the Prophet's Family." My voice faltered, but I carefully mouthed the words. Rulon's daughter Rachel, whom I had always looked up to as Warren's assistant and a teacher, held my hand as we sang. We never spoke about it, then or even later, but I loved her forever for that gesture of kindness.

The weekend of the wedding, I helped out where I could, though I ducked out of much of the socializing. Later, I happened to walk past the kitchen, where I overheard my sister-wife Mother Ruth commenting to Mother LaRue that the two of them had been put out to pasture.

"It's only a matter of time for the others," she said plainly. That struck me hard. I could see how they were suffering from the pain of growing older as their husband added these new, exciting young brides to the family. They had done their duty—even bore him children and raised them. Yet day in and day out, he rarely acknowledged them.

As I pondered this, I realized I didn't want to set myself up to be hurt like them—nor did I want to hurt another wife. I decided to set aside my own desire for love. That night I slammed the door shut on my heart and locked it tight.

Rulon and I headed to Salt Lake City with Helen and her sister to make their debut there. My honeymoon was over, and I would be heading back to Alta to teach. It had been decided that Rebecca Fern Steed would go by "Fern" because she had a middle name. I didn't let it hurt to have the young wives come up to Salt Lake with us. I didn't let it hurt that I was to be a Hildale overflow wife because Rulon had so many wives. I consoled myself with the fact that now that there were twenty-one wives, I would have to be on duty with the Prophet even less often. This unrealistic expectation would prove to be my downfall. I soon learned I would be forced to be with my aging husband twice a month or more. Out of the twenty-one wives, thirteen of us were among the group of Rulon's "young wives." It made me sick and a little angry inside to realize that he stayed only with his young wives at night—from Ora on down. He didn't bother to bed or sleep with or even hold any of his older wives.

Warren Jeffs picked us up from the airport in the Town Car, and we settled into the backseat. My new relationship with my former principal was awkward. He was now my son, but I still called him Uncle Warren. It was strange to hear him call me "Mother Becky."

Warren peered into the rearview mirror to see me sitting beside Rulon.

"Ooooh, Father!" he snickered, "there you are with your new young bride! Why don't you give her a *big* kiss?"

I was shocked by Uncle Warren's words, but even more so when Rulon put his arm around me and began to kiss me in front of everyone—and not the matter-of-fact kisses I had experienced so far. I pulled back from his slobbery lips and tongue with hot embarrassment and shame, as the girls to the side of me giggled nervously. I kept my eyes to the floor of the car almost the entire ride home, but at one point I glanced up to see Warren grinning lasciviously at me in the rearview mirror. *The man who taught me that men and boys were snakes!* I hated the confusion in my brain, but also I hated him in that moment, and how he made me feel dirty.

CHAPTER 7

For the Pleasure of the Gods

Once I'd settled into the Hildale house, I turned my attention back to Alta Academy, where I continued to help out as an assistant teacher, flying back and forth weekly in the Learjet with Rulon. I was still considered a Hildale overflow wife, since I had to share a room in Salt Lake when I came up to teach.

All too soon, my next turn on duty with Rulon arrived, which provided a crash course of a different sort. That evening, after getting Rulon settled into bed, I climbed in, and again he demanded that I lie right beside him. This time he tried to reach his hand down my nightgown, which I had sewn very carefully and modestly in accordance with church teachings. He became angry that the neckline allowed access only above the top bra line, but I was relieved until he began to fondle and pinch me through the fabric. Not only was it painful; I was embarrassed and felt dirty again. The next morning after I went off duty, I took the longest shower I had ever taken in my life. I went about my day as a zombie, pitching in where I could and wanting the buzzing in my head to stop.

The following morning I woke up late and lay for a long time in my own bed, the pillow covering my face. Throughout my life, despite all of the trauma and abuse I'd faced, I had never felt without hope. Not until now.

An hour later I looked at the clock. It was almost noon and I was still in bed. And yet there was no reason to rise. I was not on duty with Rulon. I was not on kitchen duty or expected at school. In fact, if I died right there in that bed, I thought, no one except Christine would even think to come looking for me. I knew I was being overdramatic, but it didn't ease the loneliness.

Finally, I made a decision. I realized that whether my life was going to matter to anyone, anywhere, it was up to me. Somehow, somewhere, *I would give meaning to others.*

For the next several months, I threw myself into teaching as a measure of sanity. I was trying to decipher my purpose in the Jeffs family, especially what role I had to play with my husband. Every time I was on duty, he took more and more liberties, demanding I do as he asked. I could not wait for each shift to be over, and to be able to breathe for a week or two.

Seeming to appreciate my decorum at church and in meetings, Rulon frequently asked me to accompany him in public. I was happy to please him in this safe capacity, and when we were in the midst of the people, I loved being able to interact with them. It was about this time, however, that I discovered a deeper, darker truth about the Jeffs family and the hierarchy of the Priesthood leadership.

One of these telling episodes occurred in 1996, the week after all our people gathered together for our annual April Conference in Short Creek. The sermons from the pulpit with Rulon and the other leaders were just what I had expected: we were admonished to be a God-like people. Every one of the talks contained calls for repentance and continued morality, and the day was generally concluded with exhortations to be the caliber of people that would please the Lord—and the stern warnings of what would happen if we were not.

Before the leaders scattered back to their homes, I accompanied the Prophet to a luncheon for our leaders at his favorite Chinese restaurant, located near 8600 South and 1300 East in Sandy. The proprietors of the restaurant called him "Grandpa" and scurried about to cater to his needs. Rulon; LeRoy Jeffs; Warren Jeffs; Winston Blackmore; another well-known Priesthood leader, Ron Rohbock; and my sister-wife Naomi and I were ushered over to a private table in an isolated corner of the restaurant. As soon as we sat down, our waitress rushed to fill our water glasses and take our order. She was wearing bright red lipstick, which was doubly banned in our religion because it was makeup and it was red. She was also extremely well-endowed, which was clear from her tightly fitted shirt. To make matters worse, as she bent over to talk to Rulon, who was hard of hearing, her cleavage was on display.

Our orders taken, she rushed to the kitchen, and Warren and LeRoy were suddenly at it, saying things like "Did you see how big her boobs are?" and "Did you see those things in my face?" I was shocked. Warren Jeffs, who for all of these years had been piously telling my cousins, brothers, and friends *never* to look at any part of a woman's body or allow lascivious thoughts to enter their minds, was speaking in a way I had never heard before.

Ten minutes later, every one of these "holy, God-like men" was still on the same topic.

"My wife's boobs are so big," chuckled LeRoy, "she says she has to buy an over-the-shoulder boulder-holder." Everyone, including Rulon, joined in the laughter.

"Make mine a pebble holder," giggled Naomi. The Prophet, still laughing, turned to me.

"Hers are pretty good!" he said, and proceeded to grab my breasts and begin fondling them. I pushed his hands away, trembling with shame and embarrassment, as everyone else at the table erupted in laughter.

Weren't these the same men who in conference on Sunday had been condemning people for their immoral desires? And yet my husband, the great "man of God," had publicly humiliated me. I was sickened by the double standard the powerful benefited from. Had they caught a group of young men talking like that at Alta Academy, those boys would have been expelled immediately—not just from school, but from the church and society, too.

The men continued, now talking about the bodies of *other* FLDS men's wives, many of them women I was related to by blood or friendship. I sat there silently fuming until the waitress brought the food and they finally shut up. *What do they say about me when I'm not here?* I wondered.

From that point on, I busied myself with teaching school so I always had a reason not to accompany the Prophet to any more meetings. And whenever possible, I slipped out of being on duty with my husband.

*   *   *

When I didn't have to deal with Priesthood leadership or Rulon in the bedroom, I found that I could enjoy much of life as the Prophet's wife. I started teaching with Mother Paula, my sister-wife, and I could tell we were having an impact on the schoolchildren we worked with. Paula, my first cousin and Uncle Merrill Jessop's daughter, confided stories to me of her early life. Her father married four women, and Paula and I had both seen ugly ramifications of sister-wife jealousy and vicious infighting. Sometimes, like in the case of Merrill, men used these jealousies to gain further control over their wives and children. Paula once stood up to her father, calling him out on his treatment of her mother, Ruth. While this altercation didn't change the dynamics of her home, it had changed something inside of her. She carried a level of self-respect that most FLDS women did not.

I think having come from similar circumstances, we had great compassion for the children in our classroom who reminded us of our siblings. Together we sought to love, validate, and strengthen all the children in whatever way we could.

In the Prophet's home, I was becoming much closer with my sister-wives. I discovered there was a strict if unofficial pecking order that I'd only had a glimpse of before I married into the Jeffs family: a hierarchy among the older wives, who had borne Rulon children, and a hierarchy among the younger wives as well.

Ora had been the first of Rulon's newer, younger wives. She had enjoyed only several months with him before he married again. Naomi, however, had enjoyed over a year as the Prophet's newest darling before he married Mary Fischer and Marjorie Fischer. That had seemed unfair to the others, especially since Rulon seemed to want Naomi by his side wherever he went. I soon discovered there was much more to it than her sweet manners.

When Mother Ruth had to be moved to the bottom level because climbing stairs had become too strenuous, Naomi was moved into her old room across the hall from Rulon—to the chagrin of several wives, particularly Mother Ora. But in the Prophet's household, wives were not allowed to have disagreements, so animosity manifested itself in unusual ways.

Earlier that year, before I had joined the Jeffs household, Ora had designed and sewn two matching dresses. They were quite stylish and daring for our people, with low-waisted bodices that looked like jackets over short (three inches below the knee!) green pleated skirts. Ora had presented one as a gift to our sister-wife Cecilia, whom I adored. Cecilia, also a newer and younger wife, was thrilled. She was lean but had womanly curves and often couldn't quite fit in the dress.

"Just 'cause you can button it up," Cecilia had said, winking at me, "doesn't mean you should wear it. I can only wear it on a skinny, skinny day!" Recently she had given it away to stick-thin Naomi, and Ora had come unglued.

"If you're not going to wear it, give it back!" she spat. Cecilia had been horrified, her tender heart never meaning to offend. She quickly realized the rivalry between Ora and Naomi, and her story had been a friendly warning for me to tread lightly.

All in all, the wives got along amazingly well, bonded together in their strong desire to please the Prophet and be an example to the community. I had come to realize that Rulon was not always easy to satisfy, with his superstrict schedules and high expectations. On a deeper level, Rulon had never gotten over the loss of his first wife. At the urging of his young wives, he would tell us about Zola, the daughter of a high-ranking official in the Mormon Church.

"I remember walking her up the stairs when I took her home the first time," Rulon would relate. "When she turned to say good night, I gave her a peck, and ran down the stairs, knocking over a garbage can on the way out!" We'd laugh and laugh, but we couldn't help but notice the longing look in his eyes. His face and his voice never reflected such yearning in speaking about his other wives, even Mother Marilyn, Warren's mother. Zola and her father had a strong testimony of the mainstream Mormon Church, which had shunned polygamy and extremism. She divorced him, refusing to join Rulon in the Work. He never saw his first wife again.

One Saturday afternoon when work meeting had ended and it had finally grown quiet on the Prophet's estate, Naomi asked me to go for a walk. Young, with strawberry-blonde hair and lovely features, Naomi was also rail thin, probably only ninety-eight pounds in her layers of clothes. I knew little about her, except that in the Jeffs hierarchy of wives, Naomi was definitely near the very top.

"I don't know *why* Uncle Rulon favors me," Naomi said, as we made laps around the property. Her voice was very sweet, but her eyes told a different story. I had seen that she was passive-aggressive, not letting anyone tread on her territory as a favored wife. Naomi shared some stories from her point of view, and like Cecilia, I began to realize there were more undercurrents of jealousy than I had thought.

"One time Mother Julia came to me, after Uncle Rulon and I had only been married for a few months," explained Naomi, sounding innocent. "She asked me, 'What do you *do* with Father, specifically?' I said, 'Well, I just do whatever he wants me to.' But Mother Julia insisted, 'I need to know exactly, because I want to keep him alive and happy.' So...I told her exactly what I did...and guess what? She got kind of mad at me! 'You do *that*?' she cried, and I responded 'Well, he *is* my husband, Lord, and Master.'"

She looked at me, waiting for me to respond, but I couldn't meet her eyes. I did *not* want to know the specifics. I suddenly understood the term "sugar wife" and realized what Naomi was. She did whatever it took to please Rulon in the bedroom. I shivered, also realizing that I had no desire to earn that title with the Prophet, not after what I had already experienced.

"Mother Julia may have been mad at me that day," Naomi continued, "but later on, she came back and confided something in me." Her voice got really low, and she glanced to make sure we couldn't be overheard. "You know that she only had two children with Rulon?"

I nodded.

"Well, Mother Julia said, 'Do not *ever, ever* tell Father no. I did once, and he has never come to me again!'"

I was shocked. How could he withhold his affections, as well as the prospect of more children, from someone like Mother Julia, who adored him and their children, just because she had said no *just once*? It was simply cruel.

Naomi shrugged it off, saying that *she* would never tell the Prophet no. As we made another lap around the yard, I began to realize that Naomi had come with an agenda for our walk. Her first goal seemed to have been sorting out what kind of competition I was in the bedroom. Now that she realized I was not in the running for Rulon's sexual affection, I think she decided to take me on as a pet project, to teach me to be *more* satisfying to the Prophet in the bedroom.

That was confusing to me, but I guessed that by making the Prophet happier, she would maintain her spot on the top rung. If she could train me to do things Rulon wanted, he would be pleased, and her influence inside and outside the bedroom would be magnified. Not just one of many wives, Naomi seemed determined to have influence even when she was off duty. I was not happy about where this conversation was going, but Naomi persisted.

"You know how very important it is to please Father!" she began. "We must do everything we can to make sure he stays virile and healthy!" Her tone was instructional at first but became slower and more sensual. "Now, he really likes you to rub his chest. Fondle his nipples. Then make your way down his tummy, and slowly move in. He likes you to stroke..." I blocked out the rest of what she said. I hated the feel of Rulon's hands on me; I hated when he shoved his tongue down my throat, or tried to stuff himself inside me. I couldn't imagine doing what she was describing. Though my mind was far away, I got the gist of it: I was supposed to be more aggressive in bed, though I was admonished not to be too aggressive, as that was also frowned upon.

What I was not prepared for, however, was to discover shortly afterward that it wasn't only Rulon's edicts to me in the bedroom I was going to have to handle. Just as Naomi wanted to nose her way into our intimate relationship, so did Rulon's son Warren.

CHAPTER 8

Destroyed in the Flesh

As my principal, Warren expected me to check in like a wife would do to her husband. I still had no desire to waste hours of my time in his hallway. Anytime I didn't want to be obedient to him, Warren noticed and made it difficult to enjoy my work. I felt suffocated by his double standards for men and women, and for his personal behavior and what he expected of his pupils. When he went on a rampage expelling students and getting after some of my brothers again, I wanted to yell, *You hypocrite!*

In public, I put on a brave face, but Mother Paula saw right through me. She took me for a walk one afternoon, enjoying a warm rock by the edge of the water near the irrigation pond. There I confided in her more than I ever had to anyone, opening up to her about my struggles with Warren.

"Uncle Warren is not your husband, Becky. He cannot dictate what you do unless you allow it."

I stared at her. No one had ever said anything even remotely like that concerning Warren. I had been taught to obey him without question. She planted the seed that it was literally my choice if I came back that fall or the next to teach at Alta Academy. While my heart hurt to think about leaving my students, I suddenly felt an enormous sense of relief.

To be free and away from Warren sounded more delicious than anything I could imagine. But I didn't know if I had the courage to go through with it. Somehow I felt constantly under Warren's thumb.

I helped Christine choreograph the operetta, our yearly music and dance performance that the chorus class did each spring for the community. I went through the motions and did what I could, though I felt like a zombie on autopilot. I had realized that if I left teaching at Alta, I would have very little reason to go on. Sure, I would be free from Warren, but I would also be away from anything else that gave my life meaning. That evening I was leaving the grocery store when I ran into my beloved aunt Martha, who had moved with her family to Colorado City when the Prophet had entrusted a new calling in the church to Uncle Jim. I greeted her enthusiastically. How I had missed her!

After hugging me, my aunt stepped back and looked at my face. Unlike anyone except Paula, she saw past my smiles to the dark circles under my eyes and the pain behind them.

"What is happening with you, Becky?" she asked. In that moment I knew I could trust her. I took a breath and laid my soul bare, confessing to my aunt all of my pent-up sadness and the fact that I was just another body in Rulon Jeffs's home.

Aunt Martha listened to me sympathetically, then looked directly into my eyes.

"You need to get involved in the community. Find somewhere where you belong, Becky, or it will kill you. You're so very young, with a whole life to live. You must find a place where you are needed, and you need to give and serve until you forget yourself."

I went home that night and crawled into bed, curling up into a fetal position. I knew she was right, but where could I give of myself that it would make a difference? Where could I be so needed as to forget my worries? And where Warren couldn't crush me?

The next day I arrived early to the operetta rehearsals. Christine was just as creative and energetic as ever. After a little while, I noticed several points at which things were not operating efficiently, or where the teens and children felt a bit confused in the production. I threw myself into the day and directed the participants without encroaching on Christine's toes. Before the day was over, I could tell my help was making a real difference.

That night, I again climbed into my bed exhausted, but with excitement in my bones. I might be powerless to change Warren's mind about the worthiness of my own brothers, but there were young people in need of help right where I was. One of them, Samantha, came to talk to me afterward about struggles she was facing in the community and her family. We talked for a long time and became fast friends.

At the next practice, I watched carefully. Many of these kids were just numbers in their households, too, and several of them sat very low on the hierarchal totem pole in our society. When we praised them for a job well done, I saw them shine with a new light. I could validate them, and most important, I could love them.

Three hundred fifteen miles away from Salt Lake City, I had found my home.

I kept flying back and forth between Short Creek and Salt Lake City, to stay involved with the practices but teach school during the week. Our first performance of the operetta *In Grand Old Switzerland* was a monumental success. As usual, the entire community came out, and they enjoyed the fresh spin that Christine and I had put on it, especially with the dancing we'd added to the production. What gave me the most pleasure was not the delighted applause from the audience, but the radiant smiles of the cast. I was hooked.

That summer of 1996, Christine and I choreographed our first dance of young daughters of the community for the 24th of July Pioneer Day Celebration. Costumed in sweet white dresses with blue-and-white-checkered cummerbunds, straw hats, and sunflowers, the performers were a sensation, and Rulon was charmed by the singing and dancing. I loved connecting with the ladies and showing my husband that I was using my talents to please him.

There was another place I was obligated to please my husband, but I was not "living up to my duties." That very summer, Warren Jeffs put me in my place. One afternoon, he summoned me to his Hildale office to say, "Mother Becky, it has come to my attention that you do not always do your duty. You must get close to Father."

My heart fell. Getting "close" with my husband was Warren's way of talking about marital relations, specifically sex. He was damn right I was not getting close with his father! I had even told Rulon about my childhood accident with the rusty bike, because when he would get on top of me in the night, his fingers and his manhood were excruciatingly painful every time. It had been hard for me to be that open and vulnerable, but he had acted so kind at first that I thought he would understand. Before long, though, he seemed even more determined to get his way, ignoring my tears of pain, anguish, and humiliation.

When I could not devise a Priesthood-approved way of avoiding my shift, I had deciphered an ingenious way to please the Prophet while ensuring he did not touch me. Each night on duty, I would massage his sore and troubled feet until he fell asleep. Deep inside, I knew I was being manipulative in order not to be used for his pleasure. It had worked for a while, but apparently my husband was not pleased with my progress in being a "comfort wife," the term the Prophet used to describe one who would submit to all of her husband's "earthly" demands in bed.

Warren must have seen something in my eyes, for he said, more firmly this time, "You *will* get close to your husband. You must foster a serving relationship with him. If you have a problem with that, talk to him."

When I left Warren's office, I slipped back into the black mood that had threatened to take me before. At one time I had felt that it was God's will that I be with Rulon. Over time it became disturbingly clear that marriages were *not* divinely orchestrated "by God's will to the Prophet's mouth"—as reinforced by scripture and Warren's lectures and tapes—but instead decided over dinner conversations by sister-wives and power-hungry fathers.

On multiple occasions my sister-wives would take delight in going in to the mouthpiece of God to say, "Don't you think that this particular man and woman would make a cute couple?" Almost immediately, the match would take place.

In addition, many of my sister-wives had beautiful little sisters. Whether it was their idea or not, I observed fathers coming to bargain with the Prophet concerning their younger daughters.

When one such deal was struck, a father came in for his daughter's wedding luncheon proudly displaying *two* sixteen-year-old daughters, one on each arm, like a man coming to market with his finest goods. They were not twins, but from different mothers. The bride's face shone with great hope and excitement, ready to be validated and take her place of honor beside the Prophet. In complete contradiction to what was being spouted at the pulpit and in Warren's classrooms, however, the Prophet peered appraisingly at both girls.

"Which one is mine?" he asked.

The father looked at him eagerly. "Either one, or both!"

Rulon had a great laugh over that, but at that moment, I flushed in silent anger, watching the face of Rulon's new bride crumple. God had failed to send the beam of light directly to the Prophet, and he didn't even know which bride was his, despite her sacrifices and preparations for this great day. As the more submissive and obedient of the two, she became Rulon's bride while her sister was given to Rulon's grandson.

"Guess who wants to marry me now?" gloated Rulon one night at dinner not long after. Warren, a frequent guest at our table, was present.

"Who?" asked Warren.

Rulon mentioned a young girl whose father had come to visit him that day. Warren sniggered, and it wasn't lost on Rulon.

"Of course I won't marry her. She's a fat ass." Anyone who was not rail thin was often spoken of by the Jeffs men as a "fat ass" or "fat slob," making me and several of my sister wives self-conscious and self-critical. Worse, I watched more fathers frequent the Prophet's office and his table, desiring validation and standing in the community so much that they would put their daughters up on the auction block. Their biggest coup was when the Prophet would agree to take a daughter as his own wife.

Over the next seven years, Rulon would take on forty-six wives after me.

When I got married, I could not shake the feeling I had abandoned my siblings, despite it not being my choice. I kept an eye on them at school whenever possible, but disturbing reports came in of my younger siblings, especially the boys, struggling at home. As the Prophet's wives, Christine and I couldn't display any tolerance for rebellious behaviors, but whenever we had the opportunity to take the kids quietly aside, we tried to validate their good behaviors and beg them to get on the right track at school and home.

A definite rise in rebellious behavior had coincided with the arrival of my father's coveted third wife. We'd all been surprised to learn that our cousin Maggie, who was close to my age, would now be "Mother Maggie." The kids at home had been excited, and they tried to be good for the new wife. It became quickly apparent that any happiness would not last.

Mother Maggie had come from a very authoritarian home. My mother told me that Mother Maggie insisted that my father physically create order in the household. With an insane desire to please his new wife, he beat his children into submission. Mom was in mental anguish. When Irene had beaten us, our mother had looked to her husband for safety. Having him become the abuser just to please another wife broke her.

Irene sought out Maggie's sympathies, and the two combined forces against my mother. Maggie quickly showed herself to be resentful and manipulative toward my younger siblings, particularly Amelia. With Christine, Savannah, Brittany, and me all out of the house, the others were forced to fend for themselves.

Whenever I could, I would call my mother, but my father became so paranoid that she could speak to me only in the middle of the day when he was at work, or hide to talk on the phone. Speaking in code words—like *stormy* to indicate something was brewing, or *thunder* to say that my father was close by and she couldn't talk, because his temper or paranoia was flaring out of control—she filled me in about what was happening at home.

On Halloween night 1996, Cole was kicked out of the house when he attempted to save the younger kids from a severe beating. The next day, my mother called Christine and me.

"Your father wouldn't listen, and I knew if Cole tried to stay, even to protect us, he was in great danger. I had to...I had to drive him to the highway, and drop him off..." She burst into tears.

Cole was now completely alone in a wicked land. I couldn't speak. My beloved brother had been forced out of all of our lives.

A few days later, Mom received a phone call from Hyrum Smith, a well-known Utahan who worked for FranklinCovey, a Utah-based training business. Hyrum reported that he had picked Cole up from the side of the road and kindly drove him to Colorado. He said that Cole was one of the finest young men he had ever met, and that she should be very proud. We were grateful to know that Cole had arrived safely in Colorado, but the lines of communication were cut from there on out.

Cole was to be dead to us, and my brother, having no desire to "taint" us, would not contact any of us for five long years.

After Cole's expulsion, Mom finally confirmed rumors I'd heard that Trevor, Joshua, and Jordan were not only smoking; they had also started using drugs and alcohol and were going to rave parties—a word I'd never heard before she and Christine explained it. They tried to quit but were not successful for very long. The boys and Amelia all struggled with rebellious thoughts and behaviors. I knew what they were feeling, but I encouraged, cajoled, and reprimanded them. They had to be better; they just had to! The alternative—being cast out of the church into eternal damnation and becoming a son of perdition like Cole—was unthinkable. If they were having trouble now, I couldn't imagine what they were in for "out there."

Most kids who left or got kicked out of the FLDS ran into very real, very debilitating issues. Boys and girls who had lived all their lives to please their families, church, and Prophet were cut from family ties with no education. Ninety percent or more of them wound up heavily involved in drugs, alcohol, promiscuity, and prostitution, or as the victims of some kind of physical, emotional, or sexual abuse.

I was grateful the twins were working hard to be clean and sober. Joshua and Jordan had found employment with a world-famous knife maker, where they were working exceptionally hard and learning fast. But one week, I learned that Joshua had made brass knuckles, as many boys his age might forge in a shop class. While he was showing them off to one of my other brothers, Dad walked into the room and came at him with no explanation, crushing Joshua's fingers until they were bloodied and broken to punish him for having such a weapon. Our father felt totally justified in doing it, proving to Mother Maggie and Mother Irene that he, indeed, ruled his household.

In horror, Christine told Warren what was going on with our younger siblings, and he asked her to create a time line of our family and all of the abuse that had taken place through the years. She asked me to help her, as I had an uncanny memory, even for the incidents I wanted to forget. She then faxed it from Hildale to Warren's office in Salt Lake City and received a scathing response from him.

"*Never* fax a document like this again," he said caustically. "Don't you realize if it had fallen into the wrong hands, it could have brought the whole FLDS faith under condemnation?"

Within twenty-four hours, however, my father was the one con-demned and relieved of his Priesthood. Our mother and her children were packed up and sent to stay at Grandfather Steed's ranch in Widtsoe. This was a devastating shock. We were supposed to be a "forever family." I think Mom had hoped that the Prophet would step in and sternly lec-ture my dad, Maggie, and Irene to stop these abusive behaviors. She'd wanted to keep her children safe but had never expected this result.

With Rulon's permission, Christine and I immediately drove up to meet our mother and siblings at the ranch. We did our best to calm their fears, but I could read the misery in each of their eyes. Many fami-lies were already living in the overcrowded buildings on the ranch, so the only place for all of us to stay was bunked together in one large and crowded room. We had only a wood-burning stove for heat, so it was either blistering hot or bone-shaking cold. We were all expected to pull our weight on the farm, even in below-freezing temperatures. We cooked, cleaned, mucked stalls, and watched over livestock, among other arduous chores. Several of my siblings became ill, with Elissa catching the very worst of it.

A few weeks in, Mom received a phone call and asked me to stay with the kids while she and Christine were escorted to a mysterious meeting. We didn't hear from them for weeks. Tensions were running high among all the family members. While Grandfather Steed was alive, he had certainly been strict and severe, but music and laughter had pervaded the ranch. Now, many of our cousins saw fit to preach the word of God to my four younger and "wicked" brothers, Joshua, Jordan, Zach, and Levi. One night I walked out to the barn to discover that the twins were secretly plotting to run away. I stopped them, but I could hardly stand to hear the boys confide in me their open, bloody psychological wounds. They felt betrayed and abandoned by our father because of his behavior, especially since his new marriage, and knew that our mother had no power to protect them. I had felt a lot of judg-ment over my younger siblings' rebellion and use of drugs. The more I learned about the traumas they'd experienced, the more I understood.

As December turned to January, the situation remained strained, exacerbated by the fact that though pneumonia wracked Elissa's ten-year-old body, she was still expected to do heavy chores in the freez-ing cold and was getting worse. Without warning, our parents suddenly showed up together at the end of the month, ready to take everyone home again—and to start over. I was overjoyed; not only had they reconciled, but Mother Irene had been forced to leave our parents' home. It was something we had secretly hoped for as children but never thought would happen. Part of me felt sorry for her, until my memories of all the beatings flooded back.

Before they left, my father took me aside privately. He was furious with me for helping Christine with the time line that had prompted the Prophet to dismiss him from his family.

"That's no one's business, Sis," he said angrily. "You girls lied on that time line and you see how it's ripped our family apart. The things you wrote—"

"—should never have happened, Father, but they did," I retorted angrily. It had already sent me over the edge to have to write down all the things in black and white about what my father had allowed and later perpetrated. It had been harder still to have to hear more horrifying stories from my younger siblings. But for him to deny everything? To act as if we were the ones perpetrating lies? I had never stood up to my father, but I did now, fire in my eyes.

"Don't you *even* try to act all innocent!" I retorted. "I now know things about your younger children that were never even written on that sheet! What kind of a father are you? You'd better make sure nothing like this *ever* happens again!"

Suddenly he drew his hand back as if to strike me. My heart faltered.

"Go ahead," I said, trembling, my fear mixed with fury. "I'm sure my husband would like to know all about *this*." My father's face filled with more cold malice, but he lowered his hand, then turned and stalked out to his car. I watched out the window as he put on a false smile for my mother and the younger kids. As they drove away, tears for each one of my siblings and my mother welled up within me as I prayed. *God be with you till we meet again. Dear God, please.*

As I settled into Hildale as my permanent residence, I reveled in my freedom from Warren. Nineteen ninety-seven was a pleasant, relatively peaceful time for me in the Prophet's Hildale home, interrupted only by Warren's visits from Salt Lake.

One morning I was in the kitchen, the smell of yeast strong in the air. Three or four of my sister-wives and I were on kitchen duty, baking enormous quantities of delicious bread to feed the veritable army lodged in our home. Normally I loved baking bread, but on that particular day I was distracted by a young visitor, one of Warren's newest wives, to whom I was sending waves of silent, yet tender compassion as she baked alongside us. Warren had been stalking her since their arrival. Because Stacey wanted nothing to do with him, he pursued her relentlessly, despite many, many wives at home hungry for a crumb of his affection.

When Warren popped into the kitchen, eager to see his new wife, he greeted the other women and turned to me.

"Mother Becky," he said, nodding in deference. My stomach twisted when he winked at us, then slid his arms around Stacey's waist. For him, this was all fun and games. His face and body were animated as they often were when showing off in front of his father's wives. The more Stacey refused to play along with him, the more ardent he became, forcefully turning her around to face him and trying to French-kiss her in front of us. The young girl turned her face away, and a familiar and sickening metallic taste filled my mouth. I was biting my lip, knowing too well that feeling of not wanting to be kissed, touched, or fondled in front of other women. I yearned for him to stop as we all looked away. He finally did stop, like an insolent toddler whose toy had been taken from him. He picked up a freshly baked loaf of bread that had not yet been cut or bagged.

"She'll get it," Warren said to the rest of us nonchalantly, tossing the bread up into the air two or three times. Then he stopped and laughed. "She just needs to be *bred*!"

At that moment, he thrust the loaf at his wife's chest and smirked at her before walking away. Poor Stacey was horrified, still holding on to the bread in her humiliation. I seethed inwardly. To an FLDS man, if a woman was in any way rebellious, the solution was to get her married and keep her pregnant. Then all of that rebellion would be "bred" right out of her.

I watched Stacey over the next several months having to submit to her husband, her light growing dimmer as the hope and fire in her eyes waned. I wondered how many times in the last few years I had looked into my own eyes and seen that same surrender of life force.

In statements eerily reminiscent of Home Economics classes at Alta

Academy, Warren would constantly admonish us as the Prophet's wives to seek to be "close to Father." That was the term for being sexually intimate.

"To follow the Prophet means eternal life," he would somberly intone, once again wielding the salvation stick. "Not following the Prophet means death." Church leaders often spoke of "spiritual death"—an eternal life devoid of hope. It was what we all feared most.

While living in Hildale, I became closer with my sister-wife Cecilia, who had so offended Ora by giving away her dress. Sunny and sweet, and stunningly beautiful, she had been highly sought after in her day, before her father gave her to the Prophet. Like me, she had begged for her freedom, but her father wouldn't listen. She had become Rulon's fourth "young wife." It was the only thing I'd ever heard her quietly complain about, and only rarely.

Cecilia's sweet disposition—and likely her curvaceous figure—ended up getting her into a lot of trouble. We were admonished to keep our distance from all men, but it was not unusual for several of Rulon's young wives to have a "favorite son" to help out, or to take them into St. George for shopping, of course in a small and respectable group. While this commingling would not have been tolerated otherwise, it was allowed here because the Prophet's family was considered beyond reproach. Before I was married to Rulon, Cecilia had gotten involved with Warren's younger brother Darren. He had used the secret panels of the Salt Lake property meant to protect us from a government raid as the way to access her secretly. Their tryst discovered, they had confessed and repented.

Apparently, Darren was soon married off, but Warren's youngest brother, Morgan, then sought Cecilia out, and they got into trouble both in Salt Lake City and Hildale. When Cecilia and Morgan's flirtation was discovered, Warren came down to Hildale to investigate and pulled me into his office to interrogate me. I had been oblivious to all of this. I adored Cecilia, who was like sunshine to me in a very dark world. I had never seen this in her, nor had I looked for it.

The two were never excommunicated or publicly humiliated, I believe in part because of Cecilia's marriage to the Prophet and her father's standing in the church. I was also unsure of Cecilia's degree of guilt. I had seen Warren blow similar things out of proportion. Whatever the case, Warren's insinuations made their actions seem as immoral as death. I was embarrassed at my naïveté, but Warren insinuated that on some level I had to have known.

"What is it within *you* that needs cleansing?" he asked me as I sat in a chair opposite him. I hung my head. Certainly I was secretly angry with my husband for forcing sex on me, but I had never, ever harbored the desire to have an affair! Still, after I left Warren's office, I began to brutally beat myself up inside. I was already painfully aware of my character flaws. But when I got quiet, the only thing I could think of that needed cleansing was my sexual abuse as a child. What Sterling had done to me when I was small had made me feel unworthy of marriage to the Prophet. I spent a considerable amount of time feeling stained, defiled, and dirty, and I had a strong desire to be cleansed.

That opportunity came a short while later. In January 1998, Parley Harker, the First Counselor in the FLDS Presidency and next in authority to the Prophet, died, and Warren was called to fill his position. This was a colossal event in the church and in the hierarchy of power. For his first few months in his new role, Warren was jubilant and seemed like another person. I began to see him actually treat the people with kindness. At one point, I almost thought I could actually like him as a leader, if not as my "son."

His words, however, had still struck a chord deep inside of me. It was our custom to fast and pray at least once a month for one day about any areas in our individual lives that needed additional strength, but I went without food for several days, trying to wrap my head around Warren's admonition: *What within you needs cleansing?* The question had haunted me for months.

Although I was not fully aware of most of their histories, I discovered that Cecilia and a few of my sister-wives had asked to be rebaptized. Baptism by immersion meant to fully submerge the body in water so that it could be cleansed from all sin. This generally took place in a large basin or pool of water blessed for that express purpose.

Most members of the church were baptized at eight years of age, as it was considered the age when one can tell right from wrong. As a child, I had been baptized by immersion in the font at Alta Academy, where we also attended church. I had made a holy covenant with God and Jesus Christ to always remember him, and to keep his commandments so that I could always have his Spirit to be with me. Something within me broke open years later as an adult. Perhaps a rebaptism was the way I could be fully released and absolved of what Sterling had done to me and of my angry thoughts toward my husband. Perhaps being cleansed from this early trauma might assist me so that this persistent presence of evil that Warren saw in me would go away. Perhaps then the Spirit could always remain with me, and enable me to perceive evil and keep it from me at all times.

I asked to have a private consultation with Rulon. For the first time in my life I shared the story of what Sterling had done to me, shaking uncontrollably the whole time. I was afraid the Prophet would be angry and force me out of his house, but instead he was kind. When I suggested rebaptism, he said that it was not necessary, but if it made me feel better, he would permit it. I stood up, my heart filled with joy. I would be clean and absolved of all sin, finally free of what Sterling had done to me!

A few days later, Warren arranged for my rebaptism in the font that had been installed in the basement of the Prophet's Salt Lake home, the same one I had been baptized in as a child. Cecilia had talked to me about her rebaptism, and she waited with me until the Priesthood leaders were ready for me to descend into the water. Uncle Wendell, LeRoy Jeffs, and Warren were all present, though none of them asked me any questions. Dressed all in white, I simply stepped into the water and was immersed fully under it. Under the authority of the Priesthood, I was baptized. Warren and another Priesthood member confirmed upon me the Gift of the Holy Ghost. I was free! I had not told anyone else about my rebaptism, but for the next few months, my feet felt like they had wings. My life took on new meaning, and I taught with greater power and love.

In the midst of what felt like a new beginning for me, deeply disturbing news from my childhood home arrived. Mother Maggie was still causing major havoc, and to make matters worse, Mother Irene had been allowed to return. Dad, in his attempts to please Maggie, was doling out corporal punishment again. Trevor and Amelia had rebelled and been forced up to Canada for reform. Both had been drinking beer and going to rave parties, and Amelia had kissed more than one young man. My heart hurt for both of them. On my visits to Canada I had seen the way the people treated those who had been sent to the youth camps, and witnessed the backbreaking work they were forced to do.

Amelia was not to go to Uncle Jason's, but had to work her guts out in the wood mill and was also expected to cook for and clean up after other work crews after her shift ended.

Unable to do anything constructive for them, I threw myself into helping Christine with the *Pride of Avonlea* operetta. We choreographed the production together, and I played my violin in the orchestra as well as worked directly with the youth. This year, one participant was a painfully shy young man with thick glasses and drooped shoulders who had trouble making friends. We had been working with him week after week, and it was wonderful to see him start to hold his head erect and perform with confidence, grace, and skill. I said a prayer of gratitude every day for this opportunity—and I prayed daily that someone, somewhere, would show up for my brothers and sisters in a similar way.

I would soon get to see many of my siblings when everyone came down to the annual April Conference. Short Creek swarmed with the excitement of friends and family arriving. Christine and I tried to spend one-on-one time with visiting siblings, and we were both very troubled by the stories they shared with us.

As was the custom, I had sewn a special dress for church: a pastel brocade fabric for the bodice and yards of soft, chiffon polyester. I had noticed that new trends among the community often followed my new dress patterns. This dress was by far one of my most elegant, and I was secretly proud of my new creation.

I met my mother and sisters in the side hall just a few minutes before church was to start. My sister Allyson, who was then about four years old, looked up at me with big, shining eyes. I hugged her with all the love I had for her, and I invited her to sit with me in the section reserved for the Prophet's wives. This was a big honor, to be in front of thousands of people being seated in the meeting hall. Ally hadn't been feeling that well, but she brightened and nodded her head.

My sister and I took a deep breath and gracefully walked across the front of the church crowd to our seats. I had never liked being a part of the processional of the Prophet's family, but it had become a necessary part of my life. We sat down and Ally was jabbering happily away when suddenly she stopped midsentence. I watched her face turn a sickly shade of green, and a helpless look came into her eyes.

"Becky, I don't feel so good!" Abruptly she leaned over and started vomiting in my lap, right before Conference was about to start! She continued to heave repeatedly, and I looked down, wondering what to do. My sister-wives scrambled around for tissues, but despite this and the number of layers I was wearing, my lap became wet. Knowing that a line of ladies would soon be suffering from the smell, I gathered the corners of my skirt in one hand, took Ally by the other and stood up just as the crowd was being directed to sing the opening hymn. We had just stepped out of the door of the main meeting hall when Ally turned and looked at me, happiness in her eyes.

"Becky!" she cried loudly. "I feel *sooo* much better!" I couldn't help but giggle and smile at her as we went back to the Prophet's home and my room, where we both showered and changed. It was much more fun for us to listen to church, which was always broadcast over speakers into everyone's rooms on the Jeffses' property anyway. I would miss seeing friends and family, but I was also grateful not to have to face the forced formality of sitting in line after the service, greeting each visitor who stood in line for hours just to shake the Prophet's hand.

Therefore, two weeks later I was delighted to be engaged with my people in a serving way that I loved. The cast presented our *Pride of Avonlea* operetta. My eyes shone with love and appreciation for what each performer had brought to the stage, and I loved looking out at the people and seeing the absolute joy upon their faces. In the FLDS, our lives were filled with so much work, damnation, and end-of-the-world destruction; it was delightful to have something to celebrate. Sherrie and Ally were able to come, and I saw firsthand how the operetta brought hope and joy to many of us, young and old alike.

After the operetta, life returned to an almost monotonous routine. During Rulon's visits to Short Creek, the chief of police and a local deputy took him out daily for lunch and provided him with an official escort as he met with the city officials—all FLDS Priesthood leaders, of course. Other FLDS visitors would come from outlying areas to meet with the Prophet and discuss matters of business and marriage plans for their daughters.

A few days after the operetta, news came from Canada. After gut-wrenching pressure and backbreaking work, our sister Amelia had finally caved. In order to get our mother, the Prophet, and Warren off her back and to survive the imminent end of the world, she had agreed to be placed in marriage. On May 31, 1998, Amelia was given to Collin Blackmore, Jason's son and our cousin through marriage.

I was happy to be allowed to go to Canada for the wedding, but when I arrived, I was shaken. Amelia had always been a spunky, free spirit, but I saw a surrender and deadness in her eyes and her soul. I pushed away my feelings and sought to find the bright side. Like my mother and Christine, I had become proficient at the skill of sticking my head in the sand, because our very survival depended on it.

During that visit, I became acquainted with several of Winston Blackmore's wives, some of whom I had met when I was in Canada as a young girl. One day when I was on duty, I had to be in the same room with Warren, Rulon, and Bishop Blackmore, who joked with the other two men.

"I have to marry off a particularly rebellious young filly," he declared. "Getting her pregnant will settle her right down."

I had not much liked Winston, but that flippant comment turned me sour. Through the years I had heard him say similar comments about women and realized he had likely made that exact same comment about my sister Amelia regarding her forced marriage to our cousin Collin. He couldn't care less about any woman; his desire was to control. That thought burned within me, but I had to hold my tongue and show absolutely no emotion.

I did enjoy meeting one of Winston's younger wives, a wonderful character by the name of Alicia Lane Blackmore. Using humor, she could get away with saying things no one else could. For example, when we were introducing ourselves she said it was so much easier going by numbers instead of names. "That's all we are anyway," she laughed. A few evenings later, when all the men were in Priesthood meeting and Cecilia and I were walking the property, I heard a high voice from across the grounds.

"Hey, Number Nineteen!" Alicia called. "How are you? It's Number Ten!" Cecilia was astonished, but I was nearly rolling on the grass, clutching my stomach in laughter. It felt so good to hear someone tell it like it was. And it felt so good to laugh.

Upon our return to Hildale, it was my turn to be on duty with Rulon again. As much as I tried, I was never off the hook from having to sleep with him, even with operetta practices or visiting Canada. I was required to do my time, and I had been ordered by Rulon to schedule my undertakings around my shifts with him. Still, the outside activities, as well as my rebaptism, had raised my spirits. I felt like I had a new beginning with my husband. I had been washed clean, I had more confidence in myself, and while I didn't look forward to marital relations, I did wish to show my respect for him.

Rulon, however, thought my newfound confidence meant that it was time to further my education in the bedroom. He made sure I knew who was in charge. He'd been known to preach, "The greatest freedom you can enjoy is in obedience." That night he forced me to do unspeakable acts, pulling at my head and my hair to make sure I did it "just right." When I didn't, he made sure I knew that, too.

"Ora knows how to do it just right," he said, moaning.

Then let Ora do this to you and leave me alone!

I was bitterly angry, and after he came I spent nearly an hour in the bathroom, silently crying. When I emerged, he was asleep. I climbed into the opposite side of the bed and continued to weep quietly. Every time I had opened myself to Rulon, showed him vulnerabilities, told him what Sterling had done to me, he still forced me to do things I didn't want to do. I had always followed the church's teachings. Why would God punish me in this way? I finally decided that I did not like God. Nor could I trust Him.

When my tears finally subsided, they were replaced by a fire in the pit of my stomach. I remembered a lesson that Warren had taught in family class to his father's wives.

> Now that you are married to our Prophet, or any wife to her husband, the keys of Elijah transplanted that branch, namely you, and now you are connected to a man that is the source of life, literally—the source of life to you. As you reach out in your faith, having it so available, so right around you, the Spirit of God will flow into you.... There begins to grow a love, such a love that will make you one with him. A wife can say to her husband, "I love you."

I could not say "I love you" to Rulon. I had loved him as a grandfather figure, as my Prophet and Priesthood Head, but I had reached out in my faith and how he repaid my trust seemed unconscionable. In my position, I could not help but see that so many women were treated in like manner or worse by their husbands.

At times when I was on duty with Rulon, I would catch wind of the Prophet's business as it concerned a young girl unhappy in her marriage. As he was acutely hard of hearing and kept the volume up loud on the telephone, I couldn't help but overhear most of his conversations. It was at these times I realized I was not the only one in my community struggling with issues of violation.

I had a cousin whose mother had been taken from her unworthy husband and been remarried to a man named Phillip. As was the custom, the woman and her children were "given" to that new man as a whole package. Phillip, who held high standing in the FLDS, began raping my cousin, his new stepdaughter, but no one knew. Once she got older, Phillip approached the Prophet. Perhaps Phillip was scared of her belonging to another man—or of her exposing his molestations.

"This girl belongs to me," he told Rulon, who without thought gave the sixteen-year-old in marriage to her stepfather—a man more than twice her age. In the meantime, she developed schizophrenia (considered an evil spirit among the FLDS, not the result of trauma). Her illness worsened dramatically after she discovered she was pregnant and her due date approached. I think she was subconsciously afraid that her child would be molested, too. In her worsening terror, she would run away in the family's minivan. I overheard several telephone conversations in which Rulon would always send a brother or other Priesthood Head to bring her back to her husband.

One day when I was on duty, Mother Norene, an older sister-wife of mine who had one of the most compassionate hearts in the whole community, came in to beseech the Prophet.

"She took the family's minivan again," Norene explained, referring to my cousin. "With no money, and no gas. She is stranded in Cedar City, and is begging for your help. She would like to come back into the fold, but she is terrified of going back to her husband."

"Tell her God wants her to go home and obey her husband!" he said harshly. With a pitiful look in her eye, Mother Norene left, resigned to share that message. It was not until later that Rulon and the community discovered that Phillip had been sexually molesting my cousin for years and that he had carried abusive behaviors into their marriage.

Rulon was furious. "He lied to me! He lied to us all!"

I stared at him, dumbfounded. As the all-knowing Prophet, shouldn't he have been aware of this before he forced her to marry Phillip? Even though I had seen suggestions and requests greatly influence the Prophet's behavior, it was daily ingrained in us that he was the mouth of God—the one and only man blessed with total, omniscient gifts of the Spirit. It shocked me that he had not seen what was happening. He was supposed to know everything about everyone! The thought was disturbing to me. *What else did he not know?* I couldn't let that thought take seed, however, or the rest of my world would violently crash down around me. Once again, I knew I had to remove all doubts from my mind or I would end up like my cousin.

Therefore, I was grateful for the distraction of the upcoming Pioneer Day theme parade, and I threw myself into working with the families and the children. I lived for the hours away from home and the presence of precious, innocent youth that I could love and serve with all my heart.

I also went for rides on our neighbor's horse, Miss Tree, and borrowed four-wheelers as often as I could. On rare occasions I would meet my younger friend Samantha, and we'd secretly spirit away in one of the fleet of minivans at Rulon Jeffs's home. She loved music as much as I did, and we would speed too fast down a deserted back desert highway, singing at the top of our lungs to the wicked and forbidden music of the A-Teens rendition of ABBA's "Super Trouper." At other times, I climbed the water tower or even El Capitan, the steep rock face that towered over the Creek. Those moments away had kept me sane when I had to face being on duty again.

Soon enough, I received my call from Rulon, to the phone in my room. "Mother Becky, it is your turn to be on duty. Come and stay with me tonight."

"No."

There was silence for several long seconds. Finally he spoke, his voice sharp. "What do you mean?"

"No," I repeated firmly, "I am not ready to stay with you again. I will not be on duty tonight." Let him withhold affections from me like he had Mother Julia! He'd been unable to have children long before our marriage. He was certainly not withholding anything from me that I wanted or needed.

A few days later Warren came down to visit on church business. He called me into his office. I knew a good tongue-lashing was coming, but I was not prepared for what was to follow. Rulon's son looked at me with the most menace I had ever seen in his eyes.

"You don't ever, ever, ever, ever, *ever* tell your husband no," Warren said spitefully. "Especially you, because your husband is the Prophet. Your husband would never do anything to hurt you."

He paused, to make sure I was really listening. "I repeat, do not say no again, Mother Becky. If you do, *you will be destroyed in the flesh.*"

CHAPTER 9

The Sweet Promise of Destruction

For the rest of the month, spooked by Warren's words, I looked for any Priesthood-approved reason to be away from home. I performed with hundreds of FLDS members in the Pioneer Day parade on the 24th of July. I also signed up for an EMT class with Christine. Warren admonished me for the amount of time I spent away from home, but as long as Rulon approved of each activity, he couldn't stop me. I went back to enduring my duty in the bedroom, though our shifts were lightened as Rulon now had fourteen young wives to please him in the bedroom. We were now on twelve-hour shifts instead, but I was never allowed any escape from duty.

I played the good wife when I had to, so I could leave whenever possible. And every day I prayed to the God I did not like or trust that he would somehow have mercy on my soul.

Then in August 1998, when Rulon was visiting Short Creek and my sister-wives and I were gathered together for family class, Rulon suddenly slumped over. We helped Nephi carry him to his bed, and the paramedics were called. As we watched, Rulon began spouting absurdities, and it was apparent he recognized only Mother Ruth. We were stunned. Nephi later announced over the intercom that Rulon had suffered a severe stroke and was receiving treatment at the hospital in

St. George. We certainly could not all visit for fear of attracting attention. Through Nephi, Warren ordered all of us to stay home from
church and to refrain from entertaining visitors. He wanted us on call
24/7 for anything he or his father needed.

In the meantime, Warren immediately flew to St. George. Upon leaving the hospital he warned Rulon's wives, "Do not reveal his condition
to the people." At that point Warren instructed every member of Rulon's
family to fast and to pray for his recovery. Although we were used to fasting once a month for twenty-four hours to pray for a specific need for the
Priesthood, this was an extended fast from food; we were allowed only
to sip water, mint tea, or apple juice. In addition, no one was allowed to
leave the property or even talk on the phone, except to tell the people
the Prophet was getting some rest. Essentially, we were under house
arrest, and the people were left in the dark about the whole thing.

Helen and I were going to miss our on-duty night with Rulon, so
Nephi arranged for us to drive down to the hospital for his EKG test.
As soon as the test was finished, Warren told us to leave, as Rulon was
not making good progress. It was disturbing to see my husband in that
kind of condition, and I couldn't help but feel guilty for all of the angry
thoughts I had harbored toward him.

Our eighty-nine-year-old Seer and Revelator had prophesized to us
that he would live for 150 years and be present to give the keys of the
kingdom to Christ himself. In tender moments, perhaps feeling embarrassed that he could no longer sire children in a society that so revered
it, he had told his younger wives that he would be renewed like Peleg
in Genesis, Chronicles, and the Doctrine and Covenants. He said that
he would father three hundred children for us. This hospitalization felt
unreal. So many stories of the miraculous healings of Prophets were
pounded into our heads daily that we genuinely believed that Rulon
Jeffs would be the next Prophet to experience life-saving and life-giving
miracles. Not a single one of us expressed any doubt. Not only was it
unsafe to do so, but we codependently bolstered one another in our
blind obedience. We sang songs about keeping "sweet," never complaining, never questioning, and sacrificing our feelings to do what was right.

Later Rulon was released into his son's custody and immediately
flown back to Salt Lake, where his son could monitor his progress. Warren also took over most of the daily duties while the Prophet was ill. To

the people, Warren announced that while Rulon had suffered a stroke, he was in great health and simply needed rest, which was not true. Word spread quickly and the people were very concerned about the Prophet's health. Some of the men in the hierarchy were concerned about Warren's leadership, but not one person dared to openly confront him. A dark sense of foreboding came over the house. My sister-wives and I continued fasting but began to grow frail as the days turned into weeks.

The next time it was my turn to be on duty with Rulon, I was alarmed at how severely the stroke had ravaged his body. Our sister-wife Mary had been watching over him almost nonstop. The Prophet was hooked up to several wires and indicators—all monitored by Mary, a registered nurse. My EMT classes enabled me to help by writing accurate medical notes for her.

When I went into an adjoining room to record medication intake, I heard voices coming from the side door near the garage where entitled individuals would come to visit the Prophet without enduring the formalities of the front room, as most visitors did. The Barlow brothers, several of the prominent community leaders who were descended from the earlier Prophet John Y. Barlow, had arrived for their regular monthly meeting with the Prophet.

Warren suddenly rushed through, accompanied by his brothers Nephi and Isaac, who had been taking orders from him since the stroke. "Do not grant them access," he said. "Do not tell them anything." I lowered my head and continued to write, shocked, as I watched them from under my lashes. They backed away from the door but perched nearby to listen. Isaac opened the door and greeted the men, though quite obviously barring them from entering.

"We know the Prophet has been ill," said Dan Barlow slowly, though authoritatively. He and his brothers were taken aback at being held at the door. "We simply wish to extend him our well wishes and prayers for his speedy recovery."

"Thank you," said Isaac politely but firmly. "The Prophet is resting and no visitors are allowed."

A strange look crossed the men's faces. The proud sons and grandsons of a Prophet stood there, stunned and angry, for several uncomfortable moments before turning away. It was a scandalous changing of the guard.

In time, Rulon's condition gradually improved, and thankfully some of the tension eased in our home. Fortunately, the rigid fasting let up, too. However, if Rulon had an especially rough night, Warren would blame the wife on duty for not having enough of the Spirit of God within her.

"What influence are you bringing around Father?" he would ask. "Can you not see? He is so pure." His insinuations frightened me. *What if Father died on our watch? Would we be blamed for that, too?*

Rulon experienced debilitating fallout from the stroke. While his physical body and strength began to slowly improve, our husband could not recognize his wives, nor call each one of us by name. Slowly, he began to remember some of his oldest wives: LaRue, Julia, Ruth, and Marilyn. Except for Mary, who cared for him daily, the rest of us became "Sweetie."

For the next several months Rulon was as daffy as a post. "I want all of my wives to dye their hair just like theirs!" He pointed animatedly to Paula and Ellen, with their jet-black hair. We all gasped at first, and then sat in shocked silence. FLDS women were forbidden to dye their hair—a vanity of the outside world, frowned upon by our leaders. Isaac quickly retrieved Warren, who put the whole thing to rest. Otherwise, as obedient wives, we would have all departed promptly to St. George for hair dye! "Everything the Prophet says is right" we had heard hundreds, if not thousands, of times in morning and family classes. *Never question. Always obey.* Still, we couldn't help but notice that our husband was not in his right mind.

"I'm not Rulon!" he began insisting stubbornly. "I'm Rudy Bagucious!" He was adamant and proud of this name in a childlike way, so it made sense when Mother Ruth explained it was a nickname his father had given him as a toddler.

One Sunday at church I was on duty with Rulon. It was part of my job that day to make sure he was not approached before his sons could whisk him away. He was not allowed to speak publicly at this point, nor allowed to speak privately with anyone. Whenever Rulon tried to speak, Warren and his brothers muted the lapel microphone he usually wore at church, and that way they completely controlled what was said.

Warren and Uncle Fred sat next to Rulon, as my sister-wives and I sat in the first few rows of seats across from the pulpit. We could hear Rulon speaking when most of the congregation could not. I could not help but see how Warren carefully used every opportunity to place responsibility for the people squarely on his own shoulders, and to bring their attention away from Rulon and back to their iniquity and sin.

"Father's condition is like that of Moses on the mountainside," said Warren, standing up to the pulpit. "We cannot understand it all, but he is in direct contact with God." Then Warren looked sternly out over the crowd, which went completely silent.

"And when you murmur you are like Moses's people, senselessly imbibing in debauchery and revelry while he is seeking only the Lord's will. It has been brought to the Prophet's attention that people are putting paper up in their windows so they can watch television and no one will know..." Again his voice boomed scathingly out across the congregation. "God and the Prophet know your sins."

When we returned home from church, dinner wasn't ready, but Uncle Rulon wanted to eat immediately and was acting cranky, like a toddler who had not had his nap. Sometimes his physical discomfort caused him to become very mean. Nephi patiently brought out Rulon's television and put on a National Geographic video about bears in the Northwest.

This bothered me, as everyone had just heard Warren literally attack the people for watching television. Why, then, was it okay for the Prophet and his family to watch?

Rulon sat, spellbound, providing commentary and clapping his hands. At one point in the show, he watched a bear catch a salmon and eat it. He suddenly leaned forward with as much force as his age-ridden body would allow and nearly toppled over.

"Oh my God!" he shouted as the bear ripped into the salmon with his great teeth. "Bears are barbaric!" Hearing Rulon's shouts, some of the other sister-wives came running, expecting the worst. Rulon asked them to stay and watch the show with him, as he continued his commentary. Nephi quickly exchanged that video for a program on nuclear war and the impending doom of the world, in an effort to placate his father until Warren came in to give Rulon a "snack." When we gathered for dinner a short while later, Rulon was slumped over in his chair. I wondered if Warren had drugged him. I paid attention and began to notice a pattern. If Rulon was really outspoken or talking crazy, his sons would intervene and fifteen to twenty minutes later he'd be asleep.

From time to time, Rulon would have periods of lucidity. Alone with

Rulon at lunch one afternoon, my sister-wives and I were perplexed when our husband began beating his fists on the table in great anger and frustration.

"I want my job back, damn it!" he cried, looking around at us. We knew what he was talking about. "Are you listening to me?" the Prophet screamed at us again. *"I-want-my-job-back!"* Each word was accentuated with another fist upon the table. Warren and Isaac rushed in to soothe him, and a few minutes later he was asleep in his chair, his mouth open in a drooling snore.

Warren could be heard to say "I am only doing my father's will" even more frequently. However, it was becoming obvious to us in the Jeffs family that Warren was now *directing* the will of his father.

The last year of the millennium turned into a living hell for the FLDS, as Rulon continued to decline and Warren began dictating disturbing doctrine about the end of the world. The term "Latter-day Saints" was coined by the early Mormons over a century prior, because they had felt they were experiencing the "last days." Our FLDS Prophets had instilled the concept of doomsday only deeper into our consciousnesses, and we all braced ourselves for the arrival of the year 2000.

When school ended in May, everyone in the Jeffs family moved to Hildale. Warren warned the people in Salt Lake City that the Prophet wanted them to sell their businesses, pack up their personal items, and move down to Short Creek as soon as possible. They obeyed and began coming down in droves. Warren had already moved down with his wives and children. In Hildale, where I'd gone deliberately to get away from him, I found myself under his constant thumb once again.

That July, my own family prepared to join us. Tempers had been running high in the Wall household for months. Our father felt that my mom's children did not honor his Priesthood authority. Mother Maggie had been feeding into that belief again, and the kids felt powerless against her manipulations.

One afternoon, Mom told me and Christine, she had been at a car wash several blocks from home when she saw Zach staggering toward her on foot. Her first thought was that his older twin brothers, or perhaps one of his other mothers, had gotten ahold of him. When she learned that it was actually our father who had beaten and bloodied

Zach in his rage, all because of a misunderstanding, she decided her children should not have to suffer any longer. She called Warren and within a day left home with her children, never to return again.

As she described the severity of Zach's injuries, I was relieved that she'd taken matters into her own hands, but my heart ached for her and her loss. My father had rescinded his right to be a father under those circumstances. The Prophet seemed to think the same way. Dad's Priesthood was revoked once more, and my mother and my siblings as well as Maggie and her children were taken from him. Dad and Irene moved down near us, but into a trailer house on the southern outskirts of town. He was stricken from the Prophet's good graces, though he was still a member of the church, having to repent from afar in order to be able to hold the Priesthood again.

That August, Christine informed me that Warren had arranged for our mother to move down to Uncle Fred Jessop's home in Hildale. Uncle Fred, the bishop of the Hildale area, often took in widows and displaced families. That didn't sit well with me, knowing that Rulon enjoyed giving women with children to Uncle Fred for marriage. Unable to have children of his own as a side effect from a childhood bout with measles, Fred had been given well more than a dozen wives with children already. I prayed that somehow my mother could simply be placed in a quiet setting where she could have time to heal and have peace without having to marry again.

Christine and I spent quite a bit of time trying to comfort our brothers and sisters. Joshua and Jordan, now seventeen, refused to come to Hildale, but Mom still had Zach, Elissa, Levi, Sherrie, and Ally with her—all of whom just wanted to go home. My fears came true when our mother was given to marry "beloved" Uncle Fred, and they were given along with her. I was most worried because I had seen several families suffer at Fred's hands, not because he was abusive, but because he was so very intolerant. Before my mother came to live with him, I saw that like many FLDS leaders, he had a double standard for his behavior and that of his people. It particularly irked me one Sunday when he spoke piously at the pulpit about the importance of being gentle with children, then that afternoon he went home, and while we were preparing a family meal, he publicly shamed and ridiculed one of my brothers in front of his very large family.

Unfortunately, Mom didn't have any recourse. FLDS women rarely, if ever, owned any property. She certainly had no means to support herself and her brood of children. And since Mom had been Dad's second wife and therefore a "Celestial bride" with a less-than-legal marriage license, she therefore had no legal way to get a divorce. Her marriage to my father was dissolved the moment the Prophet presented her and her children to Fred.

It was done.

I tried to be cheery and optimistic on my mother's wedding day. Warren performed the ceremony in Rulon's home, and everyone went to Fred's afterward for music and celebration. As I looked around the room at the other women and children, I saw that some faces were very kind, others cold or jealous, and still others just...*dead*. The things these women and children had already been through were tough to think about. Most had been taken from their husbands and fathers and given to Uncle Fred, generally for reasons of severe abuse.

I went through the line to wish Mother and Uncle Fred my congratulations. I gave my mom a huge hug and bent over to hug Uncle Fred in his chair, and he pulled me toward him, turned his face directly to mine, and kissed me right on the lips! I backed up in shock and he just laughed. *Who was this man?* If anyone else had dared to kiss the Prophet's wife like that, he would be kicked out of the FLDS in a heartbeat. Although I would come back frequently to visit my family, I steered clear of Fred whenever possible. It seemed he had that same depraved sense of entitlement I noted among most other FLDS leaders.

The night of Mom's wedding I could not sleep for worry over my siblings. Elissa, Levi, Sherrie, and Ally were still quite young. I feared especially for Zach and Levi. Hundreds upon hundreds of boys had already been kicked out of the FLDS. With very little education and nowhere to turn, their futures were very dim. We called them "sons of perdition," but we heard that the outside world had begun to call them "the lost boys." That made me mad. People on the outside didn't understand. It wasn't like Peter Pan, who didn't *want* to grow up. These lonely boys came from a culture where God and family meant everything, literally *everything*, and once kicked out they had neither. They weren't lost; they were abandoned.

Over the next few months, it broke my heart to see every one of my younger brothers end up in that category. Trevor was already gone, and Joshua and Jordan, who couldn't stand living in such an abusive environment with Dad, left to live with friends. Then Uncle Fred set up my sweet brother Zach on some trumped-up charge in order to send him to work camps in Canada. He escaped on the way there, and I didn't blame him. Still it was anguishing to imagine my little brother hiding out in Salt Lake City somewhere, perhaps sleeping on a park bench or under a bridge.

Not long after that some boys came and picked up my baby brother Levi in the middle of the night. He was only eleven. We were all distraught at his disappearance, but somehow I knew that Zach was involved and that he really cared for Levi. I prayed that they'd be safer out there than in Uncle Fred's home. Now only my little sisters remained. With the dramatic shifts within the Jeffs household and the FLDS at large, I had never felt more concerned and unsure about their future.

As the months progressed and December drew to a close, the paranoia and anxiety among the people was at an all-time high. On New Year's Eve, we had a sobering family class. I looked upon the troubled faces of my sister-wives as we listened to Warren's fateful pronouncements. Everything would blow up. California was about to drop into the ocean. Unless I was considered pure enough to be lifted up with the righteous while the rest of the world perished, I would die with them at the ripe old age of twenty-three.

Our class ended around 11:15 p.m., and there were no rumblings yet, although everyone seemed poised to spring at a moment's notice. Finally, my sister-wives and I all hugged one another tightly before going to bed. We believed we would not see one another in the morning, unless we were pure enough to be lifted up together in the eternities. I walked soberly down the long stretch to my room, locked in a distressful life review, convinced I would never be worthy of life in the eternities with the Prophet. Finally I took a long shower, to emerge into the deathly quiet of the house, the silence closing in somberly around me.

As I slipped into bed, all I could hear was the *tick, tick, tick* of the clock. I was so scared. I hadn't bothered to set my alarm. According to Warren, we wouldn't be waking up, and we all believed him. This was it. The end of life as anyone had ever known it. I pulled the blankets up to my chin and gripped the edges tightly in my fear. It was nearly midnight.

11:57...11:58...11:59...

I held my breath and waited...Then something occurred to me. *What time zone was God in?* Wasn't it already past midnight in New York? Wouldn't midnight in that wicked place have been a really great time to blow the earth away in a dramatic gesture of retribution?

I finally let out the breath I had been holding and, about half an hour later, fell into a restless sleep.

CHAPTER 10

God's Law Is above Man's Law

The next morning, New Year's Day, I greeted my sister-wives in the kitchen. We all glanced at one another, a little shell-shocked. We felt relieved until Warren told us later that day that the Prophet said that God had given us "just a little more time." The end of the world was still imminent—but we were too wicked to be saved. Once again, we needed to repent.

I watched my entire community try to come back to the grips of reality. Wholeheartedly believing we were on the brink of destruction, a wild recklessness had taken over the previous months. Why not buy large pieces of equipment, or rack up credit-card debt, if no one would be left to be accountable to after the destructions? Unfortunately, now there were actual, worldly consequences for our spiritual beliefs. With a breaking heart, I witnessed several of my closest relatives and friends struggle under the burden of confusion and horrendous debt.

The exception was the Prophet's household. We continued living as we had before, on the tithes and offerings of the people, which now unsettled me. A scripture often quoted from the pulpit was Malachi 3:8—"Will a man rob God? Yet ye have robbed me. But ye say, Wherein have we robbed thee? In tithes and offerings." Anyone who did not pay at least a tenth of every dollar that he or she earned was cheating God.

That was unacceptable. Our struggling people would take food from their own mouths and those of their children, but they would not rob their God.

Many did, however, take money from the government via welfare, Medicaid, and food stamps, especially Celestial wives and their children. Not considered legal wives, they used their maiden names to apply for benefits. Subsidies accounted for millions of dollars—much of the community's income. After how my father had raised us, it was uncomfortable for me to sit at the front of the church while the leaders taught us it was noble and holy to take government subsidies to "bleed the Beast," or run the evil government into the ground.

We were told that God's law was always above man's law, so nothing the Priesthood did was considered illegal. And whereas in Salt Lake we avoided police and government at all costs, here in our small area where nearly everyone was FLDS or had immediate affiliation to the FLDS, we were our own law enforcement and government.

Every town official, municipal director, and police officer was FLDS, subject to the Prophet's rule, not to state or federal laws. Nearly five decades previous, during the '53 raid—which was the largest mass arrest in modern American history, in which the entire community was taken from their homes—outsiders saw photos of children being ripped from their mothers' arms. It was a public relations fiasco for Arizona governor Pyle, and it caused his campaign to backfire. That was when our people had basically been left alone to govern ourselves—left in our own little niche that Arizona and Utah basically pretended didn't exist. The church and our people had taken full advantage of it. No one bothered us. We literally became a law unto ourselves.

A similar situation had taken place *within* the FLDS. Before Uncle Roy had passed, a falling out had occurred among the people regarding one-man rule. Those who followed Uncle Roy Johnson and then Rulon were subject to rule by that one man, who acted "only in the name of God, doing God's will." Now, as Rulon's health deteriorated rapidly, Warren acted more boldly in the name of his father. Respected Priesthood men were still being given little or no access to the Prophet, and Rulon was rarely making appearances at church. Questions were being asked among our people. *What really is happening?* everyone wondered.

Rulon's business had always been conducted in a fairly open manner, at least to insiders of the FLDS hierarchy. Now, however, much was happening behind closed doors. My sister-wife Mother Noreen had been Rulon's personal secretary for years in Hildale, always taking care of his needs. Abruptly, Noreen was replaced by Nephi, Warren's brother. Nephi said he was Rulon's new secretary, but it was obvious to us in the Jeffs household that Nephi was reporting directly to Warren.

One day early in the year 2000, Nephi came into the dining room and whispered something into Warren's ear. Warren turned to us.

"Uncle Dan Barlow, Uncle Joe Barlow, and Winston Blackmore are demanding to see Father," Warren said. The room went deathly quiet. "You are witnessing the suffering of the people for a Godly purpose. God knows more than we do why Father is having to be silent for so long as he communes with God. Say nothing to the people. Say *nothing*."

With Rulon's deteriorating health, we were back under near house arrest. Some could sit for long periods of silence at the feet of our sick husband while Warren taught us incessantly. Others struggled like I did. I did my best to hide my unrest and kept as low a profile as possible. When I had been very busy with the operettas, I had been given a pager so the Prophet's sons could get messages to me and Christine. I never gave mine back, keeping it hidden in my pocket. Besides the phone in my room, it seemed my only connection to the outside world, and I carefully protected it. Aside from my immediate family, Nephi was the only one who knew about it. I don't know why, but he turned a kind, blind eye, probably liking the fact that he could reach me if no one else could. I used the pager to send messages to the people I loved—my sisters, my mother, and my friend Samantha. During church services and my now-infrequent visits to Mom, I observed an extreme sense of discontent among the people. Warren could no longer silence their questions. He resorted to other means to keep our minds preoccupied with the work of God.

In the midst of the unrest, the marriage rate among our people suddenly skyrocketed. Since Rulon's stroke, Warren had sanctioned and performed only a couple of marriages each weekend in the name of his father. But by the late fall of 2000, Warren began performing as many as twenty marriages or more per week!

At first, the weddings were a great cause for celebration. Our people thrived on such unions, and as we knew all the families involved, it seemed a joyous time. For my sister-wives and me, still fasting frequently for long periods and rarely allowed out into the community, observing the marriages had become our only means of entertainment. Each morning we would race out to the front window to see which couples were being wed—most often celebrating with them in our hearts and with great hopes for their futures.

As the marriages increased so rapidly, however, the girls over twenty were snapped up quickly, and the marriages of younger girls began to take place. One morning I looked out to see Sophia, a vibrant, beautiful senior in high school whom I'd directed in multiple operettas and who was immensely talented on the violin. My sister-wives clapped and cheered as they saw who her husband would be. To my chagrin, I saw that it was Louis Barlow. Yes, she would be set for life as far as standing in the community and riches, but Louis was well into his seventies! I had to turn away.

Shortly before she exchanged vows with Louis, I was able to slip out and give her a hug. She cried a little in my arms. These life-changing rites of passage should be joyous for all the people involved. All I felt was deteriorating faith. It didn't take long to get to girls as young as twelve. Stories began running rampant among the FLDS about Jesus's mother Mary being twelve when she became pregnant. In a very twisted way, it became almost a sign of "holiness" to justify a wedding for one so young. With hundreds of these girls being married off, I could not help but feel dread and horror.

Some marriages were deliberately staged to breed out rebellion. For example, my uncle Frank Steed had a daughter, Kimberly, who had been getting into trouble for going to parties. I was shocked when I saw that as a teen, she was given in marriage by her father to none other than Jonathan Roundy—the local police officer and staunch FLDS member—the very officer who had arrested her for going to a party! The Priesthood found this amusing and I overheard several snide comments about my cousin among the men in the Jeffses' home—that she was a feisty animal needing to be put in her place, and now all her rebellion would be bred out of her from one strong enough to hold the reins.

Even more disturbing to me, I couldn't help but see that powerful men in the church were suddenly much less outspoken against Warren following their marriage to some very young lady—so young that the outside world would prosecute the men were they to get caught.

I realized Warren was skilled at creating not only collaborations but collusions. To justify such a change in marriageable ages, Warren explained, "We've got to take care of the people," as if he was protecting our way of life from the government. That was a lie. For decades, even generations, the FLDS had not allowed many underage marriages, usually waiting until a girl was close to eighteen. Warren blamed Utah and Arizona, which had begun enacting stricter laws regarding bigamy and underage marriages. Warren actually placed his people under greater condemnation due to these new laws.

We became worried since the marriages were being performed in Rulon Jeffs's home. The Prophet's son stirred the paranoia, saying if discovered we might have to go into hiding. Everyone became hush-hush about the marriages taking place. Soon, Warren had all the couples secreted across the border to Caliente, Nevada, where the underage laws were much less strict, and where Uncle Merrill could use his Caliente Hotel as a quiet place to perform the marriages away from prying eyes, especially when very young girls were marrying much, much older men.

While I had realized some time ago that matches were not ordained by God and certainly not whispered into the Prophet's ear, that message was still being taught to all of the young FLDS girls. What I saw were the wealthiest men giving the most money in tithes accumulating the largest number of young wives! Warren couldn't give their Prophet back to these men, but he could raise their standing and make them happy by passing out young women like candy.

Warren even used this tactic to pacify his own father. Whenever Rulon would start to question what was happening with his authority, he would suddenly get a new bride! Our ancient husband found it difficult to be cantankerous when he was distracted by a fresh, young bride for a time. Warren was accumulating more wives as well, ones with really good looks or really good standing, or both. They also seemed to get younger and younger.

To keep the gene pool fresher, teen and preteen girls were smuggled in from Canada to the United States and others back again in Rulon's camp trailer, equipped with a bathroom so they would never be seen in public. We did not know all the details, but from time to time as news came in, I couldn't help but see the "one-for-you-and-two-for-me" Priesthood transactions, as the men in power and standing in both the United States and Canada were definitely the ones accumulating. Even the most loving fathers found it difficult to say "My daughter is too young to marry" when Warren made a trade. Most men were unable to resist a new young wife, who could be molded to their desires before she got a mind of her own, as well as the promise of higher standing in the community and in Heaven.

Even though Warren said he was only the voice of the Prophet, no one wanted to tell him no. Very soon, they wouldn't dare to.

During that year of 2000, the U.S. Census was being taken. Warren decided our people should take its own, as our records were of earthly and Heavenly consequence and should not be left in the hands of the Gentiles (generally, we did not share accurate records with them, anyway). We included vital records such as baptisms, marriages, family records, bishops' records, and Priesthood ordinances as well as births. Several of my sister-wives were heavily involved in inputting data into the Jeffses' computers. I helped create one of the templates, and when the ladies became overwhelmed by thousands of records pouring in, I helped to sort them.

Joyful news spread among the people that we were now ten thousand strong! We were following the Lord's commandment to multiply and replenish the earth. It seemed a sign from Heaven to lend us confidence that we were indeed the Lord's people, and I strived to feel that confidence. However, over 60 percent of our population was under the age of sixteen (compared to 20–31 percent in surrounding areas), which meant that Warren had to keep thousands of young people under control.

Local police cracked down on socializing to the point that girls and boys were not allowed to gather under any circumstance except at church and work meetings. While we all knew that local authorities were under the thumb of the FLDS church, I witnessed firsthand how authorities bent the law for those on the "Prophet's errands." I had a lead foot and got caught speeding dozens of times. However, I never received a ticket, because no officer would want Rulon to hear about it. It also went the other way. For example, my brothers and other young men no longer in Warren's good graces were often pulled over, bullied, or even arrested for no real reason. Rodney Holm, a local police officer sworn to duty in both Utah and Arizona, was pleasant and soft around Rulon and Warren, but I had seen him menace and humiliate others. He had been a naughty kid himself, but now he used his badge to enforce Warren's wishes. Rodney and his sidekick, Helaman Barlow, another local policeman, broke up gatherings where FLDS teens were just trying to hang out like normal kids.

I knew a boy named Brian Steed very well. Besides the fact that he was my first cousin, I had been the pianist for their senior class program and had worked with him in three operettas. Although he constantly clowned around, deep inside he was a good, hardworking boy. One Friday evening I drove to the grocery store in Colorado City to pick up a few things, and I waved to Brian, who was in the parking lot chatting with some friends.

When I came out, I saw that Rodney and Helamen had dragged him out to the center of town, bright police lights flashing, as the officers made a big, animated show of cuffing him and throwing him up against their car under the pretense of checking him for a DUI. After hours had passed they had to let him go because they had nothing to hold him on, but the humiliation had been wrought. Years later, Brian would lose his life, and it would break my heart to see his name added to the long list of FLDS boys and young men who had overdosed on drugs or taken their lives.

Males were not the only ones to pay the price for living under such a rigidly controlled police state. Under Rulon and then Warren, local police officers would rarely interfere when a father or brother forced a runaway teen or bride back home. There was nowhere safe to report exploitation or maltreatment. From the girls I knew, often the abuse— and the public and private humiliation—became worse after returning home. It was little wonder that few women tried to leave or report it. It certainly didn't seem safe to report it outside of the community either.

My sister-wives and I were fully aware that our people were not exactly law-abiding citizens when it came to federal and state laws. Our people had a passive-aggressive, rebellious mentality against government that showed up nearly every day, in nearly everything we did. Whenever possible, we went only to FLDS doctors or those who agreed not to keep medical records on us, and we paid cash for their services.

Sometimes our ways held serious consequences, like the unneces-sary deaths we hid from the government. Although Merrill's and Lyle's boys often boasted of direct OSHA violations, our boys were well-trained with tools, and I hadn't thought much about safety on construc-tion sites until a child died on a worksite. We all grieved for him and his family. It had happened more than once, but everyone kept it quiet to avoid inevitable prosecution.

Every year, with every incident that could incriminate us in the eyes of the outside world, it seemed more and more important to keep our records safe from prying eyes.

CHAPTER 11

Another Child Bride:
Breed 'Em and Break 'Em

Though the church leadership was well-protected by local law enforcement, it seemed apparent that state and federal governments were starting to crack down on our people. Warren said we were being harassed, and nearly every Sunday in church, leaders reported on the growing external pressure we were facing from lawsuits, depositions, and tax fraud investigations. The United Effort Plan, or UEP, which had originally been set up by church officials in 1942 to control homes, some businesses, and land within the towns of Short Creek (and eventually all other FLDS enclaves), was part of living the United Order, or the Law of Consecration—the same law under which my father had signed his Salt Lake house over to the church. Loyal families did not own their own homes but rather lived in them by special invitation of the church, which owned the land. The Prophet, as president, had total control over the homes on the land and therefore all temporal, earthly blessings regarding the people.

Those at odds with the Priesthood, especially those at odds with Warren, would find themselves with no house to live in. The few brave enough not to leave when ordered to discovered they had no running water, electricity, or gas with which to sustain their families. If they still stayed, a visit from the "God Squad" usually did the trick.

Uncle Fred ran his house in much the same way, and he decided the fate of each young person under his roof with cold disregard for their wishes or needs. After my brothers were banished or escaped, Fred decided my little sister Elissa, only thirteen, was ready for marriage. When it was announced it would be to Allen Steed, I was even more appalled. Allen was not only our first cousin; he had been exceptionally cruel to Elissa the winter she was young, sick, and vulnerable on the Steed ranch. I couldn't see that he had matured much since then.

Elissa spoke with Uncle Fred several times to beg him to see reason and give her just two more years before marrying. However, he was adamant she be plucked immediately. Allen had done a lot of work for Uncle Fred, and Elissa seemed to be his reward. Fred also wanted Elissa safely married off before she could rebel as our brothers had. When she pointed out that Allen was her first cousin, Fred admonished her, "These things make no difference in matters of the Lord!" Though bloodlines among the people were usually considered in regard to marriage, if the Prophet directed it, it was believed God would honor the union. Biological and scientific issues would not come to pass as long as the couple had "enough faith." Christine, Mom, and I were highly disturbed at the whole situation, but as women we had absolutely no say.

The ceremony was to take place almost immediately following her fourteenth birthday, and Warren had already directed me to help Mom make Elissa's wedding dress. As a last resort, she made an appointment to see the Prophet, which meant that she would talk to Warren and only shake Rulon's hand. The day she came to visit Rulon, I was the head cook, and I greeted her in the driveway, hugging her and wishing her luck before returning to my duties. I was in the dining room with Rulon when Warren strode through the French doors and brusquely asked if Elissa Wall could shake our Prophet's hand. Rulon motioned for her to come in. I watched Elissa kneel before the Prophet, taking his hand, but pleading with her eyes and speaking softly to him, with Warren's narrowed gaze locked on her. I held my breath. I could tell it hadn't gone well in Warren's office.

"I'm trying to be a good girl and do what I'm told," Elissa told Rulon. "But I need more time."

Rulon smiled and patted her hand.

"Follow your heart, sweetie," he said. "Just follow your heart."

Elissa looked at me and our eyes both filled with relief. Warren looked livid.

After lunch, Elissa went back to Uncle Fred's to tell him what the Prophet had said and ask again for more time. He refused, very unhappy that she questioned his authority. He threatened that if she rejected this blessing now, she might not ever get another chance to marry—ever! For a girl in Uncle Fred's compound with nowhere else to go, this was a crushing pronouncement. Women were not allowed to live out on their own. This meant if she did not marry she would always be a ward of another man and shamed for her rebellion.

Christine and I made another appointment with Rulon to plead for more time, but when we arrived, Warren was already there. A chill ran down my spine.

Rulon sat while Christine and I knelt at his feet and recounted Elissa's story to him. He seemed very surprised that Fred was asking Elissa to marry her own first cousin. He started to become upset, at which point Warren stepped in.

"Uncle Fred has asked that this marriage happen, Father."

"Oh," replied Rulon.

"But Father, she just turned fourteen!" I exclaimed.

Rulon looked at me in surprise. "What the hell is Fred thinking?" he bellowed, and looked at Warren.

"Well, Father, he's insisting that this go on. He's asked that this happen, and we want to support him in that." Within moments it was clear to me what was happening. Warren obviously needed to keep Fred as a political ally. Rulon's eyes became clouded with confusion as Warren kept on, and within minutes, Rulon backed Fred again.

My family was crushed and I was outraged, but Mom and I finished Elissa's wedding dress, having been admonished by Fred and Warren to make my little sister happy in "her decision." Knowing that we had done all women were allowed, I did my best to convince her to be joyful at the "will of God," as I was told to say. At her fitting in my mother's room at Uncle Fred's, I struggled to pin the lace precisely into place onto the dress, as Elissa's body heaved with great sobs. I was crying inside. My only consolation was that Allen was not old like my husband and so many others. I did not like him, but I told her that they might perhaps grow to love each other. Silently I prayed that he would treat her well.

As I watched my baby sister being driven away to the Caliente Motel in Nevada, which was now seeing a steady flow of child brides, I wanted to run, scream, yell, and beat on the car. But I had to hold on to the only power I had—the buffer of my husband. If I acted rashly or disobediently, the little help I could give my mother and sisters would come to a screeching halt. Choking back tears, my mother and I soberly decorated the "honeymoon hideout"—a bedroom next to Mom's in Fred's house that was set aside for Allen and Elissa. What she was being forced to face that night was *not right*. It had been horrible for me at nineteen, and she was still a little girl.

Despite the promise he'd made to give her time, Allen forced Elissa to consummate the marriage almost immediately. Though she didn't say anything for several weeks, we could tell something was drastically wrong. Amelia, whose husband was much younger than mine, knew precisely the questions to ask when she called from Canada, especially, "What does he do when you say no?" Elissa opened up to Amelia on the phone, and Mom relayed certain details to me when I snuck over to visit. I confronted Elissa. She finally admitted to Mom and me that when she told Allen she hated him to touch her, he played on her gullibility, saying he would grow physically ill—even die—if she didn't allow him to have sex. Then she finally broke down and admitted that Allen was raping her nearly every night, often violently.

"I went to Warren about what he is doing to me," Elissa said, tears welling in her eyes again. "He said, 'Go home and follow your Priesthood Head.'" Neither Mom nor I was at liberty to tell Elissa otherwise, especially since we were married to the Bishop and the Prophet, respectively. But when I left to go back to my home and was finally alone in my room, I threw up repeatedly, so nauseated at what Allen was doing to my little sister—and Warren's callous disregard for the young girl's pain and grief.

Over the next several months, Elissa spent more and more time in Mom's room at Uncle Fred's massive house, when she could get away with not being at her husband's trailer. I visited, too, in order to get away from Warren, Rulon, and the morose thoughts that consumed me at home. It seemed like Warren had started tracking my every move, so I had to slip in and out as surreptitiously as possible. He started having spies at Fred's check on me, which made me furious. I knew because

I would come home and Warren would have "reports" on me—details that other people would report to him about me whenever I left the Jeffses' estate if I wasn't with only immediate Jeffs family members with Warren's knowledge. It wasn't just at Uncle Fred's house. Soon the God Squad was watching me around town, noting my comings and goings. I was certainly not the only one the Gestapo-type guards had their eye on, but if I wasn't where Warren thought I was supposed to be, I would hear about it.

Warren had a penchant for taking away all the things he knew gave a person joy. Soon all of my privileges had been taken. No more horses. No more four-wheeling. Warren had made sure the keepers of my keys to freedom knew to never allow me access again, at the risk of their souls.

Soon he restricted everything else near and dear to my heart, forbidding dances, operettas, plays, and even parades. From the pulpit, Warren demanded stricter rules among the people, like completely forbidding anyone to wear the color red, and reiterating that passion and pleasure in the bedroom were for *men only*. As holders of the Priesthood their passion was meant to fulfill God's will. Men could have that, as far as I was concerned, but it felt like Warren was taking every last thing from the community that gave a sense of purpose or joy.

"Times have changed," Warren said at church. "We as a people must focus on preparing. Father says we are being too light-minded. We must cut down on the laughter. We must restrict traveling for fancy and entertainment. Restrict your camping trips and remind your families that this is a time of focus and preparation."

I didn't want to be rebellious, but I was so tired of being controlled. If I could be involved in any activity outside the Jeffses' home, I would ask my husband for permission. One day I asked Rulon if I could help Christine and some ladies put on a small holiday program for the seniors in the community. Although it contained music, Rulon allowed it, and Warren couldn't override his decision. Arriving home exhausted from rehearsal one night, Christine went directly to her room, not feeling well. Heading over to check our kitchen schedule, I walked through the living room, where eight of my sister-wives, including Cecilia and Sylvia, were speaking in low voices. It seemed like cause for concern, so I quickly sat down to see what was wrong.

"I don't like it when he touches me," Andrea was saying. "And he's getting really weird and demanding."

"Yes, he is," said another, and most of the group nodded. They were obviously talking about Rulon, who had resorted to even more bizarre behavior, if that was possible. Worse, he had lost whatever minor inhibitions he once had, and was behaving in gross and lewd ways—with no regard as to who was around while he did these things.

Sylvia explained that she and another sister-wife had been in a room with Rulon when he had started to undress her, making her go bare all the way down to the waist, and expecting her to be open to his caresses.

"I kept saying, 'Father, no, no!' but he kept pushing my hands away," she said. "When the other wife went to leave, Father wouldn't let her and demanded she stay in the room as he was doing this to me!" She burst into tears.

"I can't *stand* him to touch me," said Emma, nodding. She was one of Rulon's newer wives. "He's so far past childbearing age, how can he be allowed to touch me?"

"What do you think, Becky?" Diana asked.

I stood up abruptly. I had to get out of there.

"I think you guys are going to get in severe trouble! I am going, because I don't get away with *anything*." I left without saying another word. While it was a relief to know that several of my sister-wives felt as I did, I couldn't take the chance of stirring up more trouble with Warren.

The next day flu and pneumonia hit our house and Fred's with a vengeance. I was nursing Elissa, who was in my room, and Christine in her own. They were both so sick, I spent most of the morning running back and forth between the kitchen, the bathroom, and their rooms.

"Mother Becky, call 600." That was Warren's extension. I reacted with my usual *Oh, what did I do now?* and dialed from the kitchen phone. Warren's voice came over the line.

"Mother Becky, I need to see you in my office."

"Why?" I asked. "I'm in the kitchen."

"I heard you were involved in a conversation."

"I didn't say anything," I said. "I just came upon the conversation. I didn't have anything to do with it."

"You didn't say anything?"

"Nope."

"I want you to come talk to me right now." He was fishing.

"I can't. I'm getting some enemas ready for some very sick people," I replied. It was true, but I hoped that comment would gross him out. "I'm going to have to talk to you later. I don't have time right now." I hung up on him, too sleep-deprived to care. Yes, I could have added plenty to the wives' discussion, but I was determined to be a good Prophet's wife. I might not have liked what had been dished out on my plate, but I was committed to show God that I would endure it. That day, I left the kitchen, armed with enemas, compresses, and a little more grit and determination to endure. My mother would be so proud.

CHAPTER 12

From the Frying Pan into the Fire

On the morning of September 11, 2001, my friend Samantha paged me while I was with the family waiting for breakfast prayer. Terrorists had used commercial airplanes to attack the World Trade Center and the Pentagon in the eastern part of the United States, she told me. Thousands were dying, both in the planes and in the buildings. Before we'd even had time to react, the national tragedy played right into the fears by which Warren manipulated our people.

"We should be rejoicing!" Warren announced jubilantly to his father and all of us present as he bounced in for breakfast. "Terrorists are attacking the government and are leading to the weakening and demise of the evil it has become!" I had been terribly saddened by the bits and pieces of coverage filtering in, and my heart was filled with compassion for the families whose loved ones were in the planes and the towers. *Was God that heartless in his plan to bring about the end of the world?* That thought didn't add much to my faith in this God. Or was it just that people were heartless—people like terrorists? People like Warren?

Every day, Warren was rescinding more of our personal freedoms. We had been a strict, God-fearing people, but we had been joyful, too. Now, fear, suspicion, and paranoia consumed the community, and it worsened as Warren pitted person against person in his power games. A vast, nearly tangible spiritual darkness seemed to settle over us all.

At home, there was no way for me to avoid Warren. He was the teacher for Good Words Class at six a.m. and Morning Class at eight a.m. and he taught his father's wives at family class in the evening, too. He was at nearly every meal. While the house was massive, it seemed like I would run into him or get called in to his office every day. I felt smothered, unable to quietly slip out to see my family or my friend Samantha.

One rare day when I was able to sneak away from the Jeffses' property, I went to the bike shop where my mother was having her bike repaired. I stepped inside to see that she and a young man were injecting a green, gooey slime into her tires so they wouldn't go flat, despite the nasty goat head "stickers," or puncture vines, prevalent throughout town. Suddenly the green goo spewed everywhere and I watched in amazement as my mother erupted into laughter. It was the first time I had seen her laugh in years! All I could think of was, *God bless that young man.*

His name was Benjamin Jeffs Musser. I had met him soon after I was married to Rulon, but I didn't know him well at all. Although I was known as "Grandmother Becky" to most young people in town, Ben actually *was* my grandson, in that he was the grandson of Rulon and my sister-wife Ruth Jessop Jeffs. He was a tall and lanky redhead, with the most brilliant blue eyes and the longest eyelashes I had ever seen on a man. But it was his kind countenance I really noticed. As my mother no longer had any sons to help her, Ben and his brother had gone out of their way to do special things for her on several occasions. I was most grateful for how he had made her smile. How I had missed her smile— and the smiles of all the women I loved.

Several days later was I called into Warren's office because he had "received a report" that I had been playing soccer with members of the community. Oh, I had seen the game all right. Oh, and I had longed to stop and play with three or four of my sister-wives I saw out there having a blast. And, oh, I had considered the consequences because of all the trouble I had been in, and how Warren had been clamping down on outdoor activities and sports. I had come home, only to be shamed and in distress for something I had not done when I was fighting with all my strength to do things right.

"Your reports are wrong," I said adamantly. "I did not stop and play. I knew I would get in trouble for it, so I kept driving, and came back home to my room."

"I'm glad you were not playing, then. Remember, there are no competitive games in Heaven."

I nodded, hoping he was done and I could be excused. He stared at me hard for a moment. "How have you been doing at getting close to Father?" he asked.

I shot him a look. I was incapable of lying and Warren knew it. I had to drop my eyes as he began reciting to me scripture after scripture and Prophets' quotes on obedience to your husband in every capacity.

"'Wives, submit yourselves to your husbands, as unto the Lord, for he is your lord.' 'Wives, seek not to set in order your husbands.'" He went on and on . . .

I couldn't believe it. He couldn't pin something on me I hadn't done, so he had to push the button of authority as far as sexual acquiescence and obedience to my husband. I kept my head down, biting my cheek during his twenty-minute discourse. Thoroughly pleased that he had reduced me to nothing again, he let me go.

I fled to my room to stew, but after an hour I snuck out, got permission from Nephi to borrow a family car, and drove over to Uncle Fred's, where I stormed angrily into my mother's room. Her door was already open, and as soon as I had shut it behind me to ensure I was out of earshot of Fred's family, I began whispering angrily.

"You would not *believe* what that big jerk said to me today, Mom! Warren is now dictating that I—"

My mother gave me a mortified look and frantically motioned around the corner. I'd had no idea that Ben Musser was in her room, putting up some shelving for her. Immediately I was struck dumb, not just with embarrassment but with fear. Warren had his spies everywhere.

Ben just smiled at me, then went back to work. I left for home not long after to await the fallout. But Ben never betrayed me—he just kept showing up to help my mother. I blessed him again for his character and integrity. Anyone else would have run straight to Warren in the hopes of getting into his good graces so he wouldn't be crucified himself.

In the meantime, our people in Canada were facing a variety of challenges. Calls from Amelia in Bountiful, as well as reports that Warren would read to Rulon, kept us abreast of what was happening. A few years in a row, resources had been scarce, and Winston was testing the mettle of his people so that they would be ready to endure the end of the world, the destruction of governments, and all of Warren's doomsday predictions. Amelia and her family had to survive temperatures below zero with no electricity, no gas, and little wood. Food was rationed as if a famine existed. They were growing weak.

Mom and I sent extra supplies of material, diapers, vitamins, and simple things like hair spray, which we brought in cases to the Jeffses' property; FLDS women used so much to strictly maintain the tidy yet elaborate styles that were encouraged by Warren and the rest of the FLDS leaders. Mom and I weren't allowed to compromise their fast, so we sent no food. I was furious with Winston, especially because the last time I had seen him, he was no thinner than before. He and his wives and his children did not appear weak or emaciated like Amelia and the rest of the people. I loved many of Winston's wives, and I was sure that watching their relatives suffer was just as painful for them as it was for us.

During the spring of 2002, the following year, Warren and Winston had a great falling-out. Although they had been strong allies for quite some time, both were young leaders with greatly developed egos, and they had begun to battle for control of the church. Now Winston had found a weak spot. After the world did not end in 1999, Warren had foretold the destruction of the earth at a time when all eyes would be on Salt Lake City for the Olympics: February 8 through 24, 2002. He said it would be fitting for the Lord to plan it then, when so much attention was being placed on the Mormon faith. God would smite the apostates and the wicked together, showing once and for all that the Celestial Law was the only pure law upon the earth!

Once the Olympics had come and gone, most of the people were placated—and relieved—by Warren's similar pronouncement that we were "too wicked to be lifted up" and the Lord had granted us time to repent again. I couldn't help but agree as Winston pointed out the number of times Warren had wrongly prophesied the destruction of the earth. He also publicly called Warren out for usurping authority from the Prophet. Like the Barlow boys, Winston had had direct access to the Prophet until Rulon's stroke, access that had been cut off as Rulon's health deteriorated. Winston had been forced to go through Warren to get any answers, and he was no dummy.

When we heard about Winston's pronouncements, we were all shocked, as we had been frozen into a state of mere survival. The bishop could say things firmly and boldly, with the buffer of the hundreds of physical miles between him and Warren, and his own seat of power firmly set in Canada. I don't think Winston was fully aware of Rulon's compromised mental state, or how much power Warren had gained over the local people. Warren told Winston it was the Prophet's will that he was out, stripped of his title and membership. It was clear who was winning in Short Creek—no one had the courage or authority to question the Prophet's son. But our relatives in British Columbia were faced with a very uncomfortable dilemma: *Warren or Winston?*

I was alarmed for our people and especially concerned for Amelia and Brittany. As a student of FLDS history, I knew that it was generally the families and the children who suffered most when people were forced to choose one leader over another. Just like the battle over "one-man rule" that had ripped families apart, I knew this wasn't just a battle over personalities. It was a bloody, spiritual civil war.

Rulon struggled through another series of ministrokes. His health situation was dire, and Warren mandated that my sister-wives and I stay with him 24/7. Once again we were on house arrest, left to stay with our husband while we fasted and prayed for his recovery. Warren pounded into our heads that it was our immoral desires and lack of fervent prayer keeping him ill. We had to be more righteous in our prayers, fasting, and suffering.

Warren and Rulon ate, while the rest of us fasted, having only sips of water, weak tea, or apple juice. I felt like we were the Egyptian wives of the Pharaoh, doomed to be buried alive until we perished alongside our husband. The Jeffses' home already felt like a tomb, and wherever I turned in the gloomy corridors, the darkened, sunken eyes of my sister-wives stared back at me. Several of the ladies started fainting and having severe digestive and other health problems. We spent as much time in nursing one another as we did attempting to nurse Rulon.

Finally Warren changed the edict: we were to fast every other week. Still, our long periods of fasting and isolation had taken a toll on everyone's health. Instead of getting better, we were becoming sicker, and so was Rulon. Mary stayed by his side night and day, resting only for a few hours when necessary. It wasn't helping. Not a single one of us wanted to admit it, but we were losing our husband, our Prophet.

On September 8, 2002, Rulon Timpson Jeffs passed away. He had prophesied that he would never die, and we had believed him. We all relied on the Prophet for our eternal salvation. And Rulon had promised he would be renewed! Even as we prepared for our Prophet's funeral services and the people mourned, we kept expecting Rulon to bang on the lid of the coffin and demand to be let out! But there was no sound.

More than five thousand FLDS members attended the funeral services for the Prophet. Afterward, Warren asked the people to allow immediate family to view the interment, promising that they could come and pay their respects when it was over. More than sixty of Rulon's wives, his children, and a few close great-grandchildren gathered to see Rulon's ornate wooden casket lowered into the ground. My sister-wives and I sang "A Choir of Angels," one of Rulon's favorite songs, a cappella. It wasn't until dirt was shoveled onto the enclosure that we looked at one another with wide eyes and the frightening realization that our husband and our Prophet was truly gone.

On the way home in the van, as we were coming up the hill between the cemetery and the Jeffs property, a deep and tangible fear grew within me. Most of us had remained in a state of devastation for several days and were terrified by the thought of living without Rulon. Not that living with him had been that grand, but the unknown felt much worse. For me, personally, Rulon had provided a powerful layer of protection between myself and Warren. I knew that now I would have to pay the price.

Warren's usurping of power over the last four years meant that the transition to full power was fairly seamless. The day after Rulon's funeral, he continued "speaking for Father" and then stunned the entire congregation who had gathered for instruction, song, and prayer when he curtly announced, "Hands off the Prophet's wives!" I was shocked and still numb, but so grateful. I had been old enough to remember the power plays involving Uncle Roy's wives after his death. Everyone had wanted one of the Prophet's little darlings, and within just a few weeks the women were placed with new men and families, hardly given a moment to grieve. I was relieved that Warren was granting us time and safety.

That night in family class Warren spoke for hours on how we should go on with our lives as if Father was still there, that it was what he would have wanted for us. He even said if we were faithful enough, we would see Rulon walking among us. I felt that same tremendous sense of relief. Like a nun married to Christ, I could simply be married to Rulon for the rest of my days. It might have been an odd thought for a twenty-six-year-old woman, but the idea of being bedded by any other man terrified me. Warren's proclamation settled my nerves.

Because of this, I was not prepared for what was about to happen.

The week after Rulon's passing, my sister Brittany called me from Bountiful, her voice full of concern as she told me that Winston proclaimed that with Rulon dead, Warren would have "free rein" over his father's wives!

At Brittany's words, my blood ran cold. When Rulon passed, I had been secretly relieved that I would no longer have to be violated at the hand of God. To have to face that violation again with someone else was beyond what I could handle.

"There are many of us praying that Heavenly Father will have mercy for your fate in the desert," Brittany said, but there was little comfort in her voice. "Becky, my husband has so many wives, he doesn't even bother to spend the night with just one of us!" Her voice broke. "He simply hops from bed to bed, treating us like whores—without even the dignity of holding us in his arms for even one night after relations."

With a start, I realized what it had taken from Brittany all these years not to crumble under the strain. Jason Blackmore should be taken out back and beaten with a hairbrush! I recalled how at the beginning of their marriage, he had forced her to submit before she was ready, and now she was expected to keep sweet and be grateful for any morsel of affection as he jumped from wife to wife in the night.

As I placed the phone back on the receiver, a great anxiety swelled up within in me. Christine had come into my room as I had been on the phone with Brittany, and she was half reclining on my bed.

"You don't think we'll be forced to remarry, do you?" I asked, confiding my worst fear to her. "Do you really think we'll have to be placed with another man?"

I looked into her beautiful, dark eyes, hoping for some verification that this was all nonsense and foolishness. Instead, I was shocked to see a wistful smile upon her face.

"I've actually dreamed that I would marry..." Nodding matter-of-factly, she added, "I dreamed that I would marry Warren."

"*What?*" I cried shrilly, unable to hide my disgust and disbelief. "*Warren?*" Christine was much too young and too beautiful to be a widow forever, and though I couldn't blame her for desiring a younger husband and children of her own, I was sickened by her response.

"Yes," she said, languidly. "I think it's what Father would want us to do. Don't you?" She stared at me pointedly, and I could feel my temperature rising. I had visions of Warren jumping from bed to bed like Jason. The heat moved from my head into my belly, and like a volcano, indignation burst from deep within me.

"If you think I will be part of a herd of cows where a wild bull runs rampant among us, openly mounting one cow, then moving on to another, and another, and another...well, you're wrong. I will have some dignity...and jump the fence!"

There was only one context in which I would have preferred to be treated like an animal. Why couldn't I be "put out to pasture" like the older wives after our husband's death? Those past childbearing years didn't have to face this gut-wrenching dilemma. I could easily live with Mother Marilyn, Mother Ruth, and Mother LaRue, and the other older wives. I honestly believed in my life and my religion, and I would have been content to spend the rest of my days cooking, cleaning, and serving others as long as I didn't have to go near a bedroom with a man in it.

"Why the hell would you base a decision like that off a stupid dream?" I threw my notebook on the bed, highly disturbed at all Christine was suggesting. I began having a very ominous feeling building in the pit of my stomach.

That Sunday, I was called once again into Warren's office. He got right to the point.

"Mother Christine came and talked to me."

I froze, then tried to act casual.

"Oh yeah...? What did she say?"

Warren gave me a rather sanctimonious look. "She told me everything."

My heart sank. And I was furious with Christine.

"No offense, Uncle Warren," I said. "I could not marry you, or any man." I waited for him to explode, but instead he grabbed a nearby garbage can and began clipping his fingernails over it. Aside from the *clip, clip, clip,* there was total silence.

"I know I could have been more obedient when Father was alive—" I finally began, but Warren stopped me.

"Mother Becky, I want to put your concerns to rest. No one is going to be forced into anything. This household will carry on as if Father were alive." My heart jumped in relief. He went on. "I am going to ask if you have a problem with me, you go directly to me. Don't go to Christine, or anyone else. Just come directly to me."

It took me several moments to respond. If I didn't have to run away from violation, I would no longer look for reasons to be gone. I would seriously commit myself to doing just what he asked of me.

"Well, okay then, Uncle Warren," I said. He looked up at me, surprised. "I will ask you for the same consideration. Stop fishing. Stop going to others for reports. Come straight to me, and I will tell you the truth of what is in my mind and my heart." Hopefully, he would be able to understand that 99 percent of my rebellion had been about being with Rulon in the bedroom, and that if I no longer had to worry about being raped and violated, I would be obedient to him.

I stood up to excuse myself.

"Mother Becky," Warren prompted, "what would you do, if Father's wish was now for you ladies to be remarried?"

I looked at him fiercely. "I will tell you one thing. I will not say yes to something that I don't agree with or feel I can succeed at."

In my mind, marriage meant sexual submission. I never wanted to be with another man, not ever.

Warren nodded. "I just wondered," he said. "Remember, no one is going to be forced to do anything."

For the next several nights, however, I couldn't eat or sleep. Warren began intimating that he had changed his tune. His words were in direct opposition to what he had told the people, and then what he had told me, but in a devious way.

"Ladies, consider in your heart that you might be called to do something that will not feel right to you," he said one evening in class.

"Consider it prayerfully. The minute you revolt from anything that comes from God, you will be under the power of Satan and not be able to resist. One night, Father is going to have you do some things that you may first reject. I'm telling you, be silent and pray for a testimony that you will not reject and that your heart will be open. If you are pure in heart, you will know that this is a truth. This is the next step."

I sat there, unable to believe how this man was so adept at twisting words and using our beliefs against us for his own purposes! When we obeyed him to the letter, he called us "Father's Heavenly angels." If we voiced a single fear, however, he would say that Satan was finding a place in our hearts. Of course, we wanted to be angels and keep sweet!

My head and heart hurt, my bones were aching, and I had the most awful stomach pains. I had developed ulcers like many of my sister-wives. Several sleepless nights later, I went to the kitchen to find some-thing to alleviate the pain. My sister-wife Amanda was in there, too, having the same problem. The rest of the house was silent.

I hugged her, noticing the circles under her eyes mirrored mine.

"Amanda, you don't think we are going to be required to remarry, do you?"

She started to cry. "Becky, the last time I helped Father was in the last two weeks of his life. Father was laying down, and Mary and I were rub-bing his legs to help with the pain. Suddenly Rulon pulled himself up with great strength and grabbed Mary by the shoulders. 'Mary, promise me, you will save yourself for me!' 'What are you talking about?' she cried, and he said, 'Promise me that if something happens to me, you will totally save yourself for me.' 'Nothing will happen to you, Father!' she cried. 'You are going to live for one hundred and fifty more years! You've said so.' Then Father shook her shoulders, hard! 'Promise me, no other man will have you!' 'Okay, I promise!' she said."

Amanda looked at me with the same desperation I was feeling. "Becky, I cling to that...I cling to that."

I clung to that as well.

In the meantime, many people, especially in Canada, began to mur-mur that Warren was not the rightful leader of the Church. Warren addressed these rumblings at the annual breakfast my sister-wives and I had at Maxwell Park in honor of my and Rulon's anniversary. We would have been married seven years. These breakfasts were always a special occasion, though we had them often, as we had sixty-five of Rulon's unions to celebrate. Naomi took notes as Warren spoke.

"Before Father passed on, he set in order this situation," Warren began, referring to Canada. "The opposition is going to say that it was not Father that made the corrections on Winston—that he was not able to make the decisions—that it was Warren who did it."

I looked around at my sister-wives. They knew as well as I did that Rulon *had* deferred everything to Warren.

"Thus it all comes down to whether they have a testimony of the Prophet and that he does right. I say to us, make sure your testimony burns bright. The other night I talked to you, about how Priesthood succession takes place, how the previous Prophet has already, by revelation, appointed the next Prophet. Even since Father's passing, think on the testimonies you have heard and how you felt—and why Father is doing this among you—so that his family will stand firm and not be divided. This is why you must stay close to home where the Priesthood can guide you and that you won't go off and join in all the fearful and doubting conversations among this people."

Not only were we not to question; he asked us to become "sweeter and even sweeter." I kept concentrating on the people and my desire to hold them together. But my body language could not lie. And my brain could not compute the way Warren was twisting his words to sound like the new truth.

Unbeknownst to me, on Friday, October 4, 2002, Warren wrote in his Priesthood Record:

> I talked to LeRoy Jeffs today. I told him to seek a testimony of what I was to tell him, of the Lord and Father, that some of Father's ladies would be sealed, many to myself, and I told him one to him, as far as I know now; that he needed a testimony of his own of the authority to perform that work and that it is Father's will. He immediately expressed that he believed and would support the directive, knowing that Father would tell me what to do. I said this to him as we walked along outside at the school.
>
> I just yearn none of Father's ladies will fail this test that is coming on them. But I feel like when a sealing takes place, most would

come, yearning to do Father's will. All but one seems to be converted, and that is Mother Becky.

One month to the day after Rulon died, my entire belief system was
shattered. At six a.m., Warren's voice sounded over the speaker.

"Good morning, ladies! This morning's Good Words will not be
over the intercom, it will be in the living room. All of you come up!"

Hmmmmm, I thought. I threw on one of my long dresses and socks,
not really bothering with my hair. When I arrived in the living room,
several ladies were already seated, and I chose a seat on a recliner.

Warren walked into Good Words Class, bouncing on his heels and
grinning from ear to ear as if he had won the Nevada state lottery. Most
of the ladies in the room looked at him as mystified as I was.

"Seven of you ladies married me last night. Would you seven please
stand up?" Immediately, seven of my sister-wives rose to their feet,
while the rest of us looked on in shock and disbelief. They stood there,
giggling like young schoolgirls.

I couldn't stop tears from racing down my cheeks and onto my dress.
Mother Paula, Mother Ora, Mother Naomi, Mother Melinda, Mother
Tammy, Mother Kate, and even Mother Kathy were standing. Once I
thought about it, I was not surprised to find Naomi in that first batch of
Warren's wives, but I found it significant that mothers Paula and Ora
were first—the ones who served as examples to the rest of us. And his
marriage to Mother Kathy, known previously in the community as an
avid follower of Winston, was a clever, strategic move on Warren's part.
Jubilantly, Warren described how each of these women had come to
him in private, feeling like they were supposed to be married to him.
They continued giggling as he spoke, while the rest of us sat there
bewildered.

"We are all going to go on a honeymoon trip, to play baseball at the
park. This is the next step for you ladies. This is what Father wants you
to do. These seven women came to me!" Then he told us to pray, and
Father would tell us who it was we were to marry.

"These women are so pure they received Father's revelation first.
This is Father's will, and I'm just his little boy. I'm just his little boy!"
He threw his hands up and shrugged his shoulders.

I glanced over at Christine. She had told both me and Warren about her dream of marrying him. Her face betrayed her sadness that she was not among the first seven of his wives. There would be more, though— I would bet my life on it. My stomach turned violently. Not only did our scripture forbid men from *ever* marrying their mothers; something about the whole thing just felt sick. I told everyone I didn't feel good and begged out of going to the honeymoon celebration at the park.

Up until that point, I wholeheartedly believed in my religion. I did not like Warren and I didn't agree with his maneuverings, but I believed I was in the truest church the world had ever known. Had we been told that the next step was to drink purple punch filled with cyanide, I would have done so without question.

Now I was questioning everything.

Even though I'd heard from Warren, "No one is going to be forced," there was a horrible gnawing at the pit of my stomach. Over the next several days, I hesitated to go to Good Words Class. Each day, Warren would show up with more of my sister-wives on his coattails! I couldn't help but be repulsed.

My sister-wives were disappearing, and not just from our household to Warren's. In the last week we had woken up to find Emma gone, and no one knew where she was until she showed up later with Warren's brother LeRoy. They were both thrilled, and my heart delighted that she had found a kind man, though it was sobering for the rest of us to lose her.

At church, Warren carefully used testimonies of the Prophet's last days to substantiate his power from the pulpit. He had Isaac testify how Rulon had pointed at Warren and told Isaac, "You follow that man. You follow that man." Then for the very first time, Warren had Naomi stand up to give her testimony. I could count on one hand the times that a woman had spoken in church—and I wouldn't use all the fingers. Naomi testified that Rulon had said, "If anything ever happens to me, you follow that man."

The destructions of 2000 and 2002 had never happened, but now I felt the ground tremble violently under my feet. At least with Rulon, we had generally known what to expect. Warren was a loaded gun.

CHAPTER 13

The Kiss That Broke the Spell

I awoke in the predawn hours with voices in my head, fighting among themselves:

Voice One: (brightly) You can get married. You can do this!

Voice Two: (darkly) You can never get married again. You're disgusted by men and their carnal desires.

Voice One: Sure you can do this! Look at Emma. She's delightfully happy, married to LeRoy. They look blissful together, the way you've pictured "love"...someone holding your hand, putting their arms around you just to hold you; to love you just for you...

Voice Three: (frankly) How can you do to other wives what's been done to you? You'll never be a first wife at your age, and that means stealing the attention and affections away from the other wives. You've seen it—the loneliness and anguish in their eyes. The longing to be loved...Think of Emma. Could you really do that to her? Or any of the women in the community you love? You can never be a naïve, happy newlywed—YOU KNOW BETTER!

That was my voice. Actually, I had to admit, they were all my voices— the fragmented pieces and parts of my heart pulled relentlessly in multiple directions. *God and the Prophet do right. Remember the Golden Windows. Sacrifice your feelings and do right. Put it on the shelf for now.* As in every other aspect of my life, there was no room for me and my authentic thoughts and wishes. Each day I was afraid to go to Good Words. Which of my sister-wives would have been added to Warren's entourage? Those were *our* sister-wives! We'd worked together, cooked together, laughed together, played together, composed music together, fasted and mourned Rulon's death together. We were as close as blood sisters now. He couldn't just take them away!

That night, several of us ended up in the kitchen, informally migrating in for a restless, late-night snack. We looked around the table at one another, at first afraid to speak.

"Are you married?" Charlotte asked me.

"No," I breathed. "Are you?" She shook her head. We turned to Virginia and Leona, who said no, and took a long breath. Then we sat for a while in silence as we ate. Rulon had died with sixty-four wives. Fifty-six of them were between the ages of seventeen and thirty-four. One by one, our numbers were dwindling.

For days, it was all I could do to put a little food in my body and not throw it back up. The months of fasting had extracted a painful toll on my health, and I felt sapped of all strength, though it was the emotional strain that was the hardest now. I felt the familiar itch to claim some semblance of freedom, if only for a few hours.

I thought of visiting Mom, but each of the two times I had slipped out to see her, Uncle Fred's wives and daughters harangued me for the latest news. "Who got married today? Who do you think will be gone tomorrow?" I knew I had to go someplace where I could be alone with my thoughts.

El Capitan, the mysterious red-rock mountain backdrop of Hildale, suddenly felt oddly inviting. At an acceptable hour of the morning when I wouldn't get in too much trouble for leaving, Nephi kindly let me borrow a minivan to drive to my sister Elissa's house. Elissa in turn let me borrow her four-wheel-drive truck to drive to the mountains. On the way I rolled the windows down, gulping in the crisp air as if it might save my life. It was already a stunning fall day, the kind southern Utah is famous for. The October sun felt warm, energizing, and healing, and as I began my hike, I was grateful to feel energy instead of lethargy for the first time in months. Each step I took was deliberate, and I talked to God the entire way up, like I never had before. I had been taught to pray on my knees, arms folded, eyes closed, but this was a pouring out of my soul onto the crimson dirt. I rarely stopped to catch my breath, and my shoes and socks were laced with sweat and soil. Less than two hours later, I dropped to the ground, breathless and exhausted.

As I looked down on Hildale, I couldn't help but think of what was waiting for me when I got back, and I had the sudden and reckless urge to throw myself off the cliff face. One had to be stark raving mad to throw away eternal salvation—and yet here I was.

A sudden breeze caught my skirts and my hair and soothed my sweat-stained brow, almost like someone had touched my forehead in a loving caress. For several long moments, I kept still and listened, and that was when I heard a strange yet familiar voice. It was outside of me and yet seemed to come from my very soul.

Your life is like a tapestry in the making, woven like fine silk in brilliant, dynamic colors…yet with a pattern you cannot yet see. Trust that your life is just beginning, Becky. Trust that many more colorful threads are about to be added, and patterns you've never dreamed of.

An intense peace filled my body and began to wash over me as I felt an emotion I hadn't experienced in years. It was hope.

On my way down the steep mountainside, I thought of all the connections I had among my people. Whom did I feel safe with? My mom, my little sisters, and Samantha were the only ones I could trust. Then my thoughts turned to Ben Musser, who had kept my confidence when he could have ratted me out. We had talked a few times since then, when he did things for my mother, and a couple of times he had been allowed to fix a few things for me as well. We had kept our distance, and everything was strictly platonic, but he had made it clear he was a safe, listening ear. He was refreshingly conscious of me. Not my looks. Not my title. Me as a person. I realized that the element of connection that I felt with him was in fact *safety*. Never had I felt that way with any man in the FLDS, not even my own father.

I had started to sense a shift in the community, one that made me feel like I was on display along with my sister-wives. When Mother Emma married LeRoy, it opened us up as possibilities for men other than Warren. Even Seth and Isaac had changed their attitudes toward me, using a much warmer tone. My cousin David Allred had done the same.

I was finishing up the last of the projects that Rulon had given me his blessing on before he died. Nicole, a friend I had made in the FLDS musical community, had tried to warn me.

"Becky, be careful. There are many men who would love to have you."

"What? No. *No, no, no!* No one is getting me," I said vehemently.

"Becky, even Harold is acting differently about you." I was shocked. Harold was her beloved husband. People I had always seen as "safe" were suddenly eyeing my sister-wives and me as an opportunity to gain status with Warren and with God.

I found myself wishing I could marry someone like Ben—or at least someone like him who was a friend to me, but I knew that simply wasn't an option. Warren would never permit it. Of course, I didn't wish a marriage like that for Ben, because I was seven years older. Surely a marriage to "Grandmother Becky" didn't sound appealing to him in any way.

Several months previous, I had been shopping with my sisters in St. George when I saw a cool snowboard bag on clearance. It was red and black, and as a seamstress with an eye for fit, I knew instinctively that it would fit Ben's snowboard perfectly. I had put it away for a while during the warm weather and planned to give it to him at Mom's as a thank-you gift before the snow fell.

However, now I was waiting for the other shoe to drop. Most of the young wives had been whisked away to Warren or other waiting men. I had the sense that my few remaining personal freedoms were about to disappear, through marriage to Warren or someone else. Christine wanted badly to marry Warren, so he withheld his affections from her. Because I didn't want to, he continued to pursue me. Warren always knew everyone's hot buttons, and boy oh boy, did he know how to play them. El Capitan had given me hope, but I'd still been too many days without sleep, without proper food, and under incredible stress.

Anxious to give Ben his gift before it was too late, I quietly gave him a quick call from the phone in my room, and we decided to meet at the narrows in the canyon—far from the prying eyes of Warren and his minions. I drove up the beautiful red-rock canyon narrows, my heart beating wildly. It wasn't wise for me to meet Ben. I just wanted to give him the bag, thank him, and get out of there. Suddenly I saw his car. No one else was in sight, so I took a deep breath and pulled up about fifteen feet away from his vehicle. We got out of our driver's seats at the same time, and I watched him as we met in the middle between the two vehicles. He grinned widely as he greeted me with one arm and hugged me around my shoulder. As it was rather unusual to receive a hug from a man, I stepped away quickly, grabbing the gift from under my other arm to hide my discomfort.

"I found this for you," I said, smiling genuinely at him. "I hope you like it." Ben looked at the bag in astonishment.

"Wow, can I pay you for this?" he asked.

"No, no!" I cried. "I just wanted to thank you for everything you've done for my mom."

"She's a great lady."

"Yes, she is."

"What I want to know is, how are *you* doing?" He peered into my eyes when I didn't dare to answer, and I noticed a stubbornness within him I hadn't seen before. "Don't let anyone force you into doing anything you don't want to do, Becky."

I started to tear up. "I don't know what I'm going to do!"

"I'm sure sorry you have to go through this," he said. I closed my eyes against the pain and Ben gave me another hug as I quietly wept. Then suddenly I felt a strange feeling upon my lips. Ben was kissing me! His lips were soft and tender. It was a young man's gentle, questioning kiss.

Before I knew it, I was kissing him back. Within seconds, something had changed dramatically between us. We pulled apart and looked at each other like two little kids who had been caught with their hands in the candy jar.

"I'd better go!" I cried. He nodded, and I ran to my car. I jumped in, did a U-turn like a madwoman, and flew down the road. I looked in my rearview mirror and saw Ben waiting—a wise move, as it would not be good for both of us to emerge from the canyon at the same time. I sucked in a deep breath.

He had kissed me! And I had kissed him back!

What did it mean? Why would he do it? Kissing the Prophet's widow risked Ben's status and his very salvation. His salvation!

It hit me. The angels had seen us! Rulon, wherever he was, had seen it, too! I felt so very guilty. Here I'd spent my entire life avoiding any compromising situation, only to blow it like this. I spent the car ride home talking to Rulon in my mind.

You can be mad at me if you want, but Warren is doing the same thing—but with many of your wives! If anyone else was doing what Warren is doing, they would be slammed, hard. You know my heart, Father. You know I've never done anything like this before. Why can't I just marry someone like Ben? He might not be the holiest, with little or no standing in the church, but I would be happy. I don't care if I attain a lesser glory.

I started in toward town, passing people and feeling a sense of shame. What would they think of me if they knew what I had done? I had broken a rule, but much more important, I was feeling untrue to myself.

When I arrived home, I went straight to my room, avoiding everyone. I was actually expecting lightning to strike, for Father to come back from the dead and cut me down. But there was no lightning, and no knock on my door. I took a breath and said a little prayer: *God, if you let me off this time, I will* never *do that again.*

Before dark I went to my mom's for a short visit. We were both very concerned about Elissa and her time away from Allen. She had been spending nights in her truck to keep away from him. Mom and I knew that Warren was aware of it and was trying to force her home. Mom was giving me whatever bits of news she had on my brothers when the pager in my pocket suddenly went off.

It was Christine's number, next to a "911." That meant, *Call home* now!

Immediately after, Mom's phone started ringing. Mom mouthed to me, *Should I tell her you're here?* I shook my head no.

It was almost a relief to know that I'd been caught. I had never been a good liar, and I didn't want this hanging over my head any longer.

My mother's eyes got bigger and bigger as she listened to Christine, and my heart fell. Still, I wondered, how had they found out? Then I remembered that Uncle Wendell's company, Western Precision, had been having their annual company outing that day, and there must have been some people hiking around. It wasn't like Ben and I had hidden behind trees. We hadn't gone up there to hide anything—until the kiss. She put down the receiver slowly, and looked at me.

"Did Ben Musser kiss you?"

"Yes, he did. It's true."

"Oh, Becky!" She started to cry. "I never should have let him come around. I'm so sorry for any part I played in this!"

"Mom, it's not what you think!"

I tried to explain to her that it had been a simple kiss and that I had left immediately after. That it meant nothing. But in my heart I knew I meant something by it. And I knew he did, too. Part of me felt justified, and part of me felt relieved. The test was over, and I had failed. But at least it was over. My sister-wives and I were all being auctioned off anyway. What did it matter? I had based my whole life on God's directive, only to discover it was actually man's opinion being labeled as God's will.

Mom couldn't hear a word I said. Rarely had I seen her so distraught. I left, knowing what was awaiting me at home. But it wasn't me I was worried about.

My pager buzzed with a message from Ben, written in the numerical "textese" that people in Short Creek used with pagers. I deciphered the message. *Dad knows.*

My head got hotter as I drove. If Ben had kissed anyone else, he might have gotten spanked. But because it was me, the repercussions would be extreme. Warren had once made a flippant comment and the words burned into my brain: *You don't know what you do to men when you smile at them, do you?*

I arrived home with my head still hot and I slipped down to my room. I had never meant for this to happen. Taking a breath to steady myself, I placed my keys on my bedside table and dialed 600 on my room phone.

"This is Mother Becky."

"Come see me right now." Warren's voice was very grave.

"All right." I hung the phone up slowly and walked down the hall. It was only just after eight p.m., and yet the house seemed so dark and deathly quiet. I felt as though the whole world was listening to my footsteps. How many of my sister-wives already knew?

I began to ascend the salmon-colored carpet on the staircase toward Rulon's old office, in which Warren had ensconced himself shortly after his father's first stroke, when it had become apparent Rulon could no longer take appointments. It had remained his to run the church from.

The moment I stepped into the office, Warren started firing questions at me: "Did Ben Musser massage you? Did he lay on you? Did you lay on him? Did he fondle your breasts? Did you touch his genitals?"

"No!" I recoiled. I hated how he could take something pure and make it so dirty. "No, nothing like that! It was just a kiss."

As I looked at him, I couldn't help but think of the huge number of my sister-wives Warren had kissed in front of all of us in the last few weeks alone.

"Well, you didn't break your marriage covenant," he said nonchalantly. That meant I had *not* committed adultery. I exhaled softly as Warren continued. "But you cost this young man his salvation because he was willing to do this. He will no longer be trusted by the Priesthood. I am gravely concerned that you are comfortable around the spirit that will lead to apostasy. I detect the seeds of apostasy in you, Mother Becky. I am giving you one week to be married. Next Monday night, you will come and tell me who you are going to marry."

He let that sink in.

"Choose wisely," Warren said, stabbing his finger at me. Then his face softened behind his glasses and he shrugged his shoulders like a little boy. "And it doesn't even have to be me..."

I wanted to vomit. Is this what he had done with my sister-wives to manipulate their choices? I had seen the Jeffses' behaviors as husbands. I would not marry a Jeffs, and certainly not Warren.

"Please," I begged, tears in my eyes, "please do not do this to me." Warren knew—he *knew* I struggled with marital relations! And still he was forcing me.

Suddenly the fire that I was known for welled up inside of me, and I could not stop it. My head pounded with the heat.

"I will not say yes to something I don't agree with, Warren."

"You'll be blessed if you do," he said flippantly, shrugging. Then he turned to look at some papers on the side of his desk as if he had become bored by the discussion.

"I've heard that before!" I snapped, my tone insinuating many things. I couldn't believe my audacity, but there it was before me. My father and mother. Uncle Fred and my mother. My marriage to Rulon.

Elissa's situation. The list of supposed blessings went on and on and led only to heartbreak and denial.

Finally, Warren looked up. "You know that this is what God and Father want," he said.

"No, I do not. I do not know that this is what God and Father want for me."

Warren's eyes turned to steel, filled with cold malice.

"*I. Will. Break. You,*" he said, with deliberate pronunciation on each word. "And I will train you to be a good wife. You have had too much freedom for too long, Becky. No matter who you marry, I will *always* have jurisdiction over you."

The reality of his words sank in. I was enslaved to Warren Jeffs, who had just claimed my life, my marriage, my body, and my soul. The buffer of Rulon was gone; any rights had disappeared just as surely as if I were bound, hands and feet. I thought of all the times I had disobeyed Warren. He would show no mercy now.

When I rose to leave, he stopped me.

"I want to know where you are at all times, Mother Becky," he declared. "I want to know who you are talking to. If I don't know, do *not* go."

"Please, do not do this to me, Warren," I beseeched one last time. "I'm begging you." He looked up at me for a less than a second.

"You *will* be remarried. One week from today."

Warren's words continued to follow me as I stumbled into the corridor. I barely made it into my own room, blinded by tears. Christine came in, crying and apologizing for any part she might have played, but I did not feel her words or her tears. After she left, I glanced at the heavy oak door I had once been so glad to have, and realized it was holding me prisoner. I wished I had never kissed Ben, nor disgraced him or his family.

As I flung myself onto the bed, I wished desperately that I had just done it—just flung myself off the sheer face of El Capitan. Now I had one week to choose a husband. In absolute agony, I felt as if I were already falling to my death.

Over the next few days, I felt like the walking dead. All roads seemed to lead to a hopeless future. One night, just four days before I was to be married, I went into my bathroom to get ready for bed, glancing into the mirror. My eyes were sunken and colorless, surrounded by graying, sallow skin. Months of fasting had played havoc on my body, but it was my spirit that felt broken. It reminded me of a critical question I had asked Warren when I was in high school.

"If God knew who was going to make it and who wasn't," I asked naïvely, "why would he send all of us here, including those who wouldn't?"

He looked at me curiously, and then replied in his usual authoritative manner. "So you can prove it to yourself."

After all the years of striving, I was tired. *Dear God, if this is Heaven, then give me hell!*

Suddenly I had a vision. It felt like déjà vu, because I had dreamed snippets a few times over the last six months. In a split second, I saw with great vividness another bathroom countertop—only this one wasn't grayish-green Formica; it was bright turquoise. I didn't recognize it at all. I was alone in that bathroom, and yet I was not alone. I didn't see anyone else in the mirror or beside me—but somehow I knew I was *not* alone.

In a flash it was gone, but the feeling remained. No longer lonely, I lay upon my bed. Trying to look at my options with less fear, I kept coming up against a door I didn't dare to open. If I did, I would have to rely on the kindness of the outside world. That thought petrified me, nearly as much as marrying again. I couldn't begin to think of how to live among murderers, rapists, thieves—the wicked, corrupt, ignorant, and unkind people of this world.

Wicked…unkind…Was that really my experience? Memories flooded my mind: neighbors after our house fire…my violin teacher, Mrs. Guertler…Brian Lewis and Peter Prier…

A memory I had carefully tucked away whirled into my consciousness. Walking into the Sears department store in St. George as a young bride, searching for vacuum parts. Briefly separated from my sister-wives, I strode alone into the appliances section, where I was unexpectedly mesmerized by a vast sea of televisions, which displayed the most striking black woman on every screen. It was sacrilegious to watch, but the woman was captivating. Even as cloistered from the world as I had been, I recognized the face of Oprah Winfrey. Interviewing a woman who had become a foster mother to a whole neighborhood of cast-off children—transients, runaways, children of addicts, and so on—Oprah was celebrating her generous heart, and even gifted her with items that would serve her hodgepodge family. I was floored.

Those two beautiful women completely refuted everything I had ever been taught about the outside world—especially about black people! Warren said blacks were from the seed of Cain, and he used words like "uncouth, wild and ignorant, immoral, and filthy," saying they were cursed, loved Satan, loved evil, and that not one soul was clean, pure, or righteous. He had been wrong. At the time, I had to put that knowledge on the shelf with so many other things that did not mesh with our teachings. Now I took a long, hard look at all the things that Warren had said were absolutely true that I knew were not. I pulled that nugget of wisdom regarding Oprah and the lovely people I had met in the outside world off the shelf and tucked it into my heart, where it belonged.

If I was going to leave, I would have to take a chance on the kindness of strangers, and that outside world, whatever it held for me. Once again I thought of Warren, but this time I felt a fire ignite in my belly. My spirit was not broken! I would not allow myself to be broken.

In the predawn hours of Sunday morning, I put a note on my bed for Christine, my mom, and my sisters. Taking an exit to avoid the cameras and any of the men on security patrol, I pushed the heavy oak door quietly behind me until I heard the latch click shut. My heart pounding, I walked as casually as I could, as if I was out for a stroll on the grounds. I made my way around the side of the massive Jeffs mansion, then turned abruptly toward the fence. The gates were locked, as I knew they would be. I looked back toward the Jeffses' property. Most of the lights were still off. I couldn't see anybody looking, but even if they had been, it was now or never.

Long skirts and all, I scaled the tall fence that protected the Jeffs family from "outsiders and wicked apostates."

In doing so, I became one of them.

CHAPTER 14

Escape

Right before dawn, avoiding security cameras and the prying eyes of any early risers, I slipped over the Jeffses' six-foot-high, wrought-iron gate. The spikes at the top were tricky to manage in my long skirt, yet nothing compared to the half-mile walk I had to trek to meet Ben, fighting my urge to bolt back to my sister-wives, whom I was having great difficulty leaving. I finally reached the back side of ALCO, an FLDS-member-run business.

Ben was nowhere in sight.

He couldn't do it, I thought numbly. He had accidentally slept in that morning, causing me to pace my room for hours until I had finally heard from him and was able to leave the property, trusting he would be here. Without Ben, all was lost. I had no escape route and no time for a new plan. Between the horror stories I knew from the inside and the police in Warren's pocket, I could not win on my own.

Just then, Ben rounded the corner in his brother's shimmery gold truck, loaded with a minitrailer from his previous employer, Reliance Lighting. My heart flooded with relief.

"I'm sorry for being late," he whispered, as he opened the door for me to hop in, his eyes filled with remorse at the fear he knew he'd put me through for the second time that morning. "How are you?"

"Scared to death!" I replied, trembling in both relief and fear. "Let's get out of here!"

My heart continued to pump wildly as we passed our neighbors' homes on the way to Highway 59, which would draw us toward Las Vegas. The cover of darkness was lifting, and so was my determination. If Ben hadn't been driving, I doubt I would have had the courage to continue. We stayed on the main highway bordering Utah, Arizona, and Nevada so as to draw no attention to ourselves, not stopping for fuel until we made it past the farthest outskirts of Vegas.

In the silence of the growing light, I stole furtive glances at Ben, whom I barely knew. I had just left everything and nearly everyone I'd ever known, and so had he. I tried to fathom why in the world he would do this for me.

The last few days had been the most tumultuous of my entire life, bar none. Secretly, I had called an aunt who lived in St. George. She had left the FLDS over "one-man rule" years prior, but it was too dangerous for her to take me in. Deflated, I had known that anywhere I went for asylum, my host and I would face spiritual, mental, and perhaps even physical danger. How could I do that to anyone? After my vision in the bathroom, I had no longer felt alone, but it had been unclear as to whom I could seek help from. I had gone to bed that night, only to be awakened by the ringing of the phone in my room.

"Is this Rebecca Wall?" The male voice on the line had sounded vaguely familiar, yet I couldn't place it.

"Who is this?" I had whispered, no longer groggy. It was not appropriate for any male to call me at two a.m. I was already in enough trouble!

"It's Cole, your brother."

"No way!" I had cried. No one had seen or heard from Cole for five years. Cautiously, I had lowered my voice back to a whisper. "It can't be. Tell me something only Cole would know." There had been just a slight hesitation.

"Do you remember at our old house, when we started that fire that almost burned down the shed...?"

"Yes!" I had squealed, slapping my hand over my mouth. It had to be Cole. We had never told a single soul about that close call. "How did you get my number?"

"You sent it with a gift you made for me." I was amazed, as I had sent that gift years before on a wing and a prayer, not knowing if the last address anyone had was accurate. In all that time, miraculously I had never switched rooms and had kept the same phone number despite Rulon amassing forty-six wives after me. Most of the wives had frequent room changes and had changed numbers accordingly.

"Becky," Cole had said urgently, "I've been keeping an eye on what's going on down there. Don't get remarried!"

I then told Cole I was being forced to marry almost immediately. I shared that I had already decided to leave but was unsure how, as it seemed unsafe for anyone to shelter me.

"You can't stay anywhere near Short Creek," he had said. "They'll get you." With a sudden urgency in his voice he had cried, "Come to Oregon!"

During that call, Oregon had sounded foreign and so far away. Even now, the thought of it frightened me. But knowing the history of our people, I realized it was likely the only way to escape the clutches of Warren for good. So now I was on my way to my brother's apartment in Coos Bay, by the sea. Cole had talked to me for several hours, describing everything he'd been through since he was kicked out from our home and the FLDS. He hadn't always lived in Oregon, but described how he had become so ill his doctors believed he wouldn't live. He had dragged his body to his car, and drove and drove until he reached the sea. Although my brother had begun to heal his body, he was still very weak, and I heard that frailty in his voice.

Cole had promised he would come to get me before Monday but had been so ill he couldn't keep his promise. My adrenaline was on high for two days waiting for his call, wondering if he had been caught or hospitalized in his weakened state. He had finally phoned in the night to tell me he was sending friends for me, but they couldn't arrive until it was too late. By that time, in my sheer desperation, I had called Ben and confided the whole story to him over the phone.

"Let me help you," Ben had begged. "Let me help get you out of there."

"I can't let you do that." I didn't want that, either. It was one thing for my brother to help me escape, but both Ben's and my reputations would be ruined beyond repair if we escaped together.

"My days are numbered, anyway—" he began.

"Because of me!" I had cried.

"I'm the one that kissed *you*, remember?"

That was when Ben had given me details of Warren's confrontation with him. Warren had asked him the same dirty, degrading questions he had asked me. When Ben answered honestly, Warren had told him he detected the seeds of apostasy in him, too. We both knew those were Warren's code words for "expect major consequences."

"You see," Ben had added to me, "I'm on my way out, anyway. I can't stay here any longer. Let me help you."

I hadn't known what to say. Ben had already scandalized himself and his family, but he would place himself in very real danger if he had the audacity to turn against Warren and escape with the Prophet's wife. How could I let him do that? I didn't know, but I had to keep planning on leaving. It was the only thing keeping my will alive. For the next two days, I attended every meal and class so it wouldn't occur to Warren that anything was different. As Monday had approached with no word from Cole, I had felt even less sure but began packing anyway. It had been agonizing, deciding what to include besides my violin. I knew nothing about Oregon, except Cole had described it as cold and blustery in November.

Carefully, I had selected only a few favorite long dresses from the closet, so that it would still look full. I couldn't leave all my photos and scrapbooks behind, as my family and friends were too precious. Neither could I leave my sewing machine, nor the boxes of material in my closet. Besides music lessons, I had felt that sewing would be my only way to make a living on the outside. That thought still terrified me.

Making sure my room looked as if everything was still intact, I'd had to sneak the most important items out without being seen, then hide them somewhere off the Jeffses' estate. Though not a liar or a thief, I'd had to steal my own belongings away to claim my very life. I borrowed one of the estate's minivans to smuggle my items off the premises and into Elissa's shed.

The secrecy had been killing me, but I couldn't tell a soul. Elissa was miserable, and Ally and Sherrie were not safe. Every night I'd been suffering from nightmares about what Warren would do with them in his lust for power and bartering of young brides. I longed to take them with me, but Cole had warned that taking any of them, including Elissa, would be considered kidnapping because they were underage. We would have the police and the FLDS looking for us. Brokenhearted, I understood, but I would never forget the look on her face when she had surprised Ben and me just the day before as we loaded his truck at her shed. Tearfully she begged me to stay. Would she ever forgive me for leaving?

Now as Ben and I raced to Oregon, I tried to concentrate on the road, but all I could think of was Elissa and the people I had left behind. I had worked for so many years to be an example to my family and my community, and the thought made me want to stop and go back. Driving through the desolate landscape skimming the north end of the Mojave National Preserve, about a hundred miles south of Death Valley, I balked, thinking if I returned now no one would have to know.

Finally the knowledge of my destiny under Warren Jeffs flooded my being and brought reason. As much as I wanted to, I could not go back. I glanced at my watch, realizing at this time our entire community would be in Sunday School. I thought how unfair it would be for my dear friend Samantha to have to learn of my leaving from another source. Since I had cleared all of the messages from my pager and left it in my room in Hildale, I used Ben's phone to text her: "Good-bye. I love you."

I found out later that Samantha got up from Sunday School and immediately tried calling my room three times, with no answer. She then called Christine, who was absent from church that day, and asked her to check on me. I couldn't blame her. Anyone with that kind of information who didn't report it would be under harsh scrutiny, and Samantha had a standing in the community and a husband to protect. When Christine couldn't get me to answer the door, Nephi and Isaac found a key to unlock my room, where they found my letter of explanation.

Warren was adamant in the order he issued to the community: find us before nightfall, "to save that girl's soul before she commits adultery." All of Warren's brothers and several members of the God Squad were sent on a massive manhunt for us, scouring Colorado City, St. George, Cedar City, and the surrounding environs. He used the threat of adultery to get the men to move quickly, as a woman's virtue was prized among the FLDS. However, Warren was also very concerned about something else, though I wouldn't understand that until much later. As

the former Prophet's widow, I knew far too much about the inner working of the Jeffs family and the true undertakings of the FLDS. I was a
dangerous liability to the new Prophet.

Within an hour of my text to Samantha, Ben's phone started ringing—
first his dad, then his mom. He ignored both calls. Next, Nephi's number showed up on caller ID as we were getting gas in a small town in
California. Though the calls unnerved us, as we got farther away we
were able to distract ourselves with the beautiful change in scenery.
There were lush fields of grapevines, even this late in the season, but we
didn't stop. We flew across the road as if the devil himself was chasing
us. It was already getting dark when Ben's brother Scott called.

"Dude!" he cried to Ben, who finally answered his phone. "This is
huge, what you've done. Everyone's calling me—Mom, Dad, Uncle
Nephi, and Uncle Warren—and crowds of people are coming out
here!" Scott had finally gotten tired of the hordes of searchers and
screwed shut the door of the shack he'd been sharing with Ben.

Both Ben and Scott were very young, and I felt bad that he was having to face the brutal buffetings of family members and strong-armed
church leaders because of me. The manhunt had become more intense,
and it was a good thing Ben had left no evidence, because they scoured
all the areas he had been. Had they found the MapQuest map on the
computer's history or a printout in the garbage can, we would have been
stalked down and brought back. I knew how it worked. They would have
separated us right away, then manipulated us, telling me things like
"Ben doesn't *really* want to be with you," and saying the same to him
about me. They would have finally forced me into a marriage designed
to break the rebellion out of me, while Ben would have been tossed to
the wolves to join the thousands of "spiritually dead" lost boys.

Ben grew more and more nervous. He didn't let me hear all the voice
mails being left, or the awful things they were saying about both of us.
However, I could tell by his face that certain ones were getting to him.
He shared the message from my mother and sisters. Mom's teary message demanding that Ben bring me back immediately broke my heart.

"Remember the Golden Windows, Becky," she sobbed.

Ally, now eight, was not as sensitive. "You can go to hell, Ben! You
can go to hell for what you've done!" she screamed.

Ben turned the ringer off, and I cried quietly, not knowing if my mother would ever speak to me again. I knew that she secretly stayed in touch with my brothers to check on them, and I hoped she would be able to forgive me enough to do the same with me. I finally succumbed to exhaustion as darkness engulfed us. A while later, Ben stopped and gently woke me.

"The ocean is over there, Becky," he said. I noticed he didn't call me Grandmother Becky or Mother Becky.

"Really?"

"Yes. Do you want to see it?"

"Heck, yeah!" I had only ever seen the Atlantic, and only once, when I had briefly visited Florida with two sister-wives and Warren's brother Wallace for his business. This was so exciting, I could hardly stand it.

We parked and I raced to the water's edge in my long skirt. I took off my shoes and felt the sand and then the water through my nylons. Suddenly, a huge wave came in and I had to pick up my skirts and run! Ben laughed as I kicked the water high, and made a face at the surprising saltiness of the sea. If this was what freedom tasted like, I was beginning to think it was worth it.

All too soon, we had to get back on the road, stopping only for fuel and to eat. People in the rest stops and restaurants stared curiously at our attire and my hairstyle. As we whipped through the forest between Northern California and Oregon and came upon the most incredible pine trees, I experienced an unexpected stirring in my soul. Even though it was dark, it was like I could *feel* their ancient presence. Finally, Ben and I pulled into Coos Bay in the middle of the night. It was largely deserted, although the sight of a man washing his car in the chilly night air reminded us this wasn't Hildale anymore. I was suddenly overcome with anxiety. What would my adored big brother think of me now?

As we ascended Cole's stairs where he waited at the top, I tried to hide my shock at my brother's appearance. His longer hair was unfamiliar to me, but his drawn face and haggard frame made me swallow. His skin was ashen, and his under-eye circles were darker than those of my sister-wives after months of fasting. For the first time, I realized how sick Cole truly was. As he embraced me, I felt something thaw inside and realized that when he disappeared years before, part of me had gone missing, too.

I introduced Ben to Cole, who graciously welcomed us both inside his apartment, which smelled like wheatgrass. He explained he had to do horrific colonic cleanses, but they were sustaining his life. Given the late hour, he showed us the two separate couches where we would sleep. Gratefully, I slipped beneath the thin blankets and had only a moment to be grateful for safety before I was out.

The next morning, after Ben and I unloaded the trailer, Cole took us for breakfast. It was so strange to walk into a restaurant where people didn't know me, didn't step aside in line in deference to my position, and didn't open the door for me. My ego wanted to say, *Don't they know who I am?* The rational part of me shot back, *Of course they don't!*

Cole couldn't eat anything on the menu, so while Ben and I ate, he told us his story, including some of the very intensive historical and spiritual research he had done on the FLDS. He felt that our beliefs were not based on any form of truth. Ben and I had already partially come to that conclusion on our own, but Cole's bold words sounded almost like blasphemy.

Then he challenged me. "Becky, where do you want to live?"

I stared at him. "I don't know. Where do you think I should live?"

"That's not my decision. It's yours. Where do you want to live?" he repeated.

I turned to Ben. "Where do you think I should live?"

"Rebecca!" Cole rebuked me. "I'm talking to *you!* Where do *you* want to live?"

I was silent and frightened for a long moment. "Ummm, well, Colorado might be nice."

"No, I don't mean in the States. I mean Fiji…or Australia…or Europe. What would you like to see? Where would you like to go?"

It was too much for me. I remembered when my sister-wives and I had received a free geographical encyclopedia CD in the mail. I had begged Seth to put it on the computer, but he had snidely declared that women didn't need to know geography. Suddenly not only was I facing freedom, but Cole was expecting me to contemplate choices and decisions I had never been allowed to make.

"It doesn't matter where you are, whether you are part of the Work or not, Becky," he said. "You need to decide what is okay for you, and what is not okay—regardless of what anyone else is doing. You need to decide your code of conduct, right here and now. If you don't, this world will *shred* you."

I sat in stupefied silence. My compass had always been set by others. I had witnessed people leave the church without a guiding light or moral code. Almost all of them had fallen prey to drugs, alcohol, promiscuity, or crime. Now that I was out, what was my North Star?

It felt much too soon and dangerous to go back to Utah, but Ben had promised to return Scott's truck and the trailer, and Ben was nothing if not an honest soul. That afternoon we drove back, taking comfort in the fact that no one except Scott would expect us to return. Still, as we left behind water, pines, and lush growth for the desert again, fear gnawed at me. It wasn't a topic of polite dinner conversation, but we both knew that girls in my community had been forced back to their families and some quite literally held captive until they could be "sweet" again.

During the drive, I became aware of a new tension between us that lasted all the way to southern Utah. Every time Ben moved in his seat, I was excruciatingly aware of the ripple of muscles along his arms and legs, his red hair gleaming in the fading sunset. When he would beam a reassuring smile at me, I felt a little thrill before reality set in. Until Ben had kissed me in the canyon, the only place he held in my world was as a friend. Now when I would look at him or think of him, my head kept spinning.

As if he could read my thoughts, Ben gave me a mischievous look, then suddenly reached over and took my hand. We sat there, hands clasped in the space between us, the warmth from his suddenly spreading up my arm. I didn't understand this feeling. I dropped his fingers and looked out the window. Ben glanced at me but didn't push it.

Our hearts were both heavy at what we had done. So many people were angry and horrified with us. The calls hadn't stopped. And it wasn't as if gold was at the other end of the rainbow: Coos Bay in November was humid and cold, with a chilling wind that had whipped through our bones. But along the way, Ben and I began to talk seriously and decided that no matter what, we were not going to live in Utah. All it held for us now was a dead-end road, a life of misery and manipulation.

The sunrise was bright and beautiful, and the air warmed considerably by the time we met Scott in St. George to exchange vehicles. Scott brought Ben's Chevy Blazer and promised to take back the trailer to Reliance Lighting. Then he gave us an update on what the new Prophet was saying about us.

Using his old tactics, Warren had warned the people that anyone who associated with either of us would be considered traitorous and deeply immoral. Our families were not to contact us—their eternal salvation was at stake. I was concerned for Scott, but he laughed it off. He was on his way out, too, and he knew it.

Once we said good-bye to his brother, Ben and I realized our mutual exhaustion. Neither one of us had slept well since before the escape. To attempt a trip back to Oregon now was to risk our lives.

At a small Motel 6 in St. George, Ben paid for a room with cash. Seeing him pull out his lean wallet made me hang my head. We had been using his money for gas, food, and now for a hotel, and I had no resources of my own to contribute, which upset me. We reached our room in silence and I stopped short as I saw that there was just one queen-sized bed. I knew I would be damned to hell for all eternity just for crossing the threshold.

Ben set down our small bags and approached me gingerly, until he stood right in front of me, blocking my view of the bed. He took my hand in one of his and lifted my chin with the other. I began to tremble, but he held my gaze, and a part of me felt spellbound by his blue eyes as he placed my hands, one at a time, behind his neck. Then he slowly put his hands around my waist. I was suddenly very aware of his wide, strong shoulders. These were not the muscles of a frail old man. His breath grew warmer, and his lips touched mine. An electric shock went down my spine.

I stepped away. *Did I love Ben?* I looked at him, and then at the floor again. Perhaps not in the girlish, Disney-movie sense of the word. But what I felt for Ben far outweighed anything I had ever felt for Rulon, and my feelings were based on an emotion I hadn't had for any man in the FLDS: *respect*. I genuinely esteemed Ben for his kindness toward my mom, his sacrifice in helping me escape, and his commitment to his brother. Finally, I respected him for not forcing himself on me the way I had seen Warren, Jason, Winston, and so many others do to their women; the way Rulon had made me prostitute myself to submit to him, and to keep sweet about it.

Yes, I realized, I respected Ben. If that wasn't a basis for love, then I didn't know what was.

Ben silently bridged the space between us once more, his eyes pleading.

Trust me, they said gently. There was a glowing ember that I didn't want to admit had begun to rise in my own body from the moment I first felt his breath upon my face.

Our eyes continued the conversation.

Please don't hurt me.

I won't. I promise. I really do.

Early the next morning, we left town before most townspeople were up and about. Despite the security I had felt in Ben's arms through the night, I couldn't help but feel like a dog running away with my tail between my legs. *Was I now everything Warren had told the people I was? Immoral, an apostate, evil?* My actions weighed heavily on me, making me feel physically ill. But Ben continued to be kind. Although he had gotten what he had wanted, he didn't push me away, like I'd seen so many men do once their wives were off duty. Instead, he looked at me with great affection and shyly grinned at me from time to time. He gently took my hand and held it for long periods. Once, he brought it to his lips. My nausea began to subside. The farther we drove from southern Utah, the better I could breathe. It didn't matter that the air was getting colder. We hadn't been struck by lightning. The road hadn't yet cracked open to swallow us whole.

Ben thought it wise to take a different route back to Coos Bay. We made our way along the coast, taking in giant redwoods, the likes of which I had never seen before. We got out of the car and I began to run between the trees, my feet soft on the padded forest floor. Ben laughed and chased me. He snatched up my hand, and I stared as a patch of sunlight illuminated him. Here I was, in this beautiful place, with a man who *wanted* to be by my side. My eyes filled with tears. This was what Christine had always longed for: to walk in nature beside the man she loved. Instead, my sister was soon to be one of Warren's entourage, following him from room to room like a puppy. Christine deserved real love, as did every one of my sister-wives. Ben noticed the change in my mood, but I didn't withdraw my hand. He kissed me on the cheek, and I smiled at him. Slowly, I was becoming convinced that life would be okay.

CHAPTER 15

The Truman Show

Once back in Coos Bay, we began to explore the gorgeous scenery of the Northwest. The area was full of windy, scenic byways, with breathtaking ridges of pines, slick rock, sand, and sea. The first time I crossed the massively tall bridge and saw enormous piles of clamshells dumped from barges, I was smitten. Chilly air still bit into my bones, but now it felt cleansing. I knew instinctively that it was going to take a lot to heal from my past, and the ocean quickly became my greatest ally. I could get used to the chill, and live each day among the lush foliage and under the sky, which was deep turquoise until the fog rolled in late in the afternoon, muting the colors and details of shops, houses, and even people.

When I wasn't at the beach or in the forest, though, I was paralyzed in fear of the outside world. I had no idea how to do my hair, how to dress, and what customs, holidays, or social rituals to follow. I was still wearing long dresses, the only clothes I owned, and poufing my hair, so Cole decided to take me shopping.

"Buy whatever you want," he said. With literally no idea what to choose, I ended up with a jogging suit and a shirt in the shocking and once-forbidden shade of red. Afterward, Cole brought me to a hair salon. I was terrified: I had never cut my hair, except to carefully trim the ends. I wasn't facing the mirror, but I blanched as I saw yards and yards of my rich brown hair hit the ground. The stylist did some things with a blow-dryer before turning me around.

I gasped. My hair had been chopped to my shoulders, but it was the way she had styled it that took my breath away. When I got home, I shyly walked through the door. I saw appreciation shining in Ben's eyes. Even though it felt so foreign and naked, I thought perhaps I could live with short hair.

However, the only product I had ever used was hair spray—and lots of it! The next day, I woke up and brushed my hair, and it didn't look anything like it had the day before.

"I don't have any idea how to do my hair!" I cried to Cole. "Everything I do looks wrong."

"Tell you what," he said, winking at me. "Whatever feels right to you—do the exact opposite. Then you'll be fine!" He turned away, laughing, but I shut the door on him and silently sobbed. Men didn't understand that a woman's hair was considered her glory. Not only was mine gone; it now looked ugly and made me feel that way inside. For days, I cried in private, feeling homesick and missing my mother and sisters and friends desperately.

In the meantime, our thoughts were consumed with survival. Ben and I couldn't allow ourselves to wear out our welcome with Cole, and we needed to start earning money immediately. We went looking for jobs around Coos Bay and adjacent North Bend. Two weeks and countless applications later, I finally got a job offer from Elizabeth's, a fine-dining establishment off Highway 101, and Ben was hired by a downtown restaurant called the Cedar Grill.

November went by in a whirlwind. Everything was new, exciting, thrilling, and sobering to me. I began reading voraciously, following Cole's recommendations. I was fascinated by the philosophies of successful people like Stephen Covey, Joe Vitale, and Deepak Chopra. Excitedly, I sat on Cole's front porch and called my mother for the first time, anxious to share with her what I was learning in life and through books. While she was glad to know I was safe and relieved I had reconnected with Cole, she was negative about everything else, telling me I was trading my salvation for material goods.

"Honey," she said, "you're talking about stuff—only stuff. Do you know what you are trading for stuff?" She was more closed off than I had ever heard her. Warren's warnings had clearly affected her. I knew she had been ordered not to talk to me, and that I was supposed to be "dead" to her. She risked her FLDS membership and salvation by the very act of communicating with her apostate children. People had been kicked out for less.

I watched a little television, surprised and often scandalized by how different it was from when we were kids. One night Cole and Ben and I watched an R-rated movie in which a man and a woman had sex, and I became alarmed when they started making noises—loud ones! I didn't know people did that when they made love. Did everyone in the outside world do that?

I did take comfort in something familiar when I discovered that Coos Bay was actually a very musical area. Ben caught me dancing across the kitchen one night in pure joy because I had discovered a local teacher who taught the harp—an instrument I had always wanted to play! I began taking lessons and took to it as naturally as I had the violin. It soothed my soul to play such a graceful, ethereal instrument, especially on rainy days—since I had moved from the state with the least amount of rainfall per year to one with nearly the highest. When dull, gray days would begin to drive me insane, throwing myself into my music seemed to magically make life balance out again.

As November morphed into December, the weather worsened, but my love for Ben only grew. When the two of us talked about life, he used the word *us*, which was comforting. Cole had noticed that Ben and I were getting closer and was emphatic that Ben was welcome to stay as long as there was nothing sexual between us. Unfortunately, it was a tough promise to keep. We both wished to honor Cole's request, but we felt magnetically drawn to each other.

Meanwhile, still weakened, Cole spent his time sleeping, reading, and watching movies. One particularly blustery day, he insisted that I watch a movie called *The Truman Show*.

The main character, Truman Burbank, is adopted as a baby by a television studio. As he grows, every important person in his life is simply an actor; every part of his life is a set—but he doesn't know it. Whenever he wants something the production team can't provide, he's told that it's just not available. "Why would you want that?" different characters ask him. "Your life is so perfect the way it is." When he has inklings things just aren't right, he finally faces his dread fear of water, and sets off in a boat for the horizon. Barely surviving a violent and horrendous storm manufactured by the producers, Truman discovers the horizon is actually a painted backdrop. Only then does he realize that his entire life has been a complete lie—set up for the camera and the benefit of strangers, the viewers. Full of that realization and the bitter disappointment of his false relationships, he walks off the set and into his new life.

As the credits rolled, I sat dumbfounded. Within a few moments, though, I rose from the couch and began pacing furiously, not just upset but enraged! The movie was a mirror of my own life. Before every decision I'd ever made, I'd asked myself, *What would the Prophet have me say? What would the Prophet have me do?* For every question, there had been an appropriate, programmed answer. I was never allowed my own opinion; I had never developed the ability to choose.

All of my people were like that, too. How had our belief system become so screwed up? I gave myself permission to look deeply at polygamy in a way I never, ever had before. All of a sudden, nothing seemed holy about the structure that must be in place for polygamy to work. Why would God put a roughly equal number of males and females on the earth if he wanted a polygamous society? This structure meant that women didn't get the time, affection, and validation they so crave. And because only a select number of male leaders are righteous enough to receive multiple wives, not only do an extraordinarily high number of young men get kicked out, but the marriageable ages of girls becomes increasingly younger as demand intensifies.

Throw all of these factors into a climate in which the leaders make the people feel as if they can never question those leaders because that means questioning God himself, and then one has a recipe for spiritual abuse. Those who admitted the truth of it were labeled as "darkened," "taken over," or "possessed." How many times had I heard "They can't see the truth because they've turned away from it"? The leaders made it shameful and dangerous for us to question polygamy, out loud or in our hearts.

Every way that I examined it, polygamy was neither healthy nor holy.

Why could no one see it? Because they would not—unless like me, they were denied the good graces of Warren Jeffs and experienced a rude awakening!

For days I was furious, and all I knew was that I did not want that perverse dictator Warren directing my show from his self-righteous pulpit. I felt intense shame and self-hatred for what I had allowed, especially Elissa's wedding and the nightmare of her Priesthood-dictated honeymoon. Now more than ever, it felt like a cocklebur in my heart.

CHAPTER 16

A Few Drops of Water

I awoke several days later feeling like the walking dead, bone tired and incredibly nauseated. I figured my emotional turmoil had taken its toll and I had finally succumbed to the flu spreading at work. I took a day off, yet the symptoms persisted. I began to wonder if something else was going on. I had never known what birth control was. At Short Creek, trying to "outdo" God's natural laws was considered evil, and I hadn't needed it with Rulon. Although I had been extremely naïve, I had seen enough friends and family struggle with pregnancy to understand the signs.

Oh my God! I can't be pregnant!

I ran to the bathroom, heaving. With the vomit came the emotions of shame and guilt I'd been holding in. I couldn't help feeling that I had become everything Warren said that I would be.

Perhaps even worse, I had betrayed Cole's one request of me. Ben and I had tried staying away from each other, but our love had grown along with our desire to be together. Being alone each night in the living room had been a test we had been unable to pass.

"You okay, Sis?" asked my brother, shuffling by the door as if on cue. Hurriedly, I collected myself, leaning against the sink for support.

"Sure," I said mustering false cheer. "Thanks for asking." Inside, I was devastated. What would Ben think if I were pregnant? Would he want a baby? Would he leave me?

From Short Creek, Scott and others gave us reports on what was happening with our families and close friends. It cut us both deeply to know the lies being publicly spread about us. Warren had become quite paranoid, placing more cameras on the Jeffses' property and more fences and security around it. He said it was to keep the wicked *out*, but I knew it was just as important to him to keep the people *in*. I'd had a hard enough time escaping. How would any woman flee Warren's clutches now? Despite the painful fallout, I had never been more grateful that I had found the courage to leave when I did.

It had only been six weeks since we'd left, but we were now adjusting to a world oblivious to my sister-wives and their plight. Ben and I went to his company Christmas party, where I clung to him like a mouse. We hadn't dared tell anyone where we came from. Instead, we were like ducks, calmly swimming new waters on the surface, but paddling like hell underneath. Our first Christmas was a culture shock, as we witnessed warm traditions and gift giving, feeling poor and unsteady in our new environment. Except for work parties, Christmas had been just another day, until Ben woke me that morning.

"Merry Christmas!" he said, grinning, and placed two wrapped presents in my lap.

"But I didn't get you anything!" I said, shocked and saddened. I hadn't any money to buy anything for him or for Cole. In Rulon's home, the only celebrations we had were anniversaries, and not even birthdays were acknowledged. I opened my gifts, a calendar and a pair of pajamas, with tears in my eyes. To be acknowledged like this was very touching to me. As the days passed, I missed my old life like crazy, but I couldn't help but see the beauty and majesty in the differences of the people and the customs outside of the FLDS.

A couple of days later, I had a dream. We were young students in Warren's classroom where he had been teaching us Priesthood History and about the government coming after the Prophet during the destructions. "Are you willing to stand by the Prophet? Are you willing to die for the Prophet?" My classmates and I quickly took a stand. Certainly we would give our lives for the Prophet.

I woke that night gasping, unable to get the dream out of my head.

Just two months earlier, I *would* have been willing to die for the Prophet. I'd been sure. So how would I know if I was making wise choices from now on?

The next morning, wrapping myself in extra layers and jackets, I went down to the ocean intending to have a brisk walk. Instead, I ended up sitting in the sand, watching the churning waves. I thought about a quote I had read from Gandhi: *"You must not lose faith in humanity. Humanity is an ocean; if a few drops of the ocean are dirty, the ocean does not become dirty."* Short Creek had become contaminated by Warren Jeffs, but he did not represent all of humanity, or even all of the FLDS. And just as I had made mistakes, those mistakes did not make up all of me. The tide was going out, and I had the weirdest sensation that it was pulling from me everything I was ready to release. As the waves came back in, I let them fill me with peace.

Just after Christmas, we received an urgent call from Mom on Ben's cell. My brother Joshua was in a great deal of trouble and needed our help. As a lost boy, Joshua had struggled outside of the FLDS and was often suicidal. Now, the police had caught him passed out drunk in the driver's seat of a vehicle, with keys in the ignition. He was not yet twenty-one, so unless he had family willing to take him in and give him some structure, he would go to jail. Cole quickly determined that Joshua should live with us, even though the apartment was tiny. He was still too ill to drive alone to Utah to retrieve him, however, so we arranged for the three of us to meet Amelia and Collin on their way back up to Canada, accompanied by Elissa, who was going to visit them. As soon as Ben and I finished our shifts, we began to drive through the night to Pendleton, Oregon.

I was terrified to see my younger siblings. The last time I had seen Joshua, I had been reeking of self-righteousness, trying to get him to acknowledge the error of his ways and repent. I was also nervous about Amelia and Collin. I knew from limited conversations with Mom that Amelia had been sympathetic when I left, but I was no longer one of the "righteous." I had no idea how Collin felt. My worst fear, however, was facing Elissa. I loved my little sister more than life and didn't know if she'd forgiven me yet for leaving her in that desert town with Allen.

Beyond all this, a bigger question loomed.

At a rest stop, Ben and I got out to stretch. "What would you do if I was pregnant?" I asked him hesitantly. He paused for a brief moment, and then looked straight at me.

"I would take care of you," he replied plainly. "You're not alone, Becky. I'm here."

Though I had been praying that I was not pregnant, I was filled with the relief of knowing I would not have to go it solo in this bizarre new world.

In the early morning hours we arrived in Pendleton—an old, high-desert town that reminded me of areas of Utah. Our family members had arrived a few hours before and were still asleep in their hotel. As we sipped hot chocolate in the restaurant next door, I noticed Cole was nervous. I wondered if he still felt as guilty as I did for leaving the others.

When we entered their room, the first person I noticed was Joshua. He was wearing only a thin and ragged T-shirt and thin cargo pants despite the cold, and had literally no possessions with him. Even though he was six years younger than me, he seemed frail and bent like an old man. As he hugged me, though, I saw his big, careless grin and realized that my rambunctious little brother was still there.

Next I hugged Amelia and Elissa, who were both genuinely kind to all of us. I turned to Collin to greet him, but his demeanor was cold. Of course, he was in an awkward situation. Here I was, Satan's child, with two other apostates, including the man who had stolen the Prophet's wife away from the people.

Elissa looked pale and unhappy. Her belly seemed bigger than when we had left, and I suspected that she might be pregnant, but she didn't say anything to me and I didn't pry. She did say was she was on her way to spend time in Canada without Allen, before changing the subject to Warren's crazy behavior as the new Prophet. Every Sunday the congregation kept showing up in fear of what he would do next, she told us.

Amelia was exceptionally kind. She brought me a letter from Christine. It said that she would remember the good times, love me, and pray for me always. My heart ached as I read. As angry as I had been that she had broken my confidence to Warren, I still loved her with my whole heart. I fingered the letter in my hands and wished I could express that to her myself.

Amelia and I went into the bathroom for some privacy, but I cried out a little when she pulled me close to hug me again. My breasts were excruciatingly tender.

"Are you pregnant?" Amelia whispered, her eyes wide with concern.

"I don't know," I murmured back, turning on the water so no one would hear.

"Do you think you could be? What will you *do*, Becky?"

I shook my head, tears spilling down my cheeks. Amelia hugged me again, this time gingerly.

All too soon, it was time to go, and Ben and I drove the long drive back with Cole and Joshua.

My job at the restaurant was a daily struggle. I would show up to do my very best, listening carefully to everything the owner, Elizabeth, asked me to do, but her words often confused me. Though my boss, coworkers, and I had all been raised next to one another in the United States, and we all spoke the same language, the meaning behind our words was completely different.

Every night I would come home and share my confusion with Cole, who had been out of the FLDS long enough to find my stories hilarious. I tried to laugh at myself, too, but my boss was often angry with me. She frequently drank throughout her shift, which loosened a very sharp tongue, and her criticism became almost crippling. To be fair, I had never revealed my background to her, so she had no reason to understand my mistakes. I became scared of my own shadow, and finally Elizabeth accused me of doing drugs. I assured her that was not the case, but she stayed on high alert.

I enjoyed several of my coworkers, especially Mark, a young man who exhibited many effeminate behaviors. I had no point of reference; I just knew he was a sensitive, funny guy. One evening that January, my brothers came in to see me, which caused quite a stir, as they were both exceptionally handsome. All the girls *and* Mark asked me several questions about them. No one had recognized the fact that they were siblings.

"Are they seeing each other?" Mark finally asked.

"Ewwww, *no!*" I cried dramatically. It shocked me that he would ask if two brothers were seeing *each other*. I had no idea that Mark was gay, and my naïve but passionately negative comment sorely offended him.

That night Elizabeth took me aside in a drunken rage. "What the hell is your problem? And what the hell planet are you from?"

I left in tears of disgrace and never returned. Nor did I ever have the chance to tell Mark that I was genuinely sorry. I had hated my boss but was deeply saddened at the loss of Mark's friendship.

Fortunately, I got another job at a cozy restaurant inside the Ramada Inn, where a new coworker, Carol, took me under her wing. The ladies I worked with there were more mature than at Elizabeth's, and exceptionally kind. In addition, the clientele of this restaurant was also mature—primarily busloads of elderly seniors visiting the area. I found I could more easily relate to these conservative crowds. In this gentler climate, I could decipher the meaning of language, and I paid rapt attention.

"You listen as if your life depends on it!" remarked one older gentleman at my table. I smiled shyly and laughed. I felt like it did.

Four people in Cole's small apartment caused more tension than we had been prepared for, and Joshua was struggling with alcoholism. Because of Cole's focus on health, he didn't drink but had not been judgmental of Joshua. However, the alcohol caused Joshua to behave irrationally at times. Both of my brothers began snapping at Ben for no reason, and seemed to align against him. I loved my brothers dearly but could not ignore everything Ben had done for me and my feelings for him. He and I talked about getting a place of our own, but we did not have enough money saved.

When my nausea continued to worsen instead of subside, I used my tip money to buy a pregnancy test. When I saw the double lines, my heart fell. That night I tearfully confided to Ben, who just held me for several long moments, before wiping the tears from my cheeks.

"We need to be honest with Cole," he said. I was worried. Whatever Joshua and I shared about our siblings had enraged him. Cole felt like he had failed us, especially when he heard that Joshua's twin, Jordan, had become a young, unwed father. So how could I tell him that I had become pregnant? And likely while I was under his very roof?

We decided to tell him that weekend after our shifts, but before that could happen, Cole got sick in the night and came out to find Ben and me together.

"You can leave here now," Cole thundered, angry at our betrayal. We left immediately, but Ben made me go back to Cole's and mend some fences. For three long weeks, Ben lived out of his Blazer, refusing to let me leave Cole's apartment in my condition to join him. He soon found a temporary room, for which I was grateful. Ben had become my best friend and confidant, and I cared for him more deeply than I had ever allowed myself to care for any man.

At home I still had to live with my brothers' degrading remarks about Ben. I did my best to be positive in that environment, and like Ben, worked as many double shifts as I could to save money for us. Whenever I saw Ben, he would graciously remind me that I still held the power to choose where I focused my energies. I began to think less about my brothers' unkindness toward him, and more about creating a life together.

In February 2003, Ben and I moved into our first real home together, a tiny little duplex. We had no furniture and slept on the floor, but we didn't care. It hadn't taken us long to find an apartment once we put the word out to our coworkers. Even though neither of us had a lick of credit, the landlords kindly gave us a chance. The world was supposed to be so wicked, and yet here were two virtual strangers giving us an opportunity to prove ourselves. My feelings began to change. Still, I had some vitally important shifts to make on the inside.

CHAPTER 17

Emerging Wings

I had left the FLDS to gain freedom, and yet I felt powerless in so many ways. Anguish over the fight with Cole and the way my brothers treated Ben was like a raw wound. Right next to it was all the guilt and shame for those I had left behind. I wept over my sister Elissa, stuck in a violent and loveless marriage. Amelia, who'd been in touch, had told me that Elissa suffered a miscarriage from being raped by her husband. I wept for my brothers scraping to survive like me, in a foreign world. I wept for my mom and for Ally and Sherrie, and the knowledge that my littlest sisters were in danger of becoming child brides like Elissa. I wept over feeling like I could do nothing to stop it. It was the deepest despair I had experienced since leaving.

At one point, my tears of frustration turned into a plea.

God, please, just show me a different way to live. Something, anything, has to be better than this.

Finally I got up, and sat down at my harp. My tears subsided as I became caught up in the music. I played and played, pouring my emotions out to God, and it was like a salve to my soul.

Suddenly there was a knock on the door.

Sheepishly, I made my way to the entrance, realizing that I'd been playing for hours and had probably annoyed neighbors I hadn't even met! In my head I could hear Irene screaming, *Can you please tell Becky to stop?*

I opened the door, and to my surprise, found two very lovely, smiling ladies I guessed to be in their late twenties.

"Hello there!" they cried, almost simultaneously. "We're your neighbors!" One held out a plate of cookies and they introduced themselves with a great deal of laughter. "We're Mary and Leah Houghton. We heard you playing and thought we'd stop by."

Horrified, I started to apologize.

"Oh, no!" they both said. Leah placed her hand kindly on my arm.

"We were *excited* to hear you play! We're both musicians." Their enthusiasm was contagious, and they didn't seem to notice or care that our living room had only a harp and some boxes in it.

"Rumor has it you might play the fiddle as well?" asked Mary, the taller of the two.

I nodded curiously.

The ladies went on to explain that they were part of the Little Ole Opry on the Bay, a musical group that put on two big performances a year—at Christmas and in the summer. They were already preparing for the summer concert series, and desperately needed a fiddle player!

I was dumbfounded—but quickly grew excited. I sent a silent prayer of thanks to God. He had sent me a lifeline of something familiar in a foreign world. Along with the baby growing inside me, I felt I had somewhere to serve and something to bring me joy.

Ben and I were anxiously awaiting the time when the nausea from my pregnancy was supposed to subside, but it never seemed to go away. Ben worked later shifts generally, and he usually wanted to sleep at the time I would need a ride to work, so I walked several miles there and back each day. My coworkers were appalled that he'd take the car, especially given my condition, but I was used to this treatment from a man. His needs naturally came before mine. It was how we had both been raised.

At work, Ben finally confided in his boss, Michelle, about my condition.

"Congratulations!" she cried, genuinely delighted. "I'm sure the grandmothers are very excited!" When Ben hesitated, she looked at him quizzically. "Haven't you told them?"

One of the earliest photos
I have of myself.

Practicing the violin.

On my grandfather's ranch with one of my brothers.

Always an eager student, here I am on my way to kindergarten.

All of my unmarried sisters and me in the front yard of our father's home; I'm fourth from the right.

Having just finished sewing my wedding dress in Canada, and getting ready to leave the next morning for my Utah wedding, I engaged in a little target practice.

On my wedding night with Rulon, my smile masking the fear and confusion I felt.

During a rare unsupervised visit to St. George with my mother and sisters, it got so hot that we went swimming—fully dressed, of course.

With my sisters in St. George.

On the day of the fifth anniversary of my wedding to Rulon.

One rare reprieve from my married life was weekend street hockey games with friends and family members; here I am advancing the puck.

Ben and me with Kyle on the Oregon shore. The ocean was such a healing presence for us as we built our new lives outside the FLDS.

With my Opry Band in Coos Bay after a Christmas performance.

Our wedding day at the Cedar Grill. Michelle was so kind and supportive to us both during this time.

My mother and me with Kyle in Cottonwood Park in Colorado City, the last time I saw her.

An aerial shot of the YFZ ranch during the raid.

The temple annex where I spent a great deal of time working with Texas Rangers.

For the first time ever, television news crews were allowed onto the ranch.

With Sister Mary Grace during the raid.

After testifying at the Tom Green County Courthouse during Warren's trial, I was photographed with Texas attorney general Greg Abbott.

Courtesy of the Eldorado Success

Being escorted from the courthouse by two of the attorney general's investigators after testifying against Warren.

Moments after being sentenced to life plus twenty years, Warren was led out of the courthouse for the last time.

My beautiful children, Kyle and Natalia, who inspire and astound me every day.

"Uhhh...no." He proceeded to share our story. Michelle was very understanding, but adamant we see a doctor immediately, and within a couple of days, she sent him home with a whole bag of maternity clothes. The next time I came into the restaurant to visit Ben, she greeted me warmly.

I beamed back at her. Happily, I reported that I had seen a doctor—a female OB/GYN. Michelle shared with me some of her own stories of pregnancy that helped me to realize that there was a lot of "humanness" that takes place during pregnancy and delivery. It felt so good not to feel dirty about the process. Her maternal warmth made me realize how much I longed for nurturing and to talk with my own mother. I worried about the kind of parent I would be. I still seemed to make so many mistakes.

One night I awoke to such intense nausea I barely made it to the bathroom. In tears again, I glanced into the mirror and pulled my stringy hair back from my face. Abruptly I was overcome with something else— the most incredible sense of déjà vu. It was the same vision I had experienced in my final few days at Rulon's home, and what I had dreamed several times in the night at least six months before I left. Each time it had seemed eerie, and yet, here it was—the same lights and colors I had experienced, the yellow tiles and linoleum, and the unmistakable Lake Louise turquoise-blue sink! I had never seen these rooms before Ben and I had fled to Coos Bay and then rented that duplex. I thought back to that night trapped in Rulon's home, feeling like there was no way out, until the moment I had that vision. Something very deep and meaningful permeated my soul. *The knowledge that I was not alone... had that been my baby?* That was impossible, and yet somehow it seemed very real.

I placed my hands upon my belly, which was still quite small. I felt a surge of connection, and my heart soared within my chest. Somehow, it seemed, my baby or the universe had sent messages of love and support to me, long before Rulon had passed, long before I knew I'd be a mother. I felt connected again to the larger world, and from that point on, despite the ongoing nausea, I was able to let go of the fear and get excited. To hell with what anyone else thought of my situation! I would be the mother my baby deserved.

That summer, as my tummy expanded during the last few months of pregnancy, we kicked off Little Ole Opry on the Bay. There I met the most incredible people, like the Houghton girls' mother, Martha, who sort of adopted me, too. She was the first person to whom I divulged my background and history. I was also privileged to practice and play with local favorites, like Dr. Bob, a chiropractor and passionate drummer, and a lead guitar player named Vinnie, who rocked the house. After leaving the FLDS feeling like I would never have close relationships again, I discovered a whole new kind of community. But at the end of each event at the Opry, I stood on the stage with roses in my arms to major applause, realizing that it felt empty without Ben in the audience.

While I was making new connections, Ben and I were facing some rocky times in our relationship. In our efforts to save money for our child, we spent a great deal of time apart at our respective jobs, and the differences in our ages and temperaments began to emerge. He had gained a crowd of friends at the Cedar Grill that he partied with after hours, and he began drinking regularly. At first I was invited along, but not only was I pregnant, I also worked early and long shifts nearly every day.

Shortly after the Opry season ended, we received the news from Ben's siblings in Short Creek that during Sunday services on August 10, 2003, Warren declared that the people were so immoral that the blessings of the Priesthood had been removed from them. With that, he suspended all further religious meetings, though of course his most "righteous" followers were allowed to continue to show their loyalty by paying extra tithes and offerings. He even planted huge wheelbarrows at the entrances and exits for the faithful to dump their offerings to him—and shockingly enough, they did. After being on the outside long enough to see his manipulations for what they were, I was incredulous that the people would put up with this.

We all speculated on where these wheelbarrows of cash would be spent, especially since rumors abounded that "Zion" was being created in Colorado or Texas. A few of Ben's friends and family had stayed in touch, and in May his brother Scott came to Coos Bay with two Short Creek friends to see him. Scott was on his way out of the FLDS, but his friends still had strong ties. In late summer, my youngest brother, Levi, had come to live with Cole and shared more about what was happening in Short Creek. I became worried about the fate of my family under such a dictator, and I continued to be plagued by nightmares about young Ally and Sherrie.

August 31, 2003, was my twenty-seventh birthday, and although I desperately wanted my child to have his own special day, he had a different idea. I went into an intense and difficult labor, and I was frightened to be surrounded by strange doctors and nurses. I hadn't realized how much my FLDS beliefs about medical care added to my fear. Due to Warren's influence and my natural discomfort around even partial nudity, I had only attended two births. One had been highly traumatic, and we had almost lost my mother to excessive bleeding. Ben was just as scared. I had also wanted to have a natural birth without the use of drugs.

Several hours into labor, my mother called to wish me a happy birthday. How I longed to tell her what was happening, and to have her comfort and advice. Yet I had never had the courage to tell her I was pregnant. Every time I had tried to broach the subject, she had cried and begged me to come back to Short Creek. I would not have my baby's first days tainted by rumor and innuendo, so Ben simply told her I would call her later.

In the middle of the labor, Ben asked if he could leave and went with a friend to have lunch, while I strained through hours of labor alone. I recalled that my sister Savannah had gone into labor in her garden while her husband was off gallivanting, and realized Ben was doing exactly what he had seen men do all of his life.

Finally, our baby decided it was time to come out into the world, and at the moment of his birth, I felt my whole universe shift. Kyle was the most beautiful baby I had ever seen. He had startling big blue eyes and his father's red hair. As I looked at him, all the terror slipped away. Tearfully, I felt blessed to wrap our fragile newborn in the beautiful new clothes and blankets I'd been given by my Ramada Inn coworkers at a surprise shower they had thrown me.

I didn't realize that after such a strenuous labor and delivery I should rest. Upon Ben's urgent prodding, we went home as quickly as the doctor let us. At home, Ben expected me to cook and clean along with caring for the baby. Amelia visited from Canada to help me out and make sure I got some rest, and I will never forget her great kindness and the risk she took in coming.

Shortly after she left, Ben's cousin John came to live with us, and he and Ben expected me to wait on them while they caught up on old times. While in Coos Bay I had been exposed to families in which husbands shared in the domestic duties and child rearing, but I didn't know how to broach the subject with Ben. He continued partying, often several nights in a row, and never rose to feed Kyle in the night, even when we moved to formula. During the day he helped out here or there, but only if Kyle wasn't crying.

Still, for what I knew, it was a joyful existence. Being a new mother and my involvement in Christmas Opry were both great miracles. The music helped me to feel the spirit of the season more than ever before. Any acknowledgment of December 25 had been considered devil worship in the FLDS. Therefore, it felt deliciously scandalous to bring our first Christmas tree home to our sparse apartment and put a few meaningful gifts under it.

That December, more shocking news reached us from Short Creek: My mother's husband, Uncle Fred, had disappeared in the middle of the night, taken on a stretcher by an ambulance and surrounded by men who were not in medical garb. Some said he had been called to a "great work," but no one really knew if that was the case. Warren apparently reported to the congregation a few weeks later that Fred had been released as bishop, saying that Fred was "in agreement" to his release. Yet I wondered about all the others who had begun "poofing," or disappearing. Were they all "in agreement"? I wanted to know what this meant for Mom and the girls. All we knew was that William Timpson Jessop, then in his midforties, had been named as new "caretaker" for all of Uncle Fred's wives and children, perhaps because he was a younger, easier candidate for manipulation than Fred had been.

That January Ben and I decided to visit family members in Short Creek, entering Utah for the first time since we had returned his brother's truck fourteen months earlier. It was a risk, and we didn't know the reception we'd receive, but because of our son I felt safe knowing that Warren wouldn't want me now. Most of all, we desired to introduce our beautiful baby boy to our families, who remained precious in our hearts.

Ben and I planned to stay in St. George with Ben's brother Scott and his wife, Holly, who had just left the FLDS. But first, we'd been invited by Jeffy Barlow and his wife, Roxie, to stay with them in Salt Lake City on our way down. After Jeffy had left the FLDS, he'd met and married Roxie, who was a Mormon with a contagious enthusiasm for life. What amazed me was how gracefully she wore makeup and that she had pierced her ears, and yet she didn't look like a harlot! It gave me a lot of courage to lay aside guilt for taking on some ways of the world. She was surprisingly easy for me to relate to as well. It was nice to feel connected to a young person outside of the FLDS.

That Sunday afternoon as we hung out with Jeffy and Roxie, enjoying pizza and discussing old times and new lives, we were suddenly inundated with cell calls. Warren had apparently called a special Sunday service in which he'd excommunicated approximately twenty of the most prominent and influential FLDS brethren! Many of the men excommunicated were Jeffy's blood uncles. The family that had enjoyed special privilege and status since the time of the prophet John Y. Barlow had lost all of its power. Warren had told their wives they were "released" from these men, and Jeffy's aunts and cousins had been instructed to pack up all of their belongings and leave immediately— not just the church, but their homes owned by the church. Other men were sent to "repent from afar." I shuddered. More displaced women and children who would be "given" to other, more "faithful" men.

Another shocker was that Warren had ousted four of his own brothers! Declaring them "deceivers" and "hypocrites," he said that anyone "darkened" by them would be cast out—another clear message to every member of the FLDS: Warren's was the only claim on the congregation's eternal salvation, and every individual was nothing without him. When he called for a vote against the ousting, everyone looked around, but not one soul dared to raise a voice in opposition.

The next day, as we approached Short Creek, I nearly hyperventilated as I remembered what it was like to have every action driven by fear. Ben was experiencing many of the same feelings. It was strange driving through town—so familiar and yet so foreign to us now. We visited with Mom, Sherrie, and Ally briefly, and it was a balm to my heart to see my mother hold little Kyle. I was grateful that the loving smiles on the girls' faces replaced some of the anger I had seen when we had left. We were able to stop by to see Elissa next, and my heart sank at the sight of her. It was clear that Allen was still not treating her well. I hoped my presence would show that she could have a beautiful life outside of the FLDS, but I couldn't force my thoughts or beliefs on her.

Even though my hair was shorter, I did wear a long skirt out of respect for the people. As we stepped into the grocery store, though, the aisles cleared as if we had leprosy. I was hoping to bridge the gap, especially with Ben's younger sisters working at the store. When they saw us, however, they turned around and went into the back.

"We don't serve adulterous people in our store," said one man who had been friends of my mother's family for years. I blinked back tears. The young cashier was very quiet and uncomfortable, but she did allow us to purchase food, and we left quickly.

Ben's dad worked in the hardware store behind the grocery on the same block. As we headed back there to see if we could catch him, several local police showed up and followed us around.

"David is not here," said one of the officers. "Your kind is not welcome. Leave." Everywhere we went, people pointed at us, took pictures, or followed us in menacing-looking vehicles. The God Squad had expanded its fleet since we'd been here last. Finally we made it to Ben's house, where we greeted his parents and many of his younger siblings. We noticed the God Squad stayed nearby.

At four months, Kyle's eyes remained as startlingly big and blue as they had at birth. As Ben's parents held him and played with him, they were entranced.

"I can't believe how absolutely perfect he is!" exclaimed Ben's mother. His father nodded and stared at our son with fascination and curiosity.

Later, Ben's brother Wendell informed us that as soon as we'd left, the family had had a discussion about us and Kyle.

"That child is so perfect and so beautiful," Ben's father had remarked, "the only thing I can think is that baby *must* be Rulon's boy. There is no other way." Ben's mother had nodded in agreement.

I was furious when Wendell told me. I would have expected Warren to think that, but to hear that Ben's family was saying this about their very own flesh and blood astounded me. And even had Rulon been able to sire children, he died months before my pregnancy, making it a physical impossibility.

I had tasted freedom, and to go back and witness the strict manipulation of my people broke my heart. I did not judge them, having once "been" them. But I made a commitment to assert the gift of my independence more strongly within myself. I would celebrate my liberty. I thought of Roxie and her darling earrings, and with a sense of purpose, I got my ears pierced the week after we returned. When I looked in the

mirror, though, I saw a fearful and questioning face instead of a trium-
phant one. Somehow, I vowed, I would find a way to be fully free.

As winter once again melted into our second spring away from Short
Creek, I went to work for Dr. Bob as a receptionist, secretary, and clerk.
Although he was incredibly patient and kind, he was floored by my
nearly nonexistent life skills. Ben and I paid cash for almost everything
and dropped off utility bills in person. I did not know how to balance a
checkbook, much less use any kind of basic accounting software. Fortunately, I loved learning, and it was eye-opening for me to see the medical
field from the other side. Doctors were not a part of some secret government scheme to poison, falsely impregnate, abuse, or annihilate people.

Between my work and Ben's, we no longer had to scrape to survive
day to day. Ben began looking for higher-paying construction work he
had been skilled in since his FLDS youth. We weren't wealthy, but
we had risen out of lowest hierarchy of survival—food, clothing, and
shelter—and I found myself hungry for self-actualization, including the
opportunity to educate myself. I looked longingly at college students
heading to Southwestern Oregon Community College in Coos Bay.
One day, I will join you, I promised myself.

Later that spring, Michelle asked if I would babysit so she and her
husband, Tim, could share some time away together. I was honored
she would ask, and excited to spend time with her charming kids. Kyle
loved to watch and imitate Gracie, who was two years older.

"Hey, before we leave," Michelle said, "I recorded a show for you.
Several FLDS women were on *Oprah*. I thought you might want to see
it." Surprised but appreciative, I nodded.

When the children went down for their naps, I sat down to watch.
Carolyn Jessop, a woman I greatly admired and respected, had escaped
from the FLDS and her husband, my uncle Merrill, just five months
after I left. She had the courage, intelligence, and miraculous luck to
be able to escape with all of her children intact, which I had never seen
before. Usually, a woman's children were kept or kidnapped, used as
leverage to bring her back and keep her until she was submissive again.

Flora Jessop, a cousin of Carolyn's, had escaped at sixteen from her
father's physical and sexual abuse and a forced marriage to her first
cousin. She had been active for the last couple of years in anti–child

abuse work, especially involving women and children in the FLDS. There were other women on stage, too, and I was shocked that several made broad, far-reaching statements implying that sexual abuse and physical abuse were present and pervasive in every single home.

This was simply not true: I knew for a fact that it did *not* happen in every single home. There *were* good FLDS people who cared about the welfare of their children. Abuse was prevalent, and I was glad they had the courage to address it, but I realized that anyone on the outside who watched would think every FLDS person was sick and depraved, and anyone from within the FLDS would turn away from the exaggerations. On one hand, fear and secrecy allowed abuse to continue among our people. That was not healthy and needed to be stopped. On the other hand, trying to break decades of silence through embellishment was wrong, and it detracted from the influence these women could have. The truth lay somewhere in the middle, along with dignity for people inside and outside of the FLDS.

An electric pulse ran down my spine. I felt an unexpectedly strong sense of determination. If I ever had the opportunity to speak, I promised myself that I would take it and consciously speak only the truth.

CHAPTER 18

Missing Persons

During the spring of 2004, Ben and I started getting calls asking for Mother Ora, my mother's youngest sister and my former sister-wife, who had disappeared. People thought she might be with us. I was worried. However brutal I'd had it in Short Creek, Ora had been such a strong believer. If she had left, something must be terribly wrong.

It was apparent that Ora and hundreds of others (like Uncle Fred) were being whisked off to some unknown place in the middle of the night. Diabolically, Warren had created an intense measure of control over the people through that fear and mystery. On strict orders not to reveal their whereabouts or what mission they may have been called to fulfill, the people who poofed left behind confused and frightened family members. Employers didn't ask questions. Parents did not question, either, obediently submitting their daughters in the hopes their entire family would be rewarded. One of my young, underage cousins from British Columbia poofed in just that way—and left her sisters frightened to the core.

Insidiously, when men would disappear without their wives or families, people were unsure if they had "made it to Zion" or if they had undergone Blood Atonement, a term Warren bandied about as a holy way for a man to absolve an otherwise unpardonable sin. It was a Priesthood ordinance that involved ritually giving up one's life at the hands of a Priesthood official. The details had to remain secret, however, because of the ramifications of the law for murder. The mystery surrounding the disappearance and the mention of this ordinance also caused people to be strictly obedient in fear for their lives.

It was this secrecy that compelled me to take action. If Ora was so faithful she had made it to Zion, I doubted her disappearance would have caused such a stir and so many calls. I had to be sure. If the roles were reversed, I hoped she would do the same for me.

In Eldorado, Texas, a tiny town of three thousand inhabitants over 1,100 miles and seventeen hours from Short Creek, Randy and Kathy Mankin, a couple who owned a local newspaper, reported a new FLDS development just north of town. The *Eldorado Success* had reported that the FLDS had bought land through my cousin, David Allred, and had begun building what David called a "hunting retreat." Intrigued, Kathy had begun flying over the property to take photos, and from her pictures and the local residents' reports of bulldozers and construction into all hours of the night, she had deduced that the FLDS was actually building a large, self-sustaining compound. In the spring of 2004, a series of ten-thousand-square-foot buildings sprang up almost overnight on the property. Kathy's reports had made national news, or Ben and I would probably not have known about it. Warren had kept it so secret that most of the people in Short Creek were clueless about it.

Under a lot of public pressure, David Allred was forced to admit that the land wasn't ever intended as a hunting retreat but as a small residential compound. He said two hundred members were living there, and that the secrecy had been an attempt to stave off the media frenzy surrounding the FLDS.

The name of the property listed with the Texas secretary of state was YFZ, LLC. The acronym stood for "Yearning for Zion," the title and line from a church hymn I remembered as being one of Warren's favorites. People from the local community were very concerned. The Waco tragedy that had occurred at the Branch Davidian compound a decade before was only a couple of hundred miles away. Kathy began an intensive investigation, some of which she and Randy shared with their community. I realized that because of the remote location, and the fact that the local minimum age for marriage was fourteen, Warren had found himself a little spot of Heaven.

I'd heard enough to realize I might find Ora there in Texas. However, tracking her down would mean contacting the authorities. Just the word made me tremble. How many times had I been taught of their wicked cruelty and the genocide they wanted to commit upon my people? I gathered as much courage as I could, and called the Texas attorney general's office. I got the runaround until someone finally referred me to the Schleicher County sheriff's office.

"I'm concerned about some people living close to you there...," I began, being purposefully vague. "I have a family member—one that *may* be in protective custody. Or at least I hope she is. Her name is Ora Bernice Jeffs, or Bonnie. We called her 'Ora.' Would you know anything about her?"

Across the line came the voice of a Texan who knew his business. Although the FLDS were newcomers to this area, Sheriff David Doran had studied up on my people and had even traveled to Short Creek to meet them and talk with local, state, and federal law enforcement. In his measured drawl, he asked me if Ora was FLDS, and mentioned that he had visited the ranch in person in an attempt to establish a relationship with them. "I essentially went out to welcome them and get to know them," Doran said. "I brought Ranger Brooks Long and a book of Texas law to the leaders there. We said, 'As long as you keep to these laws, y'all are welcomed here.'"

I was impressed by his careful research, and found myself strangely trusting this officer of the law. Having read up on Officer Rodney Holm's bigamy and sex charges from 2003 that had put FLDS underage marriages in the spotlight, Doran realized Warren was looking for a place away from prying eyes. But he wasn't ready to believe anything I said at face value.

He was testing me. I wasn't offended. I was testing him, too.

"I notice there are never any women present when I go out to the ranch," he said. "But Kathy Mankin and Judge David Doyle and a few others have snapped some pictures during flyovers. If you are at your computer, I can e-mail some and see if you recognize Ora in any of them." My heart beat rapidly, and I knew I had a choice—to risk or not to risk. It took courage, but I finally gave him my real name and e-mail address.

When I saw the photos, my heart melted. Someone had captured a couple of pictures of women working the ranch garden before they ran inside. In one photo, I recognized Asenath, and in another the beautiful, silvery-white hair of Mother Gloria, poking out of her straw sun hat.

How I missed her! It seemed that no matter how much time went by, my heart still longed for my people—and for them to be free.

Gingerly I asked, "Do you ever talk to any of them?"

"We see a few of the men in town," he replied carefully.

I was sorely disappointed not to discover anything more about Ora's whereabouts, but I filed an official missing person report with the sheriff. It took an even bigger risk to give out all of the personal information required on a missing person report, but Sheriff Doran gave me his word that anything I said was off-limits to other agencies and investigators.

Some months went by; then Doran called with some additional questions. The Mankins had reported that building on the Texas YFZ compound was continuing at a feverish pace, and people in the surrounding community were increasingly anxious. Then he asked me about a possible temple.

A *temple!* My mind recalled scriptures as ancient as the Old Testament, concerning the proud and beautiful Temple of Solomon, wherein lay the Ark of the Covenant; the very dwelling place of God. Brought back into Christian practice in the LDS church during Joseph Smith's time of the Saints, temples had been meant as pure and holy places to seal families together here and in Heaven. I told the sheriff that the sacred ordinances and covenants necessary for FLDS eternal salvation were meant to be made within the walls of a temple, and our people had dreamed of having our very own again. At the thought of such a building sprouting up in the Texas desert, I was actually happy for them. Perhaps a temple could bring the people hope and pride, and be a catalyst for positive and lasting change.

After that conversation, the sheriff checked in with me at least once a month. Although I was always careful with my words, I gave him honest answers. I was careful neither to exaggerate nor to extrapolate from my experiences, and I was open about the peculiarities of my people. Sheriff Doran could tell that I still considered the FLDS my family and loved them. When he gave me news about people dear to my heart, he could hear genuine delight in my voice.

I was grateful for the sheriff's information, but I didn't have a lot of time to speculate on what was happening in Short Creek or anywhere else. As soon as Kyle started crawling, Ben and I knew we were in trouble. It was obvious from the trail of scattered home and toy remnants that our son could take nearly anything apart. He was incredibly smart, and it was a full-time job just keeping up with him. Parenthood had been as life-changing for Ben as for me. While it was so rewarding, we were constantly asking ourselves, *Are we doing it right?*

That summer of 2004, Elissa came to visit. She had finally left Allen and was determined to start a new life. That was a huge step, and her courage made me proud. She had gotten involved with a young man named Lamont in the process of getting divorced from Allen, and she seemed genuinely happy for the first time in years. Cole and I spent some tender time with her and had many candid conversations that were healing for all of us.

Still, as Cole and I learned more details of her situation with Allen, we became bitterly angry. Just as Warren had controlled the intimate activities of his father's wives, he was controlling what happened in the bedrooms of all his people. Even after I had left he had admonished Elissa to "submit" to Allen sexually, and he didn't consider Allen's violence against her to be rape. At the end of her visit, Cole talked to Elissa about pressing charges against Warren and Allen. Law enforcement in Arizona was already putting a lot of pressure on her. She was now eighteen and didn't have to worry about getting Mom and Dad's permission, which they never would have granted. Although in our minds it was grossly apparent that *someone* had to do something, Elissa was reticent, and we couldn't blame her.

That September, I received a call from my uncle Dan Fischer, from Salt Lake. Uncle Dan was well loved among those who had left the Work, because he had boldly sought to assist those wronged by Warren Jeffs and the FLDS leadership. He had taken in countless lost boys and assisted Carolyn Jessop and her children with their frightening escape. Over the phone, Dan gave me a short update on recent human rights violations in Short Creek and other FLDS enclaves.

"Becky," he said soberly, "it's been said that '*all that is necessary for the triumph of evil is that good men do nothing.*' You and I, we know what's going on among our people. We know who is behind it. He will flourish unless we stand up."

He was right. But I remained silent on my end of the line. It was one thing to depart from the church, and quite another to stand up to the tyranny of its leaders.

"Becky, when anyone leaves, their hearts are so tender. They don't want to hurt anyone. When they finally get past their own hurt, and start to live and to educate themselves, they begin to realize the atrocities that happened to them and others. Once they're in a strong enough position to realize they could do something about it, however, it's past the statute of limitations."

I gasped. He was right.

"We have the opportunity to do something," Dan stated emphatically. "This is not about being hateful toward Warren. It's about stopping the atrocities."

Dan told me that Warren had skipped town amid allegations that he had repeatedly raped his nephew, Brent Jeffs, a boy we both knew. He was Ben's cousin, and I remembered him as a young, sweet kid. Brent had bravely come forward with information against Warren, along with several other young men. Strangely, some of the other accusers had died, either by suicide or under suspicious circumstances. I thought of the young men I had taught and of the young girls who had been hurt by Warren. Reports said that Warren was still sneaking into town to perform marriages, and sneaking back out in different vehicles, making sure his presence loomed large enough to keep some of the townspeople in fear of going to the authorities, and to make everyone feel that they needed to stay on his good side.

I wanted to help but wasn't sure I had anything that would stand up in court. I was also afraid of being forced into something. Despite my respect for Sheriff Doran, my distrust for all other law enforcement and government officials lingered.

Before we hung up, Dan told me about Joanne Suder, an exceptional lawyer in Baltimore who had successfully prosecuted cases against religious leaders who overstepped their boundaries, namely some officials in the Catholic Church. She was coming to Utah, and he assured me she was very warm and professional. On his assurances, I traveled to Salt Lake to meet with her, and she was everything he had said—respectful, kind, considerate of my rights and desires. She seemed brilliant and exceptionally fair as she asked a lot of deep, probing questions and gave me clear-cut options for what I might pursue to protect my mother and my little sisters.

I had good reason to be worried about them. Shortly before her sixteenth birthday, Amber Jessop, a young girl I had known from Short Creek, simply poofed in the middle of the night. Her sister Suzanne couldn't get her parents to divulge where she'd gone. Later Suzanne got one call from Amber, saying she was on a ranch in Texas and up early to feed the chickens. "You know that I've been married, don't you?" she said, but wouldn't reveal who her husband was. That November, Amber called Suzanne again, this time frightened and unhappy. She admitted she was the bride of Warren Jeffs and was in Short Creek. She said she wanted to escape. Suzanne tried to help her, but their parents pressured Suzanne to stay quiet. Local police who didn't want to cause a stir said because their parents reported that Amber was "fine" they wouldn't pursue it. I realized nothing had changed in Short Creek, and that made me afraid for my little sisters. Though they didn't seem in immediate danger, there were times I felt as helpless as Suzanne.

That fall, Ben had visited a town in Idaho, where he saw significant growth and opportunity in construction. He decided we should live there. Before we packed up, however, he asked me to take care of some unfinished business.

On November 7, 2004, Ben and I were married at the Cedar Grill. They had an elegant, winding staircase, which I descended in a lovely white dress, into a room Michelle had decorated beautifully.

I knew I should have been gloriously happy. Still, doubts kept nagging at me. Ben partied almost every night. It made him happy, but since I had no desire to participate, we had drifted apart emotionally.

I pushed these thoughts aside and did my best to enjoy the night's celebrations. For our honeymoon we went to Newport, Oregon, before returning home to Kyle. Immediately Ben moved to Fruitland to begin working, while Kyle and I stayed in Coos Bay to finish Christmas Opry and to give Dr. Bob time to find a replacement for me to train before I left. As Kyle and I crossed the border into Idaho on New Year's Day 2005, I prayed it would be a fresh, new start for our family. I gave my close Oregon friends my new number, and with a prayer of hope, I decided to leave it with Sheriff Doran as well.

Late in the evening of January 19, my mother called out of the blue. We had spoken very rarely, as the only safe way for me to contact her now was through Amelia, and that had only happened on one or two rare occasions. She assured us she was happy but could give us no more information. I was so surprised and delighted to hear from her. I readied myself for her usual judgmental comments, but this time her voice was soft and tender. She began talking about Kyle, telling me not to work too hard, and to avoid raising him in day care because he needed his mommy.

Her message seemed especially sweet and nurturing. I had missed being able to throw myself into her arms for comfort when life got hard. I missed our talks and our laughter. I thought perhaps she was finally accepting my choices as a wife and mother and giving me her blessing. I hung up the phone, holding it against my chest for a moment before setting it back in its cradle.

A week later Amelia called me, panicked. She had phoned Uncle Fred's house, as usual, asking for Mother Sharon.

"Mother Sharon?" a high and sweet voice responded. "There's no Mother Sharon here." Amelia had shaken her head, looked at the number, and dialed it again. Once again, she received the same answer, so she had me call.

"You must have the wrong number. We've *never* had a Mother Sharon here," I was told. Now, that was disconcerting.

Anxiously, Amelia and I both called people who might have known where Mom was, but to no avail. For a couple of very anxious weeks, my siblings and I tried contacting different friends and relatives. Amelia was the only one who could do so without setting off alarms. She tried talking to my mother's former coworkers and her friends in town, and she even sent some friends to visit "Mother Sharon" at her former home. The FLDS had always been closemouthed, but usually someone would let something slip. But now Mom, Sherrie, and Allyson were all gone. *POOF!*

I was beside myself with worry. On Valentine's Day 2005, I filed missing person reports for the three of them. After years of mostly trying to remove myself emotionally from the drama of Short Creek, I now kept my ear to the ground to catch any news I could. I cried many nights, wondering: Were they in one of Warren's houses of hiding? Had they made it to "Zion"? Were they being auctioned off in political trade for some old man's pleasure?

From bits of news and scuttlebutt, I gathered Warren was still on the run from Brent's lawsuit, but many of the people felt that he must be spending a large portion of his time on the YFZ ranch. Authorities in the United States and British Columbia had continued to collect criminal evidence against him. Jon Krakauer, the author who explored Mormon extremism in the book *Under the Banner of Heaven*, had been quoted in the *Eldorado Success* saying, "I don't know whether it will happen in a week or in a month or in six months, but I am confident that a felony warrant will soon be issued for Warren's arrest, which is going to make him afraid to venture beyond the YFZ gates. It also means, for better or worse, that Eldorado is going to be ground zero in the effort to bring Warren to justice." To me, those were very sobering words. Texans were not the only ones with lingering nightmares of Waco.

The week before, Sheriff Doran and Schleicher County appraisal district personnel had measured new buildings but were denied access to the temple site. The two new buildings that they documented, one a meeting hall and the other a residence, were each larger than twenty-eight-thousand square feet. All of the homes were built in a very handsome, log-cabin style, while the commercial buildings and trailers were much plainer.

Warren had turned the efforts of the faithful toward building a temple at the YFZ, as he was the only one with the authority to direct such projects. Within days of the New Year, furious and frenzied construction began, often going twenty-four hours a day and using the labor of FLDS members from as far away as Canada. Within one month of what appeared to be dedication of the grounds, the structure was totally up and framed in. Randy Mankin used a photo to determine a rough estimate of the size of the temple foundation, and guessed that it closely mirrored the original Mormon temple in Nauvoo, Illinois.

In the meantime, I was busy preparing for real estate school—my first formal education since Alta Academy—and vigorously studying property laws, which astounded me. I didn't realize that outside of the FLDS, people had so many property rights! Inside the church, people signed over all rights to land and homes. Warren, still on the run from law enforcement, had recently been removed as the president of the United Effort Plan, which controlled all the people's property. This meant that he should no longer have control of people's homes! I hoped this move would eradicate his manipulative power. Instead I was shocked to hear the people considered Warren to be a martyr like Joseph Smith, hanging on his every edict, as they were convinced he

was being persecuted on behalf of the church. They became more loyal
to Warren, and resisted changes from the UEP.

In Texas, legislators worried that the FLDS might be creating a
stronghold in Texas, and sought to increase the legal age of marriage
from fourteen to sixteen. I knew this wouldn't stop underage marriages
in the FLDS, but if Texas actually had the guts to prosecute, it might
give a little more teeth to the sentence—or at least buy innocent young
girls a couple more years.

The media was having a field day with rumors of an April 6 doomsday, and Sheriff Doran called me.

"Becky, people are going crazy here. Can you give me the background of April 6?"

"Well, Sheriff," I began, "on April 6, 1830, the Prophet Joseph Smith
restored the church. For the FLDS, it's a day of significance, as we were
taught that April 6 was the actual birth date of Christ, and the date of
his death thirty-three years later. The early church, the modern LDS
church, and the FLDS plan significant events like dedications and celebrations on that date. Why?"

"Well, we think Warren's pushing to have the temple finished by
then, although he's having some hiccups."

I went online and gasped at new pictures the Mankins had posted of
the temple rising high in the desert sky. The massive three-story building rose ninety full feet off the ground. The sheriff informed me that
the limestone they had carved from the earth wasn't strong enough, so
they were having exterior slabs shipped in. From the photos he sent I
could see that they were brilliantly white, and quite lovely.

Then the sheriff dropped a bomb.

"Becky, I know this might be a lot to ask, but would you speak with
an investigator from Arizona?" I felt a sudden chill but tried to brush it
away, remembering how hesitant I'd been to contact Sheriff Doran and
how phenomenal he'd been.

I agreed, with certain conditions. First, I would not talk about my
deceased husband. Rulon was not a perfect man, nor a perfect man
of God, but he was dead. *Let the dead lie.* The second was that I not
be forced to talk about my sister-wives. They had been programmed
and trained by their families, Rulon, and Warren to keep sweet above

all else, and no one could understand what they—and I—had been through. I would not cross that line for any authority.

Within a few minutes during my first conversation with the investigator, however, he moved directly into forbidden territory with questions about Rulon Jeffs and my former sister-wives. When I refused to answer, he tried to force information from me with threats and intimidation. I hung up and refused any additional calls from him or the state of Arizona. The investigator's behavior epitomized why I had been taught to distrust government.

That February, Ben, Kyle, and I went to Utah for the birth of Elissa and Lamont's baby, Kyson. It was a joy to be there for Elissa—to show up in the way I knew my mother would if she had been able to—and I was amazed at my little sister's strength and resilience. Kyson was a beautiful baby, and while he was not born "under the covenant" by FLDS standards, he had been conceived and born in love, and I was glad to see such happiness in my sister's eyes.

We returned to Idaho. After intensive study, I passed my Realtor's exam on March 15, 2005. I went out with my classmates to celebrate, but my heart wasn't in it. I had wanted the flexibility to work primarily from home to be with my son, and real estate seemed like an answer. It had felt good to study again, learn new things, and pass my test. But earlier that day, reports had come in from my family that Uncle Fred had passed away. Missing since his abduction, he had suddenly appeared in a city in Colorado under equally strange circumstances right before his death. Why was it that whenever I was building something in my life outside of the FLDS, something would happen to remind me of my family's plight? As preoccupied as I was with work, Elissa and I knew Mom would move heaven and earth to attend Fred's funeral, and we thought it might be our best chance to see her.

As I was heading down for the funeral, Sheriff Doran called to tell me the chief of police in Hildale, Sam Roundy, had called him saying that my mother was in town for Fred's funeral and had volunteered to clean up her missing person report. My heart flipped over in my chest, but I saw a big red flag. Sam Roundy, a long-standing FLDS member, had escorted both Rulon and Warren on numerous occasions. Would he really let me see my mom? Doran seemed to think so.

"This is your shot," he said, and I found myself trying not to speed to Short Creek.

"I'm just nine hours away!" I said. "Please let them know I'll be there."

"Sam Roundy and Helaman Barlow say they'll wait for you."

A few hours later, however, Mom called Elissa to say that she was meeting with a Washington County detective directly to clear up the report. Both Elissa and Sheriff Doran tried to get them to wait until I arrived, but Sam and Helaman pushed to have it happen sooner.

My bubble burst. The FLDS *always* played these games with the law, especially regarding apostates. I had seen it from the inside, so I didn't know why I'd let myself believe it would be different this time. After Mom met with the authorities, they determined her well-being to be fine and dropped the case.

The next day, Mom called us to assure me that the situation in Short Creek was changing and that the girls were fine. She begged me to drop the report involving the girls. Ben, Kyle, and I were with Elissa, and she and I agreed that we wouldn't drop it without talking to Sherrie and Ally in person. Mom received permission for us to meet with her at the park in Colorado City the following day but asked us to come alone.

The next day it was pouring, so when we pulled up to the park, Mom crammed herself into my little Ford Focus with us and our babies. We greeted her joyfully, throwing our arms around her neck. Her hug was genuine, as were her loving comments about the children, but the conversation shifted quickly, as she had to be back soon for Fred's viewing.

"The sheriff in Texas spoke highly of you, Becky," she said, looking at me. "I told him that you don't understand our lifestyle. I said, 'She's made her choice...And we've made ours.'" Mom had *not* changed. She was speaking for the girls. How could she know what they actually wanted? Sherrie was now only fifteen and Allyson only twelve, though they were as programmed as the rest of us had been. They didn't know about choice.

"Honey," Mom said, pleading with me directly, "can you let the others go?"

"No, not until I see my little sisters."

"They will be safe. No one will touch them."

"Mom, you know you did everything you could to stop Elissa's wedding!" I said a little harshly. "You could not stop it, I could not stop it, and Christine couldn't. If the leaders suddenly decide to marry off

Sherrie and Ally, the girls need to know they have options. I will not force them, but I will not stop until at least they know."

My siblings and I wanted to share a clear message with FLDS leaders: if they tried to marry off our underage sisters, they'd be opening the gates of hell.

My mother's response was pleasantly neutral, which softened me a bit, too.

"Look, Mom, we *might* be willing to drop the missing person report depending on how Uncle Fred's funeral goes tomorrow. As long as we can come and support you, and see Sherrie and Ally..."

Mom agreed but said it was necessary to ask the bishop for permission. She called us later that evening to tell us that William Jessop, who was presiding over Fred's funeral, had given permission for us to attend.

Elissa and I were pleasantly shocked. Perhaps things *had* changed.

The next day, Elissa and I dressed for the funeral in long skirts and sleeves, and styled our hair with a soft pouf out of respect, though mine was a bit short for that style. We arrived early, on the tail end of the morning viewing, so that we could easily get into the funeral without making any waves. When we got to the crowded meeting house, the smell of rain was still heavy in the air. Memories stirred and raw feelings of loss hit me. I still loved so many people in that town. My sister and I walked into the breezeway between the two sets of front doors, and immediately I recognized one of the security guys.

"Randall Rohbock!" I exclaimed softly, as he greeted me with a genuine smile. "It's so good to see you! Listen, we're not here to cause trouble. We just want to pay our respects and support our mother."

He nodded. "It's good to see you, too, Mother Becky. Do you have any cell phones or cameras?"

I hadn't even thought about that. I had my cell with me, as did Elissa.

"You know what? We'll take them out to the car." He simply nodded, and Elissa and I turned to head back to the car to tuck away our phones.

Suddenly a voice boomed from inside the foyer. *"Hey!"*

Even before I turned, there was no mistaking who it was. Standing there, arms folded and larger than life, was Willie Jessop, our first cousin, with a veritable army of men surrounding him. Randall shifted uncomfortably at his post.

"Who are *you?*" Willie said nastily. He knew damn good and well who I was. His sister, our cousin from my mom's side, had been placed with my father as his youngest wife. Willie had worked for Rulon as his enforcer, had been lead member of the God Squad, and was obviously still doing the same under Warren. People began to gather to watch the spectacle.

"Becky," I said simply.

"Becky who?"

"Becky Jeffs, once married to Rulon Jeffs."

His eyes narrowed. *"You're* the one causing all the problems with them missing person reports! You're not welcome here!"

"I'm not here to cause a problem, Willie. We're simply here to pay our respects. At the very least, don't hold it against my sister. I'm the one who filed the reports."

"She's not welcome here, either," said Willie, turning toward Elissa. I had been calm until then, but I felt the familiar hot fire begin to burn at his callousness toward my sister.

"Uncle William said we could come here," I countered as the crowd grew.

"He did not," Willie pronounced, loving the attention. "He would never let you in here!" I took one more look at Willie the henchman and his group of bullies. This was my sign that things had not improved. If anything, they had deteriorated.

We left the building quietly without attending the service or seeing Mom. Elissa and I decided we would not leave Hildale until we'd let Mom know that we'd been barred and therefore would not drop the girls' reports. We drove up and down the red dirt streets of Hildale and Colorado City, which were largely deserted because everyone was still inside at the funeral.

We returned to see crowds exiting the funeral as people began trudging up the hill to the graveside service. We parked and jumped out of the car, walking quickly up that same hill so that we could see Mom. Around us swarmed thousands of FLDS, in an eerie echo of Rulon's funeral. Once we reached the cemetery, I spotted Mom in the front, near the gaping hole into which Fred's casket would be lowered. When she caught my eye and smiled, I looked at her directly, without a nod of reassurance.

During the service, we received several harsh looks. One of my mother's sister-wives from Fred gave me the most withering glare. I didn't let it bother me, though. I loved these people. And unlike during my last visit, I recognized now that they could only see from the inside out. I was seeing them from the outside in. I smiled at this woman with great love, despite her confusion and dismay.

When the ceremony wound down, I slipped beside Mom, and she hugged me tight.

"Honey, I'm so glad you could get in!"

"But, Mom, they didn't let us," I whispered in her ear. "We tried, and Willie said that William would never let us in. That was my sign, Mom, my answer from God." A look of panic crossed her face, but I kissed it.

"We want you to know we love you," I said simply. "This isn't about you; it's about freedom." Elissa and I walked away to leave her and her sister-wives to pay their final respects.

CHAPTER 19

Zion Rising

That night, I called my mother to arrange to see her once more before we left town.

"Honey, why didn't you give up your phone at the funeral?" she asked immediately. "Willie told the bishop that you and Elissa were combative and refused to give up your phones."

"Ask Randall Rohbock, Mom. Then you'll get the truth."

The next day we met her at the park again. There to greet us was a large, menacing GMC truck with a lift kit, enormous tires, and tinted windows. I had dealt with the God Squad before, and while I refused to be intimidated, it made Mom very nervous. Then a car pulled up beside the truck, and the driver stared over at us. It was my cousin Russell Allred, a son of one of my uncle Richard's wives. I felt the fire rise up inside of me again, and despite Mom's protest, I got out of our car and approached my cousin.

"Is there a problem here, Russell?" I asked.

"W-well, hello, Mother Becky," he said, stuttering a little.

"I know you were sent here to watch us."

"No, no," he started to protest, and I put my hands up.

"Look. We're just here for a few minutes. Who do we need to talk to in order to placate people? We're not here to cause trouble."

"Oh no, Mother Becky, it's not a problem," he protested. But as I went back to our car, Russell stayed the entire time.

This time the weather allowed us to take the boys to the playground. As she pushed Kyle in a swing, my mother looked at us mournfully.

"Uncle William sends his apology."

"I appreciate that, thank you," I replied. "Is the truck part of the apology?"

"I have something for you," said Mom, changing the subject. She went to her car and brought back some granola. In the FLDS, when someone dies, people not only bring dinners but also bags of granola or bread to assist the grieving family. We could tell she was trying to soften us, as her conversation turned again to dropping the report, and her nervous behavior made me think that she was under orders.

"Thank you, Mom. Please know there would be no problem if we could just have contact with the girls, just once."

Resignedly but tenderly, Mom reached her hand out to caress my cheek. "I don't think your story is completely told," she whispered. Perhaps Mom hadn't believed all the vicious, ugly rumors Warren had delivered to the people when I left. "God will be the judge," she murmured, as much to herself as to me. She then glanced over at the truck and sighed quietly. She reached into another bag and presented each child with a gift.

As we drove away from the park and from Short Creek, Kyle cradled the brown teddy bear she'd given him in his arms and hugged it to himself often, naming it "Gramma." We didn't know it was the very last time Kyle or I would see his grandmother Wall.

Over the next several months, I learned what it would take to be a Realtor. Very few people in Idaho knew about my background, but my network of professional associates and friends was growing. I found myself enjoying the fullness of friendships that life had to offer. My communication skills flourished, and for the first time since leaving the FLDS, I felt confident enough to speak with people from all walks of life on a professional, if not personal, basis.

Elissa had been maturing as well, building her life with Lamont and the baby in southern Utah. One day, she called me with news that made me almost drop the phone. She had finally decided she might pursue a case against Warren Jeffs. I knew it took a lot of courage from her. She was still only nineteen, and she had endured many situations I wouldn't wish on a grown woman. She asked me to accompany her to meet with Joanne Suder in Baltimore, and I agreed. Joanne gently answered many of Elissa's questions, but Elissa still felt too scared to take action.

On the way back, we discussed the ramifications of testifying, as well as the statute of limitations, which would run out four years after the first offense in 2001 if charges were not pressed. Elissa did wish to press charges, but for several days she couldn't gather enough courage to pick up the phone. She didn't want to cause trouble or hurt our mother, and her fear of law enforcement was deeply entrenched.

Finally Cole called her and said bluntly, "Look, the only way we can stop this from happening to Sherrie and Ally is if you press charges." I volunteered to find out what she would need to do in Washington County to file. Terrified for herself, but hopeful for our sisters, she agreed.

During that summer, Ben and I watched Kyle grow—which was about all we had left in common. It had become clear to me that although my husband had no desire to rejoin a polygamous religion, part of that culture had stayed with him. He confessed to me he wanted to engage in polyamorous relationships. Soon it became apparent that he didn't want an open marriage, but rather that he wanted to experience more than one woman for himself. Confused and heartbroken, I shut down inside, and questioned my value as a woman who couldn't keep her husband satisfied. This hit home several days a week when I would arrive home from work to Ben asking if I had found another woman to bring with me. As I looked around me, I saw a pattern in many former FLDS men, as well as men in mainstream society who jumped from mistress to mistress, or one sexually driven relationship to another. I knew it was not just men, but they often played a more active role in that desire.

Was this something women just had to endure? Or was this an unhealthy, clear sign to get out of my marriage? That thought was almost as frightening as leaving the FLDS had been.

One early morning in August 2005, as we were leaving for a trip to visit family in Salt Lake, Ben fell asleep at the wheel and we got into a serious accident. To our relief, Kyle was not injured. I sustained some severe injuries to my knee, and Ben was deeply affected. The young and generally invincible man I'd married no longer seemed that way, and it seemed like a sign to stick beside him. Our marriage rebounded for a brief moment, but by the time Kyle and I went to Coos Bay to perform Christmas Opry, I was ready for a break from Ben's continued requests for lovers.

In early 2006, my little sister Amelia left the FLDS and her home in Bountiful, British Columbia, and came to live with us in Idaho. Her turmoil was written on her face, and my heart ached for her, not just because of the trauma of leaving the church but because she had young children she was trying to gain custody of. When any woman with children left the FLDS, she didn't have to take on just her former husband, but the wealthy FLDS church and its seasoned, well-paid lawyers. Amelia had a long road ahead of her.

Despite being on the run, Warren wielded tremendous power, and it felt like he could get away with just about anything. He continued to elude officials, although his brother Seth was caught trying to bring him over $140,000 in cash, multiple cell phones, and letters from loyal followers, all of which were seized by law enforcement. Seth only got his hands slapped and was let off, which made me mad. That $140,000 constituted the tithes of some very hardworking families, and Seth knew it. What did Warren need that kind of money for? I wondered. In April 2006, I read in the paper that Washington County attorney Brock Belnap had charged Warren with two counts of rape as an accomplice, a first-degree felony. Fifth District Court Judge James E. Shumate signed a $50,000 reward for Warren's arrest. I hoped that would spur someone to turn him in.

A month later, just before Ben and I bought our first home, Warren made the FBI's Ten Most Wanted list. The reward increased from $50,000 to $100,000. Warren's undercover games, his continued refusal to show up for depositions and court proceedings, and his flagrant disregard for the law had finally made him a prime target for the feds. His reckless abandon spoke volumes of Warren's desire to be known as a martyr for his people, and unfortunately, it was working. During this time, many thousands of members remained intensely loyal to him, a loyalty only intensified by their distrust of the government.

The search for Warren was heating up in Utah and in Texas. There were times that Sheriff Doran was almost certain Warren was on the ranch. Judge David Doyle and Kathy Mankin did periodic flyovers to check on the secretive sect. I wondered if they ever saw my sisters, but no news ever came in of the girls.

In the early summer months of 2006, Ben's little brother Wendell was kicked out on orders from Warren, and he came to live with us for a time. Unlike Scott or Ben, Wendell had been a devotee of Warren, secretly entrusted with the care of many of Warren's wives in houses of hiding across the West. It was in these remote and various shelters that Warren placed massive amounts of his growing harem of wives, away from the law and prying eyes. Wendell told us that Warren had been amassing even more wives than his father had, perhaps more than a hundred. He did know that some of his recent wives were as young as twelve years old. With deep sadness, I listened to stories of the twisted behaviors Warren used to belittle his wives, to pit them against one another so as to dissolve any solidarity. Wendell said that Warren kept them focused on *his* desires for them: each had to be tiny and rail thin, and ready to give herself as a comfort wife to him at any moment during his underground flight.

Wendell knew about only a small portion of Warren's activities, as the Prophet deliberately shared with each devotee just one piece of the intricate puzzle he was constructing. I couldn't be sure about his first and second counselors in the Presidency, but others were clearly left in the dark. Wendell talked of his secretive missions across the United States, following the Prophet's paranoid and urgent whims. After receiving calls in the middle of the night complete with code words, disguises, and directions, Wendell would leave in the dark, drive to whatever remote location his Prophet requested, and pick up one or more of Warren's wives to transport covertly from one location to another, and then start all over the next night. Warren had a complex system of technological communications— phone, video, and e-mails with which to give his directives to his people and to his web of personal emissaries like Wendell.

Living at a house in hiding in Colorado, Wendell followed Warren's orders to the letter, but all the secrecy was taking its toll. As a caretaker, he was required to be a father figure, strong and pure in the sight of the Lord, and not to allow his thoughts to wander in lust. Loyal and obedient to Warren's every directive, he was caught up in the web of Warren's self-created drama and mystery. Wendell struggled from the same high level of anxiety that Warren's wives did. A young man, he also missed the camaraderie of his brothers and friends, but absolute secrecy was essential for the protection of the Prophet.

Once in a while, Wendell would go out for a drink to relax or drown his loneliness. One night after a weeklong trip to Utah and Wyoming, he stopped at a bar for a couple of drinks. A few hours later, he was pulled over and charged with driving under the influence. Although he was released from jail two days later, when he went back to the house in hiding where Warren's wives resided, a stranger answered the door. His own wife and child were also missing. Frantically he put in a call to his father and to Lyle Jeffs and was coldly told to go home to Short Creek and repent from afar. He quickly discovered that not only had his wife and new baby boy been taken from him, but the bishop of Short Creek had already placed them with another man.

Wendell was not allowed to see them or know their location. All he knew was that his wife had been instructed to burn all photos and letters from him and to treat him as if he were dead. It wasn't until that moment that he realized just how thoroughly he had been used and manipulated. All he had ever wanted was to bring honor and salvation to his family. He was heartbroken. As I looked at my brother-in-law, I wondered if Warren's power to destroy families would ever end. Unfortunately, it was just the beginning.

CHAPTER 20

Purgatory for a Prophet

On August 29, 2006, I was taking a lunch break with colleagues from a real estate class when I received a call from Sheriff Doran. Quickly I excused myself to step outside.

"Becky, did you see the news? Warren Jeffs was caught last night outside of Las Vegas!"

I sat down in shock. Warren had been on the run for so long, I hadn't been sure this day would ever come. Doran told me that the Nevada Highway Patrol had pulled over a brand-new red Cadillac Escalade with paper license plates during a routine traffic stop. Warren's brother Isaac was driving, Warren was in the passenger seat, and Naomi Jeffs was in the back. The trooper did not recognize Warren but got the feeling something was wrong, because Warren was nervously shoveling his salad into his mouth and wouldn't make eye contact. Most conspicuously, the carotid artery in his neck was pumping like crazy. The trooper separated Isaac from Warren, and when they each gave him completely different stories, he called for immediate backup. From there, the officers began a thorough search of the car.

"First of all," Doran told me, "that red Escalade was a new model 2007, worth at least $55,000, and had been paid for in cash. Second of all, they found at least $54,000 in bills in the vehicle, and more envelopes with more letters and cash from his followers. There was also a police scanner, fifteen cell phones plus walkie-talkies, laptop computers, credit cards, and keys to several other luxury vehicles with them. They had wigs and sunglasses and all kinds of accessories to keep them unrecognizable." The list went on and on. Just as when Seth had been pulled over, there were multiple bundles of sealed letters to Warren pleading for his prayers for their family members.

It made sense to me that the people were corresponding with their Prophet while he was on the run. They still needed to show their loyalty, and they hoped their heartfelt pleadings to God would be heard through their Prophet.

"Becky," he added soberly, "Warren had slit the envelopes open only far enough to get the cash out. He hadn't read a single one."

I bit back the bile creeping up my throat. One part of me wanted to scream for joy that Warren had been caught, but a tear slipped down my cheek in frustration for all of the pleadings Warren couldn't be bothered to read.

I thanked the sheriff and sat for a moment, thinking. Perhaps now, the people would see Warren for what he really was. I prayed that this would be the crack in the foundation that would send his whole charade crumbling down on him and free the people I still loved. I let Ben know, and then I called Wendell.

"Remember how you said that Warren told you God will sweep the wicked off North America before He allows him to get caught?" I asked him.

"Yeah," he said, "why?"

"He's been caught."

"Are you serious?" Wendell began to laugh, almost uncontrollably. He'd been out only for a few months, and it was sometimes still hard for him to believe that Warren's words weren't the true and holy revelations as he'd always been told.

The sheriff reported to me later that ten sets of keys to other luxury vehicles had been found in the car, including a brand-new Porsche, a Cayenne luxury sports SUV valued at more than $100,000, and other European luxury cars, worth almost a million dollars total.

When Doran told me Isaac and Naomi were released without charges, I felt momentarily grateful. Then it hit me: they had known damn well that our people were going without food so the Prophet would be safe! Their hands were far from clean.

A few weeks later, Warren was extradited from Nevada to the appropriately named Purgatory Correctional Facility in Utah. At the end of the month, I was celebrating my birthday at a Realtor golf tournament when I received a surprise call from my mother, whom I hadn't heard from since the day after Fred's funeral.

"Well, hello, Mom! To what do I owe this pleasure?"

"Oh, I just called to check on you," she responded vaguely. "Happy birthday!"

"It's Kyle's birthday, too," I said, a little irritated. Had she so quickly forgotten her grandson?

"Oh!" she fumbled. "I'm calling to wish him a happy birthday, too, of course." There was a nervous silence, and I could tell something was wrong. Someone was putting her up to this, and probably listening in from another line.

"You know there is still an outstanding missing person report on the girls," she said finally, her voice shaky. "Why don't you talk to them?"

I gasped, and my heart soared. My sisters!

"Ally," I said, when she put her on the line. I let her talk for a bit, just reveling in hearing her voice. Then I said, "Remember that song I used to sing to you? 'I See the Moon and the Moon Sees Me'? Kyle and I sing that to you every night, knowing we're looking at the same moon." I could tell she was grateful, but her voice was filled with tension. Sherrie, on the other hand, sounded scripted and rehearsed. "Sure love ya. Pray for you every day." I asked them to put Mom back on.

"Okay, Mom, what's *really* going on?"

She hesitated for another moment. "Well, honey, we've gotten word that someone is threatening the Priesthood with litigation. Someone is pressing charges against Uncle Warren... is it you?"

I wasn't about to throw Elissa under the bus. In the charges she'd filed with Washington County, prosecutors were using the name "Jane Doe IV" to protect her. The FLDS knew there were several people who could have been pressing similar charges, and the less they knew the better. I had never lied to my mother, though, so I chose my words with care.

"I honestly don't know who all has charges against Warren," I said. "It could be a lot of different people. I'm not involved in the lives of all of the people who have left. But I'd like you to think about some-thing for a moment. Take away the names and the faces of the people in power. Just look at the actions. Look at the facts. Can you tell me that forcing any young girl to participate in marriage against her will is inspired? Can you tell me that is of God?"

"Honey, God and the Prophet do right."

"Mom, there is a reason it is illegal to marry twelve- and thirteen-year-olds." Silence. "Okay," I said, switching tracks. "Mom, is truth *truth*?"

"Yes."

"Okay, if truth is truth, will it be seen from *all* angles, then?"

"Yes."

"Then why are you afraid to see truth come out?"

"Honey, you know people don't understand us."

"Now, wait a minute. If truth is truth, then it will stand up to scru-tiny. Like the scripture in Matthew, 'By their fruits ye shall know them.' Look at the fruits, Mom! When Elissa was being forced to marry, did you honestly feel peace within you?" I longed to scream into the phone, *When you knew she was being raped and beaten repeatedly, was that sweet fruit to you?*

Finally, she responded: "I would rather see *all* of my children lying in a grave than for any *one* of them to challenge the Priesthood."

My blood ran cold. Her programming was so intense that to her this was the ultimate battle between right and wrong, God and man. The church would be right no matter how many lives were ruined. I got off the phone, shaking.

I decided it was healthiest to try to move on with my life as much as possible. But a few weeks later, I got a call from the district attorney's office in St. George, requesting an interview about Elissa's case with a deputy DA and a sergeant from Washington County. I was apprehensive when I met them in Boise, but they were respectful and professional.

The police sergeant, Jake Shultz, told me that growing up as a Chris-tian teenager, he loved to play basketball. In order to join different church leagues, he and his equally obsessed basketball buddies had to go to church and Sunday school.

"Mormon, Catholic, Church of the Nazarenes...you name it," he chuckled. "Every one of them had this attitude on some level: 'We're right, and everyone else is wrong and damned.' We can't all be wrong and damned, can we?" He made me laugh, which made it easier just to be there.

At first they asked easy questions about being raised in the FLDS, especially my experience as a girl in the community. When they asked if I would share my experience as a married woman in the FLDS, they both took meticulous notes.

"I can only speak for what I have experienced firsthand," I said carefully. "I don't believe one person can speak for the entire FLDS population in this regard. There are well more than ten thousand members now. Different women may have different experiences."

They both nodded, and I proceeded to explain the situations with Rulon. Every time I had tried to tell Ben about my marriage to Rulon, he had gotten so disgusted and angry with me, he'd interrupt with "Eww! Why did you let him do that to you, Beck?" as if I'd had any control over my body or my destiny as Rulon's wife.

By contrast, both of these men were exceptionally compassionate as I explained why I didn't like Rulon to touch me, and how Warren threatened my life if I said no to my husband. Finally, I explained how painful intercourse was for me because of my accident, especially because Rulon hadn't bothered to be gentle. As I proceeded to tell them about him forcing me to perform oral sex, though, I had to break eye contact. "At that time, I hadn't known that even young people did those kinds of things to each other in consensual sex. All I had ever been taught was that anything even remotely like that was bad, sick, and wrong, and then suddenly the Prophet was physically forcing me to do it."

It was hard for me to get the words out, and as I looked down, I noticed that Jake's free hand was clenched into a fist on his lap. He was shaking with rage. I was floored: except for Cole, no man had ever been angry at Rulon and Warren for what they had done to me!

Before we parted, I had gained an unexpected sense of trust in these two men. I felt like these guys would go to bat for me. What would life have been like in the FLDS if I had known that there were people like this out there? Despite my intense terror and shame, that interview was a paradigm shift. Even beyond my experiences with Sheriff Doran, I began to trust the process and what it would take to help others, especially my sisters.

Returning home, I focused on my work and family again. Ben seemed to respect me more as I began doing well in my new field, developing relationships with lenders and clients and learning the ropes quickly. Real estate in 2006 was booming, and everyone was looking for agents. But ethics and values were constantly challenged in that industry. I had interviewed with one broker who told me, "With your looks we'll make a lot of money." This seemed to parallel what I'd experienced in the church, and I stayed far away from him and his brokerage. Instead I found a firm that cared about me for who I was and the work I could perform. It was greatly empowering.

CHAPTER 21

The Witnesses Wore Red

In October 2006, Elissa's attorney, Roger Hoole, released some additional information to the public about Elissa's case against Warren. Her name was being protectively guarded, as prosecutors feared that intense pressure would be exerted not only on Elissa but on our remaining sisters, mother, and father, still active in the FLDS. It didn't seem to matter that Warren was behind bars—he was able to wreak the same havoc among the people. FLDS leaders—including the remaining members of the First Presidency and Warren's henchmen—were following his orders as if he were a free man. They all believed he would be soon.

In November 2006, I flew down to St. George to face Warren at his pretrial hearing. Ben would meet me there later with Kyle. I had to take a few days off from work, and I entrusted only my boss and two friends with the reason that I had to leave. Ben and I had continued the practice of keeping our past out of our present, and the DA's office and the Washington County attorneys had promised that my identity would be protected along with Elissa's. Names, videos, and personal information were to remain confidential and limited to the courtroom alone.

Aboard the plane, I had the eerie realization that this would be the first time I would come face-to-face with Warren since his threat to break me and my subsequent escape. Testifying was the right thing to do, but the fact remained that the people I loved with my whole heart would hate me. I was testifying for *them*, not against Warren—although they would never know that.

Amelia and I had spent a little time together before the hearing, and on a trip to the mall, we had the same wicked thought: why not dress in red, the very color that Warren had outlawed? (And, ironically, the color of the Escalade in which he'd been arrested!) Amelia bought a flattering gray suit to wear with a maroon blouse, while I bought a black suit jacket and a stunning red camisole. The lawyers and officers wouldn't see the significance. But Warren would. And more important, we would.

Greg Hoole, Roger's brother, picked up Amelia and me and took us to the courthouse. I hadn't read or seen anything on television about the trials, and it was the very first time any substantial charges had been brought against Warren, so I didn't have any frame of reference. Since the FLDS had such a strong presence nearby, armed SWAT officers in body armor escorted us with large semiautomatic rifles. While it made us feel a little better, it was an intimidating sight.

The prosecutors prepared me that day. "This pretrial is for the judge to determine if there is enough evidence to try Warren. He has hired two lawyers from Salt Lake City to represent him. They are very smooth. Listen to the questions carefully, take your time in responding, and realize they have an agenda for *everything*. They will try to put words in your mouth."

I discovered they were right. When it was my turn to testify, Warren's lawyer, Wally Bugden, got upset with my predilection to clarify yes or no questions. He tried to make it sound as though a woman in the FLDS could just flippantly tell the Prophet she didn't want to marry a man and life would go on as normal.

"There are women that say no?" asked Bugden.

"Not often."

"Well—"

"Hardly. Maybe two or three that I know of."

"Well, bear with me, ma'am. Are there women who say no? Yes or no?"

"Yes. But it is very looked down upon."

"Okay. So the answer to my question is yes? Is that right?"

"Yes."

"And you, off the top of your head, as a hostile witness not wanting to answer my questions, off the top of your head, you can say that you know two people that turned down the Prophet?"

He also was attempting to insinuate that I was always in trouble with Warren for immoral deeds, that I had gotten pregnant and had just decided to walk out the door one day because I didn't want to be there anymore.

I spoke on the stand for a good four hours, doing my best to set the record straight, especially about what I had experienced with Elissa before, during, and after her wedding, and the meanings of certain Priesthood teachings.

At one point they asked me who could have stopped Elissa's underage marriage, and I pointed a finger decisively at Warren.

"That man, right there!" I said resolutely. He looked at me in surprise, but I didn't waver. As I left, I was still full of nervous energy, but I felt very good about my testimony. As I had said to my mother: if truth is truth, it will stand up to scrutiny.

When Amelia took the stand after me, I went down the hall to wait in a small room with other witnesses and armed guards. I was told Amelia also gave a strong and succinct testimony about Elissa's miscarriage and her trip to Canada after she had been raped repeatedly by Allen.

I was in the witness room waiting for Amelia to finish testifying when Sheriff Doran called me from Texas.

"Hey, Miss Becky, are you okay?"

"Yeah, I guess," I responded. "I'm just tired, and relieved that it's over. Why do you ask?"

"I just wondered," he said, "because I just had Fox News on, and I saw you on there. They've got a video and everything, and I know how you are about your privacy."

"*What?*" I was astounded. "Did they show Elissa?"

"No, just you."

"Did they blur my face?"

"No, they showed you full on, testifying."

What the hell was this? They had promised—guaranteed—anonymity. This felt like a serious transgression, and I had to wonder if it was a display of ego by one of the agencies that had been looking for Warren for so long with no results. The Fox News video portrayed me talking about Elissa's marriage and my family's reaction to it. They quoted me as saying, "She was fourteen. It was just shocking and horrific... She didn't want to get married."

I opened the door that was being flanked by armed guards.

"I want to talk to someone from the DA's office *right now*," I said to one of them. "Somebody is in real trouble here." They quickly brought Jerry Jaeger to the room.

The video played two more times over the next hour before the DA was able to have it pulled. Given Warren's notoriety, Fox was reticent to take my testimony down. CNN played the same clip with my face blurred; however, you could still tell it was me. Finally, the stations blacked me out on the screen as they'd been ordered, and played just my voice testimony for the rest of the day.

The damage was done. Within minutes, I was inundated with shocked texts and phone calls from many people, most of whom I knew through real estate in Idaho but who had known nothing about my background. Fortunately, I had planned to go directly from the trial to see our friends in Coos Bay and perform in the holiday Opry. The Houghtons and my other very close friends knew about the pretrial and were supportive of us. Luckily the hubbub in Coos Bay died down quickly, but when I returned to Idaho, people were reluctant to let it drop.

A week after my return, I went to show a property to a client.

"Oh my God!" exclaimed the property agent. "Aren't you the girl that was married to that ninety-something guy?" I brushed it off, but he would not let it go, becoming downright vulgar. My client was so offended at his behavior he asked if we could leave, a request I was happy to oblige, and we never went back.

Before the holidays, Judge James L. Shumate had ruled that Warren would indeed stand trial on two felony charges as an accomplice to rape. Elissa had delivered a baby girl only days before the hearing and wasn't able to come to the final session. Roger Hoole contacted her as soon as court was dismissed, and he reported that Warren had had no reaction to the ruling. I wondered how he felt about facing consequences for once in his life.

Work on the YFZ ranch was progressing as if Warren had never been caught. I couldn't believe how much phone time and how many visits he was allowed in jail—enough for him to continue to run the lives of the FLDS. I thought of all of my family members who had left the church or were told to repent from afar, and I asked them all to come for Christmas. Everyone except Cole and Joshua came, even my dad and Irene. Since we'd grown up with so little, I had wanted everyone to feel spoiled. Later I realized I'd gone way over the top: presents for everyone, decorations everywhere, and absolutely no sleep. Within a few weeks the presents and food were forgotten, but I would never forget my family being together.

I no longer felt the animosity for my father and Irene I once had, and that was very healing. I could see that both were striving to live a different life from before. And I recognized that they had taken a *big* chance to come see us for Christmas, as three of his daughters—Elissa, Amelia, and me—would be testifying against their Prophet in the coming year. The fallout of my testimony on Ben's side of the family, however, was horrendous. They were ugly and nasty, and it created more strain and tension in our marriage.

The FLDS were back to manipulating laws, and the trial was delayed again, again, and again. During this time, the people at my work were paragons of kindness and generosity, but the real estate bubble was beginning to burst. With profits and glamour fading, I witnessed some people give up on life immediately, while others provided great examples of resilience and authenticity.

Warren, on the other hand, was an example of misery and false martyrdom. Caught up in life at home and trying to avoid the topic with Ben, I didn't watch the pretrials on television. Therefore, I didn't know until later that Warren had become sickly from self-imposed fasts and that he had been suicidal. He looked terrible on camera when he showed up for a pretrial, and rumors were circulating around Short Creek that Warren had renounced his role as Prophet, telling Nephi he was "the greatest of all sinners," and admitting indiscretions with a daughter and a sister. It was always difficult to separate truth from rumor, though.

Elissa and I were not allowed to discuss the case; she had been placed in the FBI's witness protection program, so we didn't talk much. However, she urgently phoned me when Warren's next pretrial hit the news. In court, Warren had tried to present a handwritten note to the judge but was not given permission to approach the bench, and his lawyers would not allow the note to go there, either. A *Deseret News* reporter took a photo of the note, and specialists determined it read: "I have not been a Prophet and am not the Prophet," that he had "failed to lead the good people of the Fundamentalist Church." Elissa and I were both floored. Surely now our people would see the truth and free themselves of this dictator? Unfortunately, word was deliberately spread among the loyal about a "government ploy" to hang Warren.

That spring I discovered I was pregnant again. While familiar feelings of uncertainty and joy rode through me, the morning sickness was much milder this time and it felt worth celebrating. I remembered my sisters when they held baby Kyle, and I wondered if they would ever see my new baby.

In June, my sisters were still nowhere to be found. Sheriff Doran and his deputy, George Arispe, came to southern Utah to meet with law enforcement officers from Arizona and Utah and learn from one another about the FLDS. Ben and I met the men for coffee in Hurricane, and Doran told us that his biggest conundrum was that the FLDS seemed like such good, God-fearing people at the mercy of a maniacal leader. Even with Warren behind bars, several FLDS leaders and their families continued to be under his spell, including involvement in illegal activities like money laundering and total disregard for the law.

Now that word was out about our testifying, Amelia and I both faced veiled and overt threats. Certain FLDS "enforcers" seemed to come and go from my little town, while someone cunningly sabotaged Amelia's car, including cutting her brake lines. Her friend, a mechanic, said she was lucky to be alive.

FLDS leaders exerted pressure on my father and active members of our families to convince us not to testify. The hardest for me was what it was doing to Ben. My husband had come to the courtroom during the preliminary trials, but because of the games the FLDS was playing, the actual trial didn't start until nearly a year later. The longer it went on, the more uncomfortable he became. It didn't help that his friends and family called him often to tell him he and our kids would burn in hell with me and my sisters for testifying against *the* servant of God.

"I didn't ask for this!" Ben cried more than once.

I understood. I hadn't, either.

One night I awoke from an intensely vivid dream in which I was fighting a medieval battle side by side with male soldiers and a woman who was dressed like a knight. Though I had read about Joan of Arc only in passing, somehow I knew it had been her. The strongest remembrance was my conviction: *If you stop now, this will have all been in vain... keep fighting, and no longer will they be able to take your sons and daughters.* I awoke with the smell of smoke still strong in my nostrils. In the real battle I was facing in the courtroom, I could not stop now. I honored Ben's feelings and his choice, but I felt a sudden, intense conviction. He didn't have to do this, but I did. Not once did I doubt from that time forward.

Finally, Amelia and I traveled from Idaho to St. George on September 11, 2007, for Warren's full trial. Elissa had brought Lamont with her, but Amelia and I only had each other, as Ben made it very clear that he wanted nothing more to do with the case. I was six months pregnant, and had grown my hair out. I'd actually gone blonde since the last trial, and as I entered the packed courtroom and they announced my name, several FLDS members gasped at me.

Once again I wore the color red: a beautiful maroon-and-red-patterned maternity dress. Warren stared coldly at me but couldn't keep his eyes off my belly. Behind him, a veritable army of FLDS men and a few handpicked women gave me menacing looks. Willie Jessop's behavior was the most egregious. When any of the witnesses was on the stand, he and the others would lean forward in their chairs, trying to make us lose confidence. After each response, he would scribble a note for Warren's attorneys and make a big show of passing it up to them. During Elissa's testimony, the prosecution finally intervened by physically placing a large person right in front of Willie, but I couldn't believe they wouldn't just remove him from the courtroom.

During my own testimony, I made sure to answer deliberately and truthfully for the benefit of every person in that courtroom. As part of the cross-examination, Bugden asked me to read quotes on the big screen for the jury from *In Light and Truth: Raising Children in the Family Order of Heaven*—the same book that had been compiled with many of my notes of sermons given. It was so uncomfortable, because Bugden had cherry-picked phrases for each quote to sound very high and noble as far as the treatment of women, and wouldn't let me interject. I was greatly relieved and impressed when the prosecution put the entire page up on the screen, and let me read and explain the whole passage the defense attorney had taken completely out of context. I looked at Warren and was surprised to see a small smile at the edge of his mouth. The student had been taught well.

After five grueling hours on the stand with only one short break, sitting that long with my big belly was taking its toll. The defense continued being brutal; Bugden and Tara Isaacson, Warren's other defense attorney, kept asking leading questions, trying to discredit me with constant insinuations or notes that Willie was writing to them. I looked into my lap and I saw that my hands were clenched into fists.

Please, please, I cried out to God. *I need help now.*

I have never been kicked so hard in my entire life. *Bam! Bam! Bam!* The baby girl in my belly kicked with such intensity it jerked my body back and my head upright. With my head lifted, I could see the back of the courtroom windows, where my reflection was lit up. Light seemed to stream through my body, surrounding me. Suddenly, I felt like my shoulders grew broader, like the hands of others were holding me up. I relaxed my fists, and from that point on, I could not be shaken.

The same peace permeated my being when I left the courtroom to wait down the hall for Amelia. I testified twice, I had told the truth, and the rest was up to the jury. The *Salt Lake Tribune* reported that a jury member had said, "Rebecca Musser, that woman made eye contact and she shot fire." Amelia's testimony was exceptional, as was Elissa's moving story in her own words. I hoped the jury would feel compassion for her—and all the girls inside that religion.

Back in the waiting room, Lamont looked at Roger and winked. "One down, one to go."

"*What?*" I cried.

"Arizona. Didn't you know that Arizona has a couple of cases against Warren? They've charged him with eight additional crimes, including sexual misconduct with minors and incest, involving two separate cases."

There was an awkward silence. I looked directly at Lamont. "Oh, no. Not me. Don't count me in for anything more. I've served my time." I had avoided any contact with Arizona unless it had to do with Elissa's court case. Not only did I not trust that state's law enforcement, but I couldn't put any more pressure on my marriage. Plus, if Warren was convicted here, it made absolutely no sense to pursue another conviction. More trials meant more legal fees paid for by the *people*. Warren certainly had not labored himself to pay his lawyers.

Later I heard that Roger Hoole had filed a civil case on behalf of Elissa and others. I understood that they wanted to strip Warren of his vast and egregious powers, but I refused to get involved. A criminal case was one thing, but in my mind a civil case would surely cause more suffering among the people.

Warren's Utah trial lasted just fourteen days. On September 25, 2007, after sixteen hours of deliberation, the jury announced its verdict. Warren was found guilty of being an accomplice to two counts of rape of a minor. He would have to wait until November for Judge Shumate to hand down his sentence.

In the meantime, he was facing a federal charge for fleeing prosecution. No longer a ward of Purgatory, Warren was taken to the Utah State Prison to await his sentence. My biggest hope was that Warren and other FLDS leaders would no longer take for granted their control of children and young women. If a girl didn't ever *know* she had a choice, she had no choice.

Though I was relieved by the verdict, it made me think of my little sisters, still within the FLDS and still under Warren's authority. What would become of them now?

CHAPTER 22

The God That Revealed
Himself to Me

The next few months went by in a blur. Amelia was fighting hard for custody of her kids, who were still among the FLDS in Bountiful. During Elissa's trial, Amelia and I had met Mark Shurtleff, the attorney general for the state of Utah. He had been polite and grateful for our testimony and said to give him a call if there was anything he could do. Amelia shared with him the plight of her children, and Shurtleff had assured her that Utah would lend a hand returning her kids to her. However, once the trial was over, his office never returned her messages, and she never heard from Shurtleff again. But Amelia would not give up.

A few weeks after the trial, Elissa shared something with me she was not allowed to discuss while it was going on. Apparently when Warren had been caught, several of his Priesthood records as the people's Prophet were in the vehicle with him, including his journals and audio recordings. While they were preparing the case, Bruce Wisan, who had been appointed legal overseer of the United Effort Plan by the state after Warren was released as head, had said to them casually, "Wouldn't it be wise for the jury to know we have an audio recording found in Warren's vehicle upon his arrest of him molesting a twelve-year-old girl?"

I stared at her. "Are you kidding?"

"No," she said, her face somber. "Judge Shumate said the material was too inflammatory." She paused, and then said, "We think it was little Merrianne, Uncle Merrill's daughter."

Merrianne. I remembered our cousin as a vibrant six-year-old in braids, with rosy cheeks and freckles. She often came to Rulon Jeffs's home with her older sisters, Maria and Cecilia, two of my sister-wives. With bile in my throat, I recalled Warren paying special attention to her like he had with Sherrie—and how I'd shielded Sherrie from contact with him. Thinking of Merrianne in that predicament made me want to cry. On top of that, he recorded it? I was sick, agreeing with Judge Shumate that the material was inflammatory, but truth was truth. Luckily, Warren had been found guilty without it.

While we were awaiting Warren's sentence, more details emerged in the media. A video recording documented Nephi's visit to Warren in prison, during which Warren had actually renounced the mantle of Prophet and given it to former bishop William T. Jessop, admitting to his own "immoral actions with a sister and a daughter." Warren had tried to commit suicide by running into walls and banging his head against them. He also attempted to hang himself but again was unsuccessful.

Warren was the last thing on my mind on November 20, 2007, the day Warren's lawyers declared that "Mr. Jeffs resigned as President of the Corporation of the President of The Fundamentalist Church of Jesus Christ of Latter-Day Saints, Inc.," and also the day he was to be sentenced. I was in labor, and the pain was intense, with nothing to alleviate it. This time, however, I had taken classes, I knew how to breathe correctly, and I knew what to expect.

I was not nearly as frightened as I had been with Kyle, and I was so grateful that Ben stayed during the entire labor, especially when I began to grow very weak. The practitioners changed how I was lying to help the baby drop into a more advantageous position. Unfortunately, her feet were tangled in the cord, so she couldn't drop far enough for me to dilate fully. Hours later, when she was out, I lay back and closed my eyes for a moment, my body trembling violently. Anxious to hold my daughter, I opened my eyes to see Ben, whose face was drained of color. I knew something was dramatically wrong.

"What is it?" I cried. "Will she live?"

"Oh yes," said the midwife, as she placed the most beautiful, beautiful baby girl into my arms. Natalia Michelle, named in honor of Ben's old boss who'd supported us so much, had the most incredible blue eyes I had ever seen, very much like Kyle's and Ben's. However, a huge dark birthmark completely covered Natalia's left eye and several inches around it. I gasped. I hoped it had to do with the difficult delivery, a bruise from the pressure—*something*? But Natalia had a large and definite permanent black birthmark. I cried as I looked at her, feeling both relief that she was here and seemed healthy, and fear about the birthmark.

The midwife was no help, as none of them had any idea what Natalia's birthmark was. She simply said, "God created her that way. She seems healthy otherwise. God bless you."

After the midwife and her helpers left, I held Natalia and buried my face in Ben's chest for a moment. Why did our baby girl have to suffer?

I felt responsible. Crazy or not, today *was* Warren's sentencing. We had heard from several friends and family members that Warren was to serve two consecutive terms of five years to life at the Utah State Penitentiary. That meant he would spend at least ten years behind bars, and some speculated he might never get out.

Had Ben's family been right? Had little, innocent Natalia been cursed because I had testified against him?

I looked into my baby's sweet face. The irony was that had Natalia been born to Rulon and me "under the covenant of Celestial marriage" in the FLDS, her birth defect would have been considered a mark of innocence and purity, a sign that she was special, blessed, and close to God. It was how the people explained any birth defect, including the recessive gene that resulted in Fumarase deficiency. Those symptoms included severe mental retardation, IQs of 25 or less, missing brain segments, epilepsy, and disfigurement. The occurrence of FD among the FLDS was the highest in the world, especially since the Barlow and Jessop lines carried the gene and there were so many intermarriages.

No doctors seemed to know what Natalia had. It wasn't until I e-mailed a doctor in California pictures of Natalia that I was able to get an affirmative name for it: congenital nevus—a benign but blood-filled tumor. It was, indeed, permanent.

Over the next two days, I would cry on and off for Natalia, while Ben became aloof and cruel about my sadness.

"What's the matter, Beck? Do you think just because you're beautiful everything has to be that way? It doesn't fit your white picket fence to have a daughter who is not as perfect as you?"

I had to realize that as a man, Ben had no way to understand how much every society I'd known placed value on a woman's appearance! Even outside the FLDS, there was still *major* emphasis on it. From air-brushed magazine photographs to music videos to movie stars to professional attire, so much of our daily life seemed based on appearance. How could she survive, much less thrive, in this world?

I was about to the get one of the biggest lessons of my entire life.

Day by day, as Natalia grew, I fell more and more in love with the adorable giant soul inside her little body. And I was not the only one.

Anywhere we went, it was as if she had pixie dust! No friend, family member, or stranger ever left her presence without smiling. After each interaction, she would turn to me, her eyes vibrantly happy. Natalia not only brought miracles—she *was* one.

At times when I looked at my daughter, I realized I had much bigger dark marks on the inside than she did on the outside. For many years I had hated myself. I'd been going through a spiritual crisis, feeling a vast and lifeless desert inside my soul. For quite some time, I couldn't even stomach the word *God*. He was the god that had demanded my total submission, the hell-and-damnation deity ready to smite me and carry me away to Outer Darkness because I had not submitted to my Prophet-husband, and then apostatized. I found it difficult to talk to friends about my spiritual hunger, since every time I opened my mouth some of the crazy things I'd been taught would come out. For example, one day I discovered that what I had been taught about Jesus—that he was a polygamist with many wives—wasn't taught in other parts of the Christian church, and my face grew hot with anger and embarrassment. It was taking a long time for my FLDS beliefs to become untwisted. I stayed away from doctrinal books and discussions, because it was too easy to get all twisted up again.

It didn't help that my hope for my people had crumbled, too. Not long after Warren's admission and video were revealed, he had suddenly rescinded his resignation. Buoyed up by the assurances of the people, who wanted to believe he was a righteous Prophet, he essentially stepped back into the role of Prophet and leader. They refused to see his true self and they stayed enslaved. I felt helpless to assist them.

As I devoured a number of self-help and motivational materials in my early months out of the church, I had come across Deepak Chopra, an author whose work and nonjudgmental outlook inspired me gently and deeply. One day, as I cleaned the house, I listened to another man with a similarly tender, open-minded demeanor. He spoke of having been abandoned by his parents, the other people who had come through for him, and the miracles that had taken place even under the most difficult of circumstances.

I stopped mopping the floor, with a sudden realization. This man had said the word *God* at least eight times, and I hadn't once felt nauseated! Amazed, I rewound the MP3 player on the computer. Not only could I stomach the word *God*; it felt good and even beautiful to me.

The man's name was Wayne Dyer. Apparently he was quite popular, but I had never heard of him. I started reading his work, and though he did not become my new Prophet—I would never fall for that again—he seemed to love more deeply, genuinely, and without judgment than anyone I had ever heard. He also had a great sense of humor. Spirituality for me had always been dark, dense, and fraught with fear, but my whole being lightened up just listening to him.

Although my strong will had helped me in many difficult situations, it also caused problems. I was scrappy, stubborn, and still angry at a lot of life. I liked to blame God, Warren, and the FLDS for my people's misery and my siblings' grief. My anger and bitterness were poisonous and exhausting. I didn't want to live my life that way anymore.

What happened next didn't help. On Valentine's Day, Sheriff Doran called to say that my uncle Merrill, the bishop of the YFZ ranch, had called him out of the blue to inform him my younger sisters wanted to get their missing person reports cleared up. I was overcome with joy after five long years of wondering and hoping, but I was nervous.

"It seems too good to be true," I said.

"Yeah, but I explained to Merrill that a family member needs to ID them. I specifically asked if they had any problem with any family member being there. He said, 'No, Dave, we just want to get this cleared up.'"

Quickly I took down all of the details I would need and booked a flight to Las Vegas, the neutral territory where everyone agreed to meet. I gathered some pictures of Kyle and Natalia and snipped a small piece of Natalia's hair for my mother, knowing I'd see her.

En route to the airport, I got a call from the sheriff.

"Becky, I'm sorry. The FLDS boys are saying if you show up, they won't. It looks like your dad will have to identify them."

I hung up the phone and drove home, my heart in pieces.

"What did you expect, Beck?" asked Ben. He had thought it was stupid to go in the first place. I knew that my mom and sisters resented me for pursuing them like I did. In the FLDS, a missing person report was considered an attack on the entire people. But I had submitted it out of love, and I longed for the chance to explain.

I decided to fax the letter that I had written for the girls to Doran, hoping beyond hope that it might reach them. It read:

Dear Sherrie and Ally,

There are so many things I'd like to say to both of you, and I would so LOVE to be able to tell you in person . . . not one day has gone by that I don't think of you, send my love and wonder how you are . . .

I know the situation at hand is hard for you to understand. I'm sure you have wondered why we haven't stopped looking for you both and Mother . . . The honest fact of the matter is that I realize that Mom cannot protect you girls—it isn't in her power to say whether or not you stay close to her, or if you are sent somewhere else, or if you are placed in marriage when it is inappropriate. She could not stop it from happening to Elissa, and it is a grave concern to each one of us.

I realize that you only know what you have been told about the situation—always remember that there are two sides to the story, and what you are being told may not be entirely true. We don't want to be harsh or hurt you in any way. We want more than anything to have communication with you both, and Mother. This is what we will pursue . . . I send only love to you—Sherrie, Ally, and Mom. I sincerely hope that you realize and feel the love each of us sends to you . . . I want you all to know that I am only a phone call away, anytime, any day. I will do anything to help you.

I LOVE YOU SO VERY MUCH!

Later Doran would inform me that he gave my letter to FLDS men to pass to my sisters, but of course they did not.

I held Natalia in the rocking chair for her nap while I cried gut-wrenching sobs, every tear burning like acid. Natalia didn't stir. When she finally woke and looked at me with her big blue eyes, I thought, how could my mother sever ties with me and my siblings who'd left, when each of us was once a babe in her arms, as Natalia was in mine?

As she fidgeted and I prepared to feed her, I noticed a CD I'd ordered had arrived. The house was too quiet, and I put it on to distract myself.

The narrator, Louise Hay, recounted how her life of unspeakable trauma had been transformed into a joyful existence. I recognized so many echoes of what I had been through: sexual abuse, forced separation of loved ones, success in certain arenas that was tempered by old resentments and pain. I realized how important it was to release those once and for all, but I knew I needed help.

Locals referred me to a nearby holistic health center, where I met an extraordinary older woman, a healer named Jane. When I first stepped into her office, she looked into my eyes and said, "Oh, honey, what have they done to you?" She didn't even know who "they" were. Over the course of time, I found I could tell her things I'd never told anyone, not even the men from Washington County. One step at a time, her counseling would transform my life—and the way in which I saw the world. And by letting go of the hate, shame, and humiliation, I made room for God.

Along the way, I discovered that I could choose the loving God who honors choices and free agency in our humanity. I also recognized that the difficulties of my journey had been some of my greatest teachers and had made me a much stronger person. Finally, this loving God, the one I'd met on El Capitan and in the hearts of gracious people around me, knew me and *loved me for me*. The threads of the tapestry he had hinted at on that mountaintop were breathtakingly vibrant and wonderful. I simply needed to learn some additional tools to recognize that beauty and to release the past. Though I didn't know it then, I would desperately need those tools for the coming months.

*   *   *

Most local physicians had no idea how to treat Natalia's congenital nevus, but after extensive research, I found Dr. Faizi Siddiqi of Primary Children's Medical Center in Salt Lake City. He specialized in treating children born with craniofacial anomalies such as cleft lip and palate, hemangioma, and tumors like Natalia's. He met with us and agreed to take her case, describing the natural phenomenon of what had happened to Natalia in the womb in layman's terms, which put to rest any thoughts of a curse.

Then came the bad news. It was unlikely this size birthmark would go away on its own, and this type had an unfortunate tendency to become cancerous. Natalia would have to undergo a series of painful surgeries.

When we finally arrived home after the four-hundred-mile trip from the hospital, I got the kids settled, then went straight up to our bedroom and got down on my knees. I did not pray to the god of judgment, hell, or damnation. I prayed to the God who had revealed himself to me in the corners of my opening heart. I asked him to pour love and strength and compassion into me. And, above all, to wrap my baby girl in the arms of his love.

CHAPTER 23

Yearning for Zion

As I picked up the pieces of my life and chose to be strong for my daughter, we had a sudden surprise. Ben's seventeen-year-old sister Kristin called him, with desperation and fear in her voice.

"Umm, Ben, I need help. Dad is forcing me to stay here and...to get married. Pllll...please, please come get me," she whispered. She explained that she had sneaked her mother's cell phone to call him and didn't know if she'd be able to again. Ben gave her some hasty instructions, and then hung up to call Wendell to formulate a plan.

Ben and Wendell left immediately for the nine-hour drive to St. George. They didn't know if their sister had been caught on the phone, but it was her one and only chance to escape a forced marriage, so they didn't have a choice.

The very next day, Kristin and a few other girls were waiting their turn at the orthodontist when she mentioned to her sisters that she had left something behind and slipped outside. Out of sight of the others, she turned the corner to find Ben and Wendell, and ran to the car. The three of them sped north to Salt Lake City, where they spent the night in a motel far off the beaten path before heading northwest to our home.

Ben and Wendell quickly realized that Kristin had been following Warren's teachings to the letter, and as a result she had very few communication skills. They had to ask her multiple questions to get a single answer, but what eventually came out was very sobering. Kristin's father often spoke of how happy she would be when she got married, but she was finally frank with him, telling him she didn't want to. He responded, "Leaving is *not* an option," and squirreled her away in a house of hiding in Las Vegas. Wendell knew all about girls in houses of hiding: their strict security, forced disguises considered "holy" to keep the Priesthood safe, and especially the fear with which each girl was controlled. Kristin couldn't even decide what to eat on her own without severe mental stress.

Ben called me a couple of times from the road, and while I was grateful to know she was safe, we were all scared that the police might come after them. At seventeen, she was still considered a minor, and we didn't know what her rights were. I had put in some calls to lawyers we knew. Her existence in Idaho certainly wouldn't be a secret for long, and we were not about to keep her hidden away as her father had done.

That Saturday, I was home with the kids when a police officer came to our door looking for Kristin, who'd been reported kidnapped. His department had been notified by FLDS leaders that we were prime suspects.

"She's not in my home," I said carefully. "You are welcome to come in and take a look." He stepped inside and looked around thoroughly as we introduced ourselves. I decided it was best to hide nothing from him. As I told him about our family's background and the call we'd received, his eyes grew large. Then I told him that, indeed, we had picked her up so that she would not be forced to marry.

"Do you think we could call to verify some things?" he asked. We went to the kitchen to call Roger Hoole, who validated what I'd said and gave us contact info for two FBI agents and a U.S. marshal. As it was Easter weekend, the information we had reported was not yet loaded in the system that Kristin was not a typical runaway or a victim of kidnapping, so he had to make further calls. I also called Ben, who let the officer talk to Kristin to verify that she was safe and exactly where she *wanted* to be. I was grateful to him. On his way out, the officer turned to me.

"If anyone shows up here," he said, "you let me know right away." I knew what he meant: *if some of the FLDS boys happened to get here before Ben and Wendell did.*

When they arrived home, I was both dismayed and joyful. It had been so long since I had seen Kristin, and I was astounded at how much she'd grown, but mentally and emotionally she was stunted, afraid to make any move. Over the next several days Kristin never left my presence except to sleep. I was in for a culture shock as much as she was, thinking of where she should have been at her age, preparing for college and a beautiful life—all of that stolen from her.

As Kristin slowly opened up about her life, I was sobered to hear how quickly things had changed. Before I'd left, Warren had already quashed sports, camping, and entertainment, in addition to music, radio, television, and Internet access (except for businesses). But now, Kristin told me, children couldn't even play with toys, go outside, or see their friends! They were allowed only to go to school, work, and home, except for church work projects that every child was ordered to participate in on Saturdays, with specific duties to be completed.

It was painfully clear that education had not improved. After Alta Academy had closed in 1999, a couple of schools remained in Short Creek, but most youth were homeschooled with special FLDS packets. While educators had worked diligently to put these packets together, their own knowledge of the outside world was dangerously limited. Kristin was two weeks shy of eighteen, but I could tell it would take at least another two years of study just to get her GED.

It had been Kristin's daily duty to serve meals to the men at Western Precision, an FLDS company with a government contract to make precision parts for the nation's defense system. This work brought in massive income to certain families and tithes for the FLDS church. Uncle Wendell, who was Warren's first counselor, loved fine food, and he hosted grandiose gourmet meals to wine and dine contractors as well as the men who worked there. Young, single FLDS women were brought in to cook and serve the meals—and so that the men could see which girls were becoming available. As Kristin described it, as soon as the girls began to develop breasts, they would be picked off, one by one.

Over the next few days, I showed her pictures of the YFZ in Texas, and the humongous temple rising into the sky.

"What is that?" she inquired.

"You don't know?" I was incredulous. It dawned on me how secret everything in Texas had remained to the "common" people.

I then showed her pictures of Warren after being caught in his red Cadillac Escalade. She gasped at his shorts and T-shirt, no long underwear in sight.

"Oh my gosh, he's got a tan!"

"Kristin, he told the people he was in hiding, but then he and Naomi bought leather jackets and leather pants and rented Harley-Davidson motorcycles. He and his entourage went to Disney World. The receipts show he spent the people's tithing on bathing suits and tanning beds and to braid Naomi's hair. This is why they don't want you to use the Internet—this is the truth and it's all over it!"

Kristin looked into my eyes. "I knew it," she said softly. "I wouldn't believe the awful things they said about you...I wouldn't believe what they said about Ben or Wendell, either. That's why I called." I breathed a sigh of relief. Deep down, this girl still had her own intellect and her own voice. It would take some time and struggle, but Kristin was going to be okay.

My young sister-in-law was still settling in when I received an unexpected call from Sheriff Doran. This time, his friendly drawl sounded very serious.

"Becky, I want to run something by you. A domestic violence hotline monitored by Texas Child Protective Services got a call a couple of days ago from someone claiming to be a sixteen-year-old girl named Sarah Barlow or Sarah Jessop—or even Sarah Barlow Jessop. She alleges that her husband has repeatedly raped and beat her, and that she is now pregnant with her second child."

I gulped and took a deep breath. I thought of all the girls I knew who would be around that age now, including Sherrie.

"The girl said she was living on the YFZ. Now, Becky, know this: regardless of what you have to say, or what your feelings are on the matter, it will not affect our decision as to whether or not we investigate this." He paused. "I'm only asking, based on your experience and knowledge of the people, do you think there could be any merit to these allegations?"

I was silent for a moment, thinking carefully.

"Sheriff, I can say that when I was growing up, it was not acceptable for men to beat their wives. We did know of situations where it happened. While Rulon Jeffs did not beat his wives, and to my knowledge

Warren did not beat his, he condoned Allen's beating and raping of Elissa, and there were other cases. From what we've learned from Wendell, and from Ben's sister Kristin in just the last ten days, things have deteriorated drastically. Unfortunately, in my estimation, what the caller described could be plausible."

I told him that Sarah Barlow or Sarah Jessop could refer to a number of different girls, although I honestly couldn't pinpoint who she was. I knew most of the players in the FLDS, but I certainly didn't know them all.

"Well, Becky," he sighed, "there is going to be an investigation on the property. The Texas Rangers will be involved."

A lightning bolt of fear shot through me. Suddenly it was 1993 again, and I was a frightened eleventh grader watching in horror as Warren brandished a front-page newspaper article about Waco. *"Seventy-six people killed—this is nothing. The government will rain down upon us with bullets and with fire, just like they have done to the Branch Davidians."*

Even in my limited knowledge of who had poofed, I knew there were many good people on the YFZ ranch, including innocent women and children. I had to remind myself that I could trust Sheriff Doran, who had taken the time to get to know these people, asked questions, and, most important, listened. Of course he wanted to do his job, but he had no desire to punish all of the people for Warren's actions.

But Texas Rangers? The name brought to mind visions of rogue, wild cowboys.

"Please," I asked quietly. "Is there any way I can speak to the rangers who will be entering the property?"

"I don't know, Becky," he replied.

"I know. I understand you have a job to do, and my heart aches for this little girl, if this is true. But I know what will be going through the minds of the people on the YFZ." I paused before blurting out, "These people have not only been preparing for Armageddon, Sheriff; they have been praying for it."

There was silence on the line. Then: "I'll see what I can do, Becky."

The next morning, I did everything I could to put Texas out of my mind as I rushed around getting Kyle and Natalia ready for the day. I took comfort in the daily routine until I received a call from the sheriff shortly after ten a.m.

"Things are heating up," he said. The NewBridge Family Shelter hotline in San Angelo had received more calls from Sarah saying she was frightened and needed help urgently. She had given a few vague but disturbing details, including that she'd had to hand her baby to another woman to hold while she was being beaten and that she'd been given sedatives. "She sounded drugged this time," Doran said gravely, and then indicated that it was almost time to go to the ranch to investigate.

"We're trying to coax some additional information so we can somehow identify and find her," he said. They had a team poring over the data they were collecting, as well as satellite shots of the ranch.

I pleaded again with him. "If there's any way I can talk to those men going on the property, let me do so." Again, he was sympathetic but made no promises. I said a prayer in my heart for the people on both sides of the line. That afternoon, the phone rang again.

"All right, Miss Becky," he boomed over a speakerphone. "I'm sitting with the officers who will be going in on the ranch. You said you'd like to speak to them. Here's your chance."

I felt tongue-tied, but I knew that this was the only opportunity I had to give these officers—whoever they were—a window into the mind-set of the people on that ranch, one that could keep everyone safe.

"This group on the ranch is considered by Warren to be the 'elite of the elite,'" I explained. "They are the upper echelon of 'God's people,' meaning that they are the most obedient. This makes them the most dangerous of all, because they will do whatever their leaders say is God's will, no matter what." I paused, praying they would understand the severity I was trying to convey.

"The way to get the upper hand," I said firmly, "is to go in as quietly and peacefully as possible. They will not expect this of you. They *expect* you to come in guns blazing, kicking down doors, pillaging and raping the women and children."

I was met with silence, but I pushed on. "You have to understand that the FLDS people have been deliberately schooled by Warren Jeffs about the tragedy at Waco. We were all told that we would be next!"

There was just one question on the other end: "Are they going to come out, guns blazing at us?"

I thought about it. "They probably do have guns. My dad had a handgun. Several are woodsmen and hunters. I don't think they will come out at you that way, though, since they believe that *God* will strike you down. But Yearning for Zion is not just a name; it is a mind-set! To them, you are the end of the world they have been waiting for, especially since Warren Jeffs, their Prophet, has been incarcerated by what they feel is a wicked government. As I told the sheriff, they have been praying for this—*hard*. Death would be a mercy to them—a way to honorably earn their eternal salvation. Please, please, do not give them what they are looking for. Surprise them with your kindness."

The sheriff took the phone off speaker.

"Thank you, Becky," he said gruffly. "Good-bye."

I put my face in my hands. I could only pray that what I'd said would somehow make a difference.

CHAPTER 24

"Forced" Entry: The Raid

The next day was one of the most stressful of my life as I waited to hear what was happening. I didn't hear from Doran until the following evening, when he called to tell me that they had visited the ranch that day, April 3, with warrants in hand, and closed off the roads going to and from the ranch. So far, there had been no altercations, but it hadn't gone well.

"Not only did we have a search warrant to find Sarah; Child Protective Services also had a warrant specifically to interview all the girls between seven and seventeen," he said angrily. "Yet Merrill and his boys forced us to sit at the gates for over three hours before they finally led us onto the property, to a schoolhouse where we could conduct interviews." Uncle Merrill had joked around with the group, cajoling them as he let three Texas Rangers and the sheriff into the schoolhouse with the CPS workers and one volunteer. Nine watchful rangers stayed outside for everyone's protection. All of them were forced to wait there for hours until a few girls straggled in.

"They tried to get us to believe that these were the only young girls on the ranch. We kept asking, 'Is this all of them?' and Merrill kept saying, 'Well, yeah, I think so...' But while we were waiting, CPS was glancing through student journals that were on the shelves at the schoolhouse, and they realized the journals contained specific entries. You know, events like a new baby in the family, or their sisters getting married—some of them at very, very young ages! Yet none of the authors of the journals, nor the girls listed in them, were within the group they brought to us for interviews! But Merrill would say, 'Oh, yeah…ya know, I forgot about her…We'll see if we can figure this out.'

"Becky, this happened over and over! Our intent was simply to get in there, find Sarah, her baby, and her husband and get them out. We hoped Sarah would see us and run into our arms. While that hasn't happened yet, there is much more going on here than we've *ever* been told. The whole place is strange, and there's a picture of Warren Jeffs on every student's desk."

I felt ill just thinking about it.

"And I'll tell you something else that Merrill lied about. Judging from the journals, there's a helluva lot more people on this ranch than just one or two hundred!" All of the rumors we had heard of people poofing from FLDS communities, and houses of hiding, made more sense now.

"We're in for a long night," Doran said finally, sounding exhausted.

"Yes," I agreed. "Yes, you are."

That same night, one of the older patriarchs on the ranch, Sam Roundy Sr., father of Sam Roundy Jr., suffered severe heart pains, and since Lloyd Barlow, the resident doctor, was busy with law enforcement, Sam was taken to a medical center in nearby Eldorado in an ambulance. One of his older wives didn't dare leave him alone in the outside world, so Deputy Arispe drove her the four miles there. When she got out of the deputy's car, she looked bewildered.

"Where are we?" Roundy's wife asked.

"You're in Eldorado, ma'am," the deputy said, tipping his hat. He realized that the speculations about the women being smuggled in at night to disorient them might be true. They had reached "Zion," and unless they'd climbed the watchtower, they would have believed they were totally isolated. All of that desert, for miles on end, would have been more than enough deterrent to any woman or child who thought of leaving.

The nine rangers posted outside the schoolhouse were on high alert. A strict no-fly zone had been established above the ranch, and all roads in and out blocked. A command post had been set up a couple of miles away, manned by sixty or so officers who were also securing a perimeter around the 1,691-acre ranch. The residents quickly realized that there were no escape routes, but rumors flew that some underage girls had somehow been smuggled out. Whatever the case, the rangers on the compound were very tense. They were fully aware that the FLDS had at least a small hunting arsenal of weapons and access to explosives used in constructing the ranch.

To make matters worse, as dusk settled young men from the ranch had scaled nearby trees wearing night-vision goggles. The rangers, equipped with their own night-vision equipment, could tell they were unarmed, though, and they weren't very good at being surreptitious— one young man actually fell out of a tree near the schoolhouse, injuring himself. The rangers ignored him and kept their uneasy watch throughout the entire night. Doran told me later that thirty-five to forty FLDS men had wandered in and out of the schoolhouse over the course of the night, as a passive-aggressive tactic.

It had been impossible for me to sleep, and I gave up even trying to go to work the next day. My every moment was wrapped in prayers and pleadings. With no word from the sheriff, I turned on the television to find the media had been alerted to the events of the previous night. The closing of the roads and gathering of so much law enforcement alerted local reporters Kathy and Randy Mankin that something was going down at the YFZ. They had cleverly devised a monitoring system to decipher radio signals between officers. Since they were close personal friends with Sheriff Doran, they were very careful about which tidbits they shared with the world, but by that morning, April 4, it had hit the national news. I was seeing only what the world was seeing, and it was disconcerting.

My phone erupted with calls from friends and family, but none of them knew any more than I did. CNN was my only source until the sheriff called around 10:15 a.m. He sounded exhausted. Indeed, their forces had been up all night.

"You wouldn't believe this, but we still haven't talked to most of those girls listed in the journals as new wives or mothers! Merrill deliberately kept most of them away from the schoolhouse, except for ten girls we were able to interview. Do you happen to know who Dr. Lloyd Barlow is?"

"Oh, yes," I said. "Lloyd married my mother's younger sister Faye while he was in med school. Once he graduated, he oversaw the Short Creek clinic and became Rulon's personal physician. After Rulon's initial strokes, Lloyd was at our estate all the time, and was at Rulon's side when he died."

"Hmm. He seemed like a decent fellow in the beginning," murmured Doran, "though it quickly became apparent to me he likes to throw his weight around."

"Well, he's got big stakes in the FLDS. His father, Alvin Barlow, was the superintendent of the schools in Short Creek and is a survivor of the '53 raid. Both are descendants of John Y. Barlow and yes-men to the Prophet."

"Interesting," Doran said. "You know, he came directly to Brooks Long, one of the head rangers of the investigation, saying that he had 'issues' with the search warrant. Brooks had him call CPS. During the conversation, using Brooks's phone, Lloyd Barlow *admitted* to delivering babies to underage mothers!

"Also, in the YFZ clinic and birthing center, two of our rangers found records of underage patients whom Barlow had treated for pregnancy. When they reported it, the ranger captains made them go back to gather up that evidence before the FLDS could destroy it all, because during the night, Ruby from CPS smelled something burning and discovered a shredder that had become red-hot from working nonstop. That discovery led us to two industrial-sized garbage bags of freshly shredded documents. Sure enough, when the rangers went back to the clinic, they discovered that some files from the illustrious FLDS doctor's office had been removed or destroyed. They had to pack up the rest to keep them safe."

I couldn't believe the nerve of the FLDS in blatantly destroying evidence.

"And still Merrill doesn't bring Sarah or the other girls! Meanwhile, CPS had discovered information in the schoolhouse about a Teresa Steed Jessop who was sixteen and already had a baby. CPS asked for Teresa and six more specific girls they had found from the school journals, but only four of them showed up, and one was pregnant at age sixteen. Plus, several girls we interviewed said there is a Sarah Barlow here on the YFZ, but Merrill never brought her to us."

Due to the large number of pregnant teen girls and the deliberate destruction of evidence, Sheriff Doran and the Texas Rangers commanders felt that it had become necessary to do a house-to-house search. As they started searching houses that morning, Doran told me, they found more pregnant underage girls who unashamedly lied about their ages, most of them looking to their husbands or fathers to supply the investigators with the years of their fake birthdates.

"I gotta tell you something you're not going to like. CPS is going to have to remove these young women into foster care—they can't let them return home to their families. Based on what we've found so far, CPS thinks that all children under the age of seventeen are in danger."

Somberly, I hung up the phone and switched on the news again. Neither the rangers nor CPS said much except that they were pleased with the nonviolent nature of the investigation so far. A few hours later, however, news crews showed large buses arriving on the compound to take the young women and children away. I watched members of my extended family and a few of the older children I knew lining up, and I rejoiced to see some of my former sister-wives with child, and others holding the hands of little ones. Motherhood was what so many of them had longed for when Rulon was alive.

Yet the scenes on the screen pulled at my heart. The images were too eerily reminiscent of the '53 raid. Memories of the terror I'd experienced as a child hearing those stories coursed throughout my body— and here I was, safe in Idaho!

Elissa, Amelia, and I got on the phone together and searched for our mother and sisters in the sea of familiar faces on CNN. We were disappointed that we were unable to locate any members of our immediate family, until we realized why: the missing person reports!

"They'll do anything to keep Sherrie and Ally from police and media, won't they?" I said to my sisters. "Otherwise, they'll have to admit they've not complied with a missing person report for three years!" We cried for all of these women, yet we were genuinely grateful to Texas for following through where Utah and Arizona hadn't had the guts.

Ben, however, was livid with me.

"Why don't you let it go?" he asked. "That part of our lives is over." It wasn't for me, though. I cared about these people, and my sisters were still missing. Sheriff Doran hadn't exaggerated about the number of people on the ranch. According to news reports, by the end of the evening, 167 children had been removed and were staying at the civic center near Eldorado, where cribs and cots had been set up for them. How the hell could CPS have prepared for this? I watched the Texas Rangers and local authorities, alert in their full body armor and artillery, as they oversaw the process, and was relieved that I never observed any one of them point a weapon at any of the people.

The next day, the sheriff called me bright and early. He and the rangers had worked through the night once again without a break. There was too much evidence of organized crime to ignore.

Doran reported fifty-two girls ranging from six months to seventeen years were removed from the ranch, many of them visibly pregnant. It was enough for Ranger Brooks Long to visit District Judge Barbara Walther with another affidavit requesting an additional search warrant. (While the first affidavit listed thirty pages of documentation from Sarah's calls, this one detailed multiple crimes of abuse and bigamy and ran hundreds of pages. The ranger had no way of knowing this would likely become the most highly scrutinized search warrant in U.S. court history.)

CPS workers finally interviewed some of the young girls who had given birth to one or more babies, but they were having great difficulty getting straight answers, even from the ones who seemed most willing to be honest. When workers asked if the girls had had sex, they'd answer no, even if it was clear they'd given birth.

"Why would they answer that way, Becky?" Sheriff Doran asked me, chagrined and exhausted. "Are all these young girls lying, too?"

"Not necessarily," I said carefully. "Although I'm sure they've been coached. The problem is the word *sex*."

"Yeah," he said, perplexed. "That's what makes the babies, right?"

"No one uses the word *sex* in that culture—except maybe a few older adults, and only referring to what *other* people do in the outside world. These girls won't know what you mean."

"Are you kidding?"

"Tell the workers to ask them if they have had 'marital relations' with their husbands."

This clarification in language worked, and the social workers were finally making a little more headway. Throughout the day, I continued to receive calls from the sheriff, asking me to explain scenarios, situations, and the significance of particular words that were flummoxing the workers.

Every development became international news, and the media

were clamoring for the story, but Brooks Long and his commanding officer, Captain Barry Caver, issued an order of silence to their ranks. They needed their officers engaged in organizing and preserving the evidence they had found rather than informing swarms of reporters. Sheriff Doran, too, refused to speak to anyone except occasionally the Mankins. Lawyers for the FLDS had already begun a campaign of protest and counterpublicity, calling the raid unjust.

Later that day, the sheriff sounded worse. "My God, Becky, we had no idea of how big of an operation this was going to mushroom into! At every turn we encounter major resistance. Get this: each time we enter a house, kids slip out the back doors and windows—going back to houses we've already searched! Now they've resorted to behaviors and rude comments that we normally wouldn't put up with on the street. And tell me, what's the deal with the little kids with notebooks and pens?"

I puzzled over his question for a moment, then exclaimed, "Oh my goodness! Are they asking for your names?"

"Yes," he said. "That's exactly what they're doing."

"They're keeping track of the damned," I said. I couldn't help but grin at the audacity of these cheeky little kids, chronicling the names of the rangers for restriction from Heaven. "You see, Sheriff, you are not only Gentiles, but they see you as persecuting God's chosen people. Your names will be kept in a book of records of those who will be destroyed in the last days."

"Well, that's a little creepy," he said, not finding the humor in it. "Today, there was this van that kept circling the compound, always as far as possible from our surveillance vehicle. We weren't sure what we would find in it. Men with an arsenal? Bombs? Cameras? When we finally pulled it over, guess what it was filled with?"

"What?" I asked, worried.

"Pregnant teenage girls! Several of them! Sadly, none of them admitted to being Sarah Barlow."

I was still uncomfortable. What if the rangers had been convinced the people in the van were a threat? Thank God the officers were more careful and compassionate than I had given them credit for.

"Becky?" the sheriff asked suddenly. "Do you think you could come down here? I'm in over my head. We all are. I think what we've got here is the biggest child custody case in the history of this nation. We've gotta have someone who *understands* these people."

I quickly agreed. We discussed possible scenarios for my arrival, and I prepared to get off the phone to make my travel arrangements. Suddenly the sheriff interrupted me.

"I have to tell you something important first. We're going to have to go into their temple."

"*What?*"

"We don't know what or who they have in there, and they're refusing to open the doors voluntarily! We know it's sacred to them. The last thing we want to do is barge in. But their refusal could mean any number of things, none of which sound good to us."

I was silent. *How long had the people dreamed of a temple?* As with the early saints, it was a symbol of their devotion to their God.

"They keep tying our hands, Becky," he said sadly. "They keep tying our hands."

Later that night, a friend still closely tied with Short Creek called me to tell me that an armored ambulance had been sent out to the ranch just as the officers were preparing to go into the temple. The ambulance had the ominous appearance of a tank, and I knew officers would send it only if it seemed necessary.

I was frightened of how the FLDS would react to law enforcement breaching their temple, and I felt completely helpless. I tried calling the sheriff back a couple of times that evening to see if anyone was hurt. He didn't answer. In desperation, I finally called Uncle Merrill shortly before 9:30 p.m., pleading with him to cooperate and be honest with law enforcement. He talked to me for a few minutes about his views on the raid, and I was relieved he didn't say that Warren wanted the men to defend the temple with their lives. Perhaps there was hope for a bloodless raid after all.

CHAPTER 25

Apostate at the Temple Gates

In the middle of my packing for my flight to Texas, Ben had nearly forbidden me from going.

"What's the deal, Beck?" he said. "Have to go off and save the world again? Testifying hasn't given you enough attention?" Swearing he wouldn't give me one red cent to get to Texas, Ben made it clear I might not have a home to come back to. I thought long and hard. These were *our* sisters and brothers and nieces and nephews, their lives and families at stake. And as Mother Becky and Grandmother Becky, I'd been sister-wife, mother, and grandmother to many of them. I was being offered the chance to help them. I had to take it.

Descending the stairs onto the tarmac in San Angelo, I looked up at the night sky. I had never seen so many stars. Sheriff Doran and another officer had come to pick me up, along with Elissa, who had arrived the day before. She'd found out I was going and asked if she could help, too.

In the car, Doran caught me and Elissa up to speed: sixty FLDS mothers had voluntarily left the ranch to be with their children, and none of the men were allowed to leave the ranch during the investigation. So Saturday afternoon had been tense as the rangers, sheriffs, and their team, armed with a battering ram, prepared to breach the huge oak doors of the temple.

As he was explaining this, we neared Eldorado and were just north of town. The sheriff zoomed close to the perimeter of the YFZ ranch. There was no mistaking the FLDS temple, lit up with huge spotlights. My heart was pounding as I took in the monolithic white building I'd seen only in photos.

The sheriff said softly, "You know, after those initial interviews in the schoolhouse, Merrill suddenly disappeared. He was still on the ranch, but other than a couple of brief phone conversations, he hadn't been in contact. So on Saturday, we had yet to find Sarah, or this 'Dale Barlow' that Sarah mentions as the husband who has been beating her. Then Flora calls me and says her sister got a call from this Sarah and she says she's being forced to stay in a cold, dark place. That could be anywhere, but we're concerned it might be the temple basement."

The sheriff pulled up next to the gate and showed his badge to the officers guarding the perimeter. We parked just off the road, and the sheriff continued.

"So when I was told that it was time to go into the temple, Captain Caver asked if I wanted to be part of it, and I said yes, being that this whole thing is taking place in my community. I was also hoping we'd find Sarah, once and for all.

"We geared up, in helmets and heavy-armored vests, but I didn't have any type of weapon as I was helping with the battering ram. As we approached the gates, the FLDS cut off all communication with us. In fact, they totally quit cooperating, which was not a good sign. We'd heard that Willie Jessop was saying the men should defend that temple with their very lives."

I shuddered.

"The FLDS attorneys told us their men wanted to do a silent protest about us entering their temple, and they stationed their men all the way around the temple walls, praying. When we breached the gate, the FLDS men stationed around the temple cried out. I've never heard anything like it. They were absolutely bawling with grief."

"You weren't struck by lightning like they thought you would be," Elissa said.

"Exactly," he continued. "They cried out that they were not faithful enough, not holy enough. It broke my heart. Anyway, we stepped onto the temple grounds and approached the stairwell. The higher we went, the more men we could see standing on top of vehicles and houses and gathering in small crowds to watch us. We knew that anything could happen, and had officers stationed to make sure nothing would. We had to walk up a helluva lot of steps in the back with the battering ram, while having to watch for attack or bombs from inside. Suddenly at the back steps, the locksmith had this panic attack and had to be given oxygen. Then it was time for us to use the battering ram."

He paused for a moment, looking up at the temple again.

"We rammed in that beautiful heavy oak door, and every time the ram hit, you could hear the reverberations half a mile away. It was so big and heavy, we had to swap guys out. We make it through those doors, and there was another heavy set behind it. We got through that, too."

He shook his head, and looked over at me. "If they had walked in with us, we could have been in and out of there in an hour or less, but every single door was locked. That looks very suspicious, and so of course, we have to force every door open, even every cabinet door. One SWAT officer cracked his wrist on one of the heavy oak suckers and had to receive medical attention. It took us three, maybe four hours to search that temple. So the team was doing what they have to do, clearing rooms. As we secured one floor, we'd be off to the next.

"All I got to say is that we felt like shit going into that special, sacred place of theirs. Most of our men are Christian or believers. We felt sick about it..." He paused and looked me in the eyes.

"...that is, until we reached the third floor."

My heart shuddered. The weekend had been particularly rough on every FLDS member: April 6, which would have been a day of historical remembrance and celebration, had seen families torn apart and their temple desecrated. In addition, their closely held secrets were quickly unraveling. Instinctively I knew I would be seeing some of those secrets in the temple the next day.

The following morning, my sister and I awoke in our hotel knowing that both the FLDS and the state of Texas were under enormous pressure. We hoped we could make a difference. The sheriff requested that Elissa and Shannon Price, a spokeswoman for Uncle Dan Fischer's Diversity Foundation, help out at CPS. That weekend, the women and children had been bused again, this time to San Angelo, fifty miles from Eldorado. They were placed in temporary housing at historic Fort Concho, under much more controlled yet somewhat primitive circumstances. By Sunday CPS realized that on a ranch supposedly supporting a total of two hundred people, *well over four hundred children had been discovered!*

CPS had another dilemma. Under Texas law, once a child is removed from his or her home, the child must be returned home within two weeks unless investigators can prove abuse. If a case involves one or two children—even one or two families—that two-week window isn't usually a problem, but they had cleared out children from an entire small city, so things would become exponentially more difficult.

Carmen Dusek, a brilliant estate lawyer whom I would later meet, was also known as a passionate family-law case volunteer. The previous Friday, Judge Walther had asked her to find family law professionals to serve as guardians ad litem to represent the twenty-five children in court. By that Friday evening, the number of children had risen to 108. On Sunday, Carmen and fellow attorney Randol Stout were told that as many as 463 children needed representation for what was undeniably the largest CPS case in Texas history. That weekend, Carmen pulled out all the stops, calling upon family members, friends, professional associates, church communities, and even strangers. Some of these volunteers were estate or contract lawyers; some had never taken a family-law class. It would take a miracle to provide representation.

"How in the world can we pull this off?" Carmen later told me she murmured on her way to the church that had donated the space to gather volunteers. "Dear God, please help us protect those children and their rights." When she pushed open the door, she witnessed the great hall overflowing with volunteer law professionals ready to represent FLDS children.

I was struck by the vast numbers of Texan volunteers coming out of the woodwork, not just attorneys. Meals were brought in from families, businesses, and churches across the state. Bedding and clothing were donated by the truckloads. Medical personnel had arrived to care for all of the women and children. I felt like I had after the fire in my childhood home, when people's caring attitudes changed my views forever. I hoped it might do the same for the women and children now in San Angelo.

Doran asked me to work the law enforcement command post on the ranch that day, and reminded me that for my safety, and to preserve the integrity of the investigation, I would have to be escorted by a sheriff or ranger wherever I went. On our way over, Doran added that they were still looking for children in hiding, and he was visibly discouraged by the fact that they still hadn't located Sarah. The antics of the FLDS people as workers attempted to catalog families were also getting to him.

"We're trying to keep them together...Why do they tell us so-and-so is this child's mother, but she runs to another woman when she's afraid? Or they identify the mother of an infant and a toddler, but she's stooped and gray to her toes!"

"Sheriff," I said gently but firmly, "prepare for this to be the pervasive attitude. It's honorable in their society to make everything difficult for law enforcement, who they believe is persecuting the Priesthood of God."

He described several kids being nasty and defiant, but then spoke of some that were curious and even relieved at their presence. "We had these red-headed boys that were inquisitive about the armored ambulance. So a couple of the SWAT guys let them check out the controls and even punch a coupla buttons—safe ones, you know—and they just grinned until an adult came and told them to get out. Another time, one of the girls got off the bus to get her shoes, and on her way back on, she whispered into one of the officer's ears, 'Thank you for coming.'" He seemed moved by that.

"We'll be glad to have your help today. The FLDS culture is more foreign than we anticipated, and there are several documents I'd like you to help us identify." We had arrived at the compound, and the sheriff drove me around the perimeter of the property to keep me under the radar. I was fascinated to see the ranch for the first time in the light of day, but a little unnerved to see such familiar workmanship firsthand. By looking at a certain building, I would know precisely who had built it, or who was meant to be living in it—or both.

At the command post, Doran introduced me to several Texas Rangers, pleasant enough but all business. Their faces were tired and worn. The sheriff had explained to me that the Texas Rangers had earned their trademark white hats—which they'd traded in this case for SWAT gear—from countless years of service in law enforcement, their skills in investigation, and their ability to defuse volatile situations. Many of them had traveled hundreds of miles to get here, and most of them had been working thirty- to thirty-six-hour shifts with only a few hours' sleep in between.

We parked, and the sheriff walked me through one of the buildings that had been emptied of people. Eerily, there was a picture of Warren Jeffs in every single room, and the aroma in the hallway was so familiar that I started to feel like Mother Becky, with long, braided hair and a prairie dress...until I was interrupted by a voice calling, "Becky— can you come and explain what this might mean?" In one unconscious moment, I had become FLDS. And one moment later I was not. The magnitude of what was about to happen hit me again.

The FLDS would never understand why I was assisting law enforcement. As with Warren's Utah trial, they would think that my intention was to hurt them. I remembered Warren saying, "The world does not know how to hurt us. It is those who knew the truth and have fallen away that teach the world how to attack us." And yet, by the time I reached the end of the hallway, a familiar fire pulsed through my bloodstream as I recalled the number of very young, very pregnant girls on my television screen. *Then you shouldn't have done this in the first place, Warren,* I thought. Only truth and courage had emancipated me from Rulon's home and Warren's clutches. I had to rely on truth and courage again for the sake of the young girls.

Three men were looking at some documents they had found— marriage records, I realized. I remembered collecting them by the hundreds at Rulon's home during an FLDS census. We had been taught since elementary school about the importance of keeping meticulous family and ordinance records, because "whatever is recorded on earth is recorded in Heaven." The officers did not understand what they were looking at. I was struck by the sobering realization that what I told these men would forever change the course of my people. Based on what the rangers had seen on the ranch already, these records of marriages would definitely be damning to several of the FLDS leaders—not just the men who married underage women, but also the men who performed the ceremonies and those who gave their young daughters to other leaders.

After leaving that building, I returned to the command post, where two rangers were getting ready to do a more thorough investigation of a home they believed to be Warren's.

"Is there anything we should look for?" they asked.

"Yes," I said. "Look for a room—a secret room, something behind a bookshelf."

They looked at me as if I had been watching too many movies. I noticed that some of the men didn't seem to believe my answers, despite my being meticulous and refusing to exaggerate. When they returned, though, they looked very serious.

"Hey, what was it again you told us to look for?"

I hesitated. "I've never lived here on this compound, but I would be willing to bet there would be a secret room of sorts in that—"

"We found it, ma'am." They both grinned ear to ear. "It's filled with boxes of documents and even safes."

I noticed several others perk up at that news, and pretty soon some of the officers who had ignored me came over with more questions.

That afternoon, at my request, a ranger quietly escorted me out to watch, from a distance, the last of the women and children being bused off the ranch. My heart leaped with joy as I recognized many of the women I knew and loved, but when I saw the looks of fear and uncertainty on their faces, I longed to comfort them. I couldn't help but notice how considerate and respectful the guards and SWAT members were, even as some of the women were blatantly nasty to them. Some of the other women seemed incredulous, and I realized that they had never been treated respectfully by a man before, and certainly hadn't expected it from an armor-clad government officer.

As the buses drove away, I walked back to the command post, where a ranger came to tell me that I was going to meet Brooks, the Texas Ranger in charge of the investigation. Sheriff Doran had coached me, saying, "He'll call a spade a spade, and a snake a snake. He's under a lot of pressure, so don't take it personal if he snaps or barks."

I waited there until a broad-shouldered man with a strong, angular jaw and a name tag saying "Long" approached me.

"Are you Miss Musser?"

"Yes."

"Come with me, please." He began walking briskly toward the temple. As I hurried to keep up with him, he asked me a few brief questions. After fumbling a bit, I realized that *he* was Brooks—Brooks Long.

"Wow, you're nicer than I thought you would be," I sputtered, and instantly placed my hand over my mouth.

As we neared the temple, I thought about what it would feel like to live here among the FLDS again. Sheriff Doran had told me that the women had likely never left the property. What would the women's schedules be like? I wondered about the structure of their days, how they socialized and conducted worship.

"Are you okay, ma'am?" Brooks's concerned voice interrupted my thoughts. "Am I walking too fast for you?"

I stared wide-eyed at Brooks, who was now in front of me. Twice now, I'd unconsciously stepped in line behind him. I had always walked behind Ben and Wendell. I had always walked behind Dad. Behind Rulon Jeffs. Behind Warren, behind Seth, or any other Priesthood leader. Even in mainstream society, I'd received the subtle message that a woman must be subservient, that she must follow and obey. It dawned on me that for the very first time in my life, I was being treated like an equal by a man!

I'm sure Brooks was unaware as something from my unconscious suddenly exploded into the light of day. That moment crossing the temple lawn would change me forever.

CHAPTER 26

Sacrificial Lambs

I accompanied Brooks up the blinding white back stairs to the temple, going as fast as I could in my heels. Glancing nervously over my shoulder, I realized what an easy target I was this high up. I had no doubt how they would feel about an apostate entering their temple—I was considered even worse than law enforcement. We entered through the split doors to the main floor of the temple, and with more than a little sadness I saw the damage of the battering ram on the heavy oak doors. I also saw the many, many locks that had to be busted open. Warren had certainly not wanted any unauthorized persons to access this place.

Now inside, Brooks first led me over to the left, to a walkway leading to a small building adjacent to the first floor of the temple, with furnaces and a laundry facility inside. There I noticed a laundry list in Mother Paula's familiar handwriting. She had made it to Zion, and to the temple. The knowledge in the pit of my stomach of what lay in this temple kept me from rejoicing for her.

Back in the main building, just past the elegant foyer, was an assembly hall decorated in soft earth tones with at least two hundred beautifully handcrafted oak chairs spread across it in formation. In one corner, a beautiful white baby grand piano rested; against another wall, an entire column of chairs sat upon an impressive platform behind a banister. Certain chairs were clearly marked for the First Presidency and the Quorum of the Twelve, as outlined in early church doctrine and scriptures. On each side, there were another thirty-five chairs, likely for the Quorum of the Seventy, who, like the Twelve, were to be traveling ministers under the President of the Church. Despite Rulon's assertion of one-man rule and Warren's continuation of it, he had nonetheless designed everything on this floor to the strictest standards of the temples of the early church, with quorums. Warren had been preparing for it on a physical, if not spiritual, basis.

Sheriff Doran joined us and we made our way up to the second level, where all of the colors transformed from earth tones to sky blue and white. Two intricate murals decorated opposing walls, one depicting a harmonious scene in the Garden of Eden, the other terrible in its ferocious portrayal of predator and prey. I didn't care for the latter, but I marveled again at the workmanship of the artist, whom I recognized from Short Creek: "Mr. Rich" Barlow, once a fellow teacher who was related to me by marriage and was Dr. Barlow's brother.

Different areas of the temple were meant to signify different kingdoms, or degrees of glory—the degrees of Heaven one would earn in eternal life. Christ said, "In my Father's house, there are many mansions," and we were taught these mansions or kingdoms were the Telestial Kingdom, the Terrestrial Kingdom, and the highest, the Celestial Kingdom. The scene of chaos was intended to portray the Telestial Kingdom—a step up from outer darkness or perdition, but not so different from what we experienced on earth, while the scene in Eden represented the higher Terrestrial Kingdom, one of peace and harmony with greater light and knowledge. Only in the Celestial Kingdom, with the magnificent light and glory of the sun, would we reside in our Father's presence and be like him, able to create our own worlds. It was what all worthy FLDS aspired to, and the only way to attain it was through the fullness of the Priesthood: Celestial Marriage. The Higher Law. The Work. Plurality.

I ascended the stunning spiral staircase next to Brooks and was almost blinded by the next level: complete whiteness, in the walls, carpets, and ceilings. We stepped into a room with muted sea-foam carpeting, but even the familiar scriptures on the shelves were bound in white leather with gold lettering: *Journals of Discourses. Sermons of Leroy S. Johnson.*

Sermons of Rulon T. Jeffs. Sermons of Warren Jeffs. In Light and Truth.
Teachings of the Prophet Joseph Smith.

I tried not to gasp. The most prominent feature in the room was a twin-sized Murphy bed that unfolded from a bright white cabinet in the wall. Kitty-corner from it was the President's desk, and to the right of it was a smaller desk. Chairs surrounded the bed in a profound arc—some taller than others, signifying those in authority. Though Warren had been caught before the whole temple could be dedicated, it was obvious from the disarray that this room had already been dedicated and used.

Yellow crime scene tape kept us from going all the way in, but it took less than a fraction of a second for my brain to determine what this was: a training room.

For a brief moment, I thought I might pass out. This room was all about total submission to your husband, your husband who owns you, mind, spirit, and body. *Good God, Warren…,* I couldn't help thinking. *How could you?* I choked back a tear but regained my composure quickly, knowing it was facts the officers needed, and only facts that could help all the girls and women now.

Brooks and Doran began asking questions. Everything I saw in the room had been hinted at in our trainings, as it had been explained to us by Warren, Rulon, or another of his sons. When Brooks pointed to a lavish crystal decanter of olive oil and a very large, shiny bowl that were prominently displayed in a glass-front cabinet, I was able to answer: "On this floor, and with that size bowl, it could only be for one thing: a ritual known as 'the second ordinance.' What you must know is that a first-time temple goer will be washed and anointed, meaning washed of all worldly essence, and anointed or sanctified as one of the Lord's appointed followers to be worthy to receive the first temple endowment, which is significant, because this is how he or she learns the precise way to get into Heaven after death.

"But way beyond that is the second ordinance, called the Fullness of the Priesthood, which is about a person's 'calling and election made sure.' What this means is that a person has been determined to be ultra-worthy in the Lord's eyes, and he is going to Heaven *no matter what.*"

They looked at me quizzically.

"I haven't personally participated in it, but remember how I explained a woman's hair is considered her crowning glory?"

Doran nodded.

"Well, my sister-wives Naomi, Ellen, Paula, and Ora all had participated with Rulon, one at a time, in this ordinance. As Mary and another woman did to Christ in Luke, in the New Testament, a wife will wash her husband's feet, anoint them with oil, then dry them with her long hair. That's why an FLDS woman is never to cut her hair."

"And the bed?" asked Brooks. "What do they do there? Pray over you? Cut a cake?" Brooks wanted lightning-quick answers, but not everything felt so cut-and-dried to me. If they were to know anything, it was important that they know *everything*—that it not be misconstrued. The people I loved would be greatly affected by whatever words came out now.

"We found a woman's hair on that bed," Brooks said brusquely, pointing to a black medium-length strand visible on the white sheet. My first thought was that it belonged to Mother Paula, but I realized it might be Ellen's or Ruthie's or any number of Warren's wives. Which one of them had been subjected to what I feared most during my married life to Rulon?

My mind went right back to family classes, where Warren first alluded to this "great blessing" we would receive at our own temple, always leaving more questions than answers. After Rulon's stroke, however, I remember him saying that as Rulon's wives, we were the most "well-taught and trained" throughout all of FLDS history, since our people had known relative peace during Rulon's reign. Warren urged us to prepare ourselves immediately for the second anointing, essentially a second endowment, and to invite angels to be with us from that point forward every time we were "with" our husband. It was to prepare us for something even greater, he said.

One night closer to the end of Rulon's life, during family class, Warren began to talk about the Fullness of the Priesthood. Rulon, who had lost his mental filter, got so excited he had interrupted Warren.

"Can't we set up a room in this house for this ordinance?" he cried. "*I need to take care of these ladies!*"

Warren about fell off his chair—and I almost did, too. Warren had taught us these principles perhaps three times before, but it had always seemed in the distant future! For the duration of that class, however, Rulon kept insisting we immediately set up, bless, and dedicate a room specifically for the "True Order of Creation." Warren kept trying to shut Rulon up without blatantly telling the Prophet no. My sister-wives and

I were dutifully taking notes, and I wondered how many of them were as sick inside as I was. Later that night after class, Isaac came to each of our rooms, asking to see our notebooks, which he took with him. I remembered being relieved, because I figured it meant we truly weren't ready.

"What we talk about in this home is sacred," Warren admonished us the next day. "If you are talking about your second endowments, even amongst yourselves, you are forsaking them, treating your endowments lightly, and you will eliminate those blessings." That was our signal to keep our mouths shut. I was happy to do so, and hoped we would not hear about it again, but that was not the case.

Now I informed the men about what we learned soon after.

"Warren told Rulon's wives, 'You are living the Law of Celestial Marriage, but there will come a time that as faithful people, we will have a temple. There you will be taught the Fullness of Celestial Marriage, also known as the Fullness of the Law of Sarah. You will have the opportunity to learn the True Principles of Creation, and true order of creating pure and holy spirits.'"

Warren said we would learn how to correct our thoughts, turning away from the carnal to be so pure and holy that angels would surround us so as to help us to conceive a child, also adding there would be certain "positions of intercourse" we would learn.

A look passed between Brooks and Doran, and it only added to the heat I felt in my face as I was reliving the horror of the training. "And if we were really pure," I added gravely, "then we could act as witnesses for our sister-wives when they received their endowments. That was the Fullness of the Law of Sarah—that not only would we agree to let our husband marry others, but that we would so graciously welcome them into the fold with the purest of hearts as we *witnessed* their endowment. That meant we had to see our husband having intercourse with other wives, and at some point, we also would be the object of that witness." I was so embarrassed to say these words that I wanted to cry. I wanted to be sick.

"I'll be honest with you," I told the two men, "I prayed that we weren't ready yet as a people! I for one knew I couldn't participate. I wanted to be considered by God as pure and holy, and I welcomed more than forty-five wives after me into Celestial Marriage with Rulon. But the thought of having my body exposed to angels was shocking enough. I knew I could not have intercourse in front of earthly witnesses, even if it meant being able to have a child. I kept that thought to myself, but I was horrified."

There was an awkward silence for a moment; then Brooks murmured to the sheriff, "If Rulon was interested at ninety, then damn well Warren and these guys are doing what we thought they were." He turned to me, much softer than he had been before. "And that desk?" he asked, pointing to the smaller one.

"Well, the clerk's desk next to the bed is where the Church Recorder—the designated Priesthood leader ordained to this job—makes a record of the training. According to FLDS teachings, a record of every ordinance must be not only witnessed but recorded and kept safe." Sure enough, to the right of the clerk's desk, there was an open white cabinet that held an electronic safe, with a shredding machine below it. Just as Warren had guaranteed that the information on the Fullness of the Celestial Law didn't leave his father's home, Warren and his minions had not taken any chances about leaking it to the outside world.

On our way out I looked back at the bed. I hadn't seen a Murphy bed since Rulon's last days, when my sister-wife Mary had nursed him around the clock. This bed looked like it was made by the same hands, and I had a very good idea of which craftsman had built it. Did that man have a clue as to what it was for? Did he know who would be victimized by the work of his hands?

Attached to that room was a doorway through which we entered a gigantic assembly room, as blinding white as the third level: white carpet, white paint, white benches, white chairs. Cleverly positioned skylights created the impression of a bedazzling pillar of light, similar to the one in our stories about Joseph Smith receiving his first visitation from the Lord. Across the expanse, three large, round white tables were set up with chairs, and the room was lined with shelves of scriptures, with pure white reclining chairs nearby.

"Now, what do you think of this?" asked the ranger.

It took everything I had not to burst out into sobs.

In the center of the room several chairs had been placed in a semicircle for the witnesses of the ordinance, including the tall-backed chairs to honor the First Presidency. There was a small desk in the corner, again for the clerk or recorder. But it chilled me to see the several chairs in the middle, near something that had obviously been so heavy it had left grooves in the carpet when it was removed. The marks had alerted the team, who'd found it in a storage closet in the hallway and set it up again on the side of the room. Brooks pointed to it, and my eyes darted from the obvious mattress to the retractable rails.

Here it was, in all white with gold hinges: the sacramental, full-sized "Heavenly" bed just large enough for two. There was no mistaking that the white, padded bench on the end was a place for observers to kneel.

Before we descended again, Brooks turned to me. "Until you told the sheriff on the phone about the beds and what they signified, all we could do was speculate—but additional evidence has begun to show up. When Caver secured this floor and called on the radio, 'Get your ass up here,' I took one look and cordoned off the crime scene. But I'll be honest—I let *all* my guys come up here to see. We'd all felt like shit coming in their sacred place, but I wanted them to see that much more than prayers was going on inside. You are validating exactly what we worried about.

"There are other parts of the temple I need to show you," he continued. "But first, can you tell me what Blood Atonement is?"

I froze.

Up until my final year in Rulon Jeffs's home, I had never heard of an ordinance involving Blood Atonement, except in reference to Jesus Christ making the ultimate sacrifice for our sins. One day, however, I had come upon my sister-wife Tammy in the hallway of the Prophet's home. She was deathly pale and holding a book open with the palm of her hand.

"Have you read this?" she asked me. I glanced at the cover of the book that Warren had suggested we all study: *Purity and the Celestial Law of Marriage*.

"Only the first few pages," I told her truthfully. "Why?"

"It talks about Blood Atonement…"

My body had gone cold. All I could picture was the painting of Abraham as depicted in the Old Testament, knife in hand, towering above his son, Isaac, whom he had tethered to an altar as he prepared to make the ultimate sacrifice—to kill his son for God.

Tammy showed me a passage from the book written by our Prophet

John Taylor. "Is this the only way for such a sinful person to have all their sins absolved before God?" she asked. I was dumbfounded and unable to answer. Just then, a door opened into the foyer, and we saw Warren's unmistakable silhouette. Tammy looked over at me, and I nodded. We figured we might as well get our answers, so we approached him and Tammy handed the book to him, open to the page she had been reading. He glanced at it for three seconds.

"Oh yeah," he said nonchalantly, and handed it back. "This was established in the early part of the church, for adulterers, fornicators, and murderers—anyone who requires a greater sacrifice to reach the highest kingdom. To sincerely repent is not enough to show God their true repentance. This ultimate sacrifice will take thousands of years off of your suffering in the afterlife." My heart had raced. Warren had already threatened that I would be destroyed in the flesh for not being a "comfort" to my husband. Would this be required of me?

Warren went on to explain that the ordinance would take place in the basement of the temple. "An executioner is ordained to hold this office as an angel of destruction," he said somberly. "Dressed in robes, he must say specific prayers, and when it is time, he must cut the person's throat in this specific way." As I watched him gesture, I could almost feel the cold steel of a blade across my neck.

"It is something we *will* do again," Warren said, then looked at me, repeating the words he had said in his office: "The Prophet holds the key to your salvation." Then he had walked away, leaving me chilled to my core.

I now shared this story with the sheriff and Brooks and told them why it had haunted me. Rumors had spread throughout Short Creek about Blood Atonement. Everyone who had left was disturbed by the number of men, women, and children who'd just poofed into thin air. Obviously most had made their way here onto the YFZ, but some were still unaccounted for. They might have been holed up in houses of hiding across the country, still awaiting the commands Warren still issued from prison. But I knew that other Mormon extremists had used Blood Atonement to excuse the ritual killings of family members, like Ervil LeBaron of the LeBaron family, who had continued to issue death sentences from behind prison walls. I had never been inclined to blow things out of proportion, but I hadn't thought Warren capable of what

I'd *already* seen in the temple. It worried me that no one could predict what he would do.

I was incredibly relieved to find there was no sign of a place for the Blood Atonement ritual when we canvassed the rest of the temple, including the baptismal font. Although several rooms downstairs were eerily empty, whatever Warren had planned for the future, seeing the beds had been enough for me for one day.

When we left I breathed in drafts of warm, spring Texas air. I would be fine with never going indoors ever again.

Late that day Doran informed me that the court released affidavits from the Texas Department of Public Safety (DPS) detailing information about Sarah Barlow's blocked calls, and it continued the international media frenzy. She had a pattern of getting paranoid, hanging up, and calling back. She'd cry, "They're coming! They may be listening…They lock up the phones…I may not have a phone…There's a guard in the guard tower here on the ranch."

It sounded all too plausible, especially as she used FLDS verbiage, but suddenly the calls had stopped.

As the officers continued to search the compound for her, Brooks, Caver, and Doran seemed worried. What if they really did have her hidden away in either the temple vault or the temple annex vault? There was only one way to find out.

CHAPTER 27

Breaching the Vault

My attempt to locate Sarah by reviewing some boxes of evidence and files that were confusing to the officers proved fruitless as well. That Wednesday, I was stationed at the temple annex building with Joe Haralson, an older ranger who had heard so many FLDS lies that he initially had very little faith in me. Ranger Haralson's wariness seemed to be justified by some disturbing news he delivered to me. My sister-in-law Miranda, who was married to Ben's brother Oliver, asked her midwife to call the authorities in Texas and provide false information: she said I was an informant with a huge chip on my shoulder, that I was bitter and hateful, and would do anything to bring down the FLDS. Her midwife swore that I had made a prank call as Sarah to spur the raid. Fortunately, I was able to set the record straight with Texas authorities, starting with Joe, and the sheriff, who had heard the recorded calls and backed me up, saying it could not have been me.

Several of the rangers got angry and prepared to go after Miranda for supplying false information. I asked them not to, but I did send her an e-mail warning her about the criminality of falsifying reports and possible prosecution. But she was only one of a slew calling with worries and fears and speculations. FLDS members in other parts of the nation and Canada were terrified as rumors abounded. My dad called to tell me that Irene's daughter Cindy had been on the YFZ, and she had told Irene that women and children were being held in concentration camps and had been made to line up and strip down in front of men who were checking them by hand for pregnancy.

I angrily refuted this rumor.

"First of all, Dad, they have made sure that women work with the women officers as much as possible. Some urine tests have been conducted, but these women have been treated with more respect than they have by their own husbands. As far as the people, if they had just told the *truth*, none of this would have ever happened! No one would have been removed—no one would have entered the temple. If anyone is to blame it is Uncle Merrill and his lies, yet still people are continuing to spread fabrications."

I filled him in on all of the FLDS misdeeds, including LeRoy Steed's flight from officers with a hard drive, and the van filled with pregnant teens. "Consider your sources, Dad. The women are not being put up in the Hilton, but they have everything except showers, and that's being fixed as we speak. They're being well fed and treated with respect. The FLDS are spreading bullshit."

The calls and speculations seemed to slow considerably when DPS revealed the discovery of beds inside the FLDS temple and suggested that it was an area where men "engage[d] in sexual activity with female children under the age of seventeen." Doran had warned me they had found even more evidence regarding the ages of some of the girls having to be "trained," most of them Warren's younger wives. It made me physically ill, but I pushed it out of my brain and focused on finding Sarah. The longer she was missing, the more we worried for her safety.

I was looking over a list of properties rangers had found, and then the bus lists, and realized that though several of the women had changed their names, there were often enough clues so that I could guess who they were.

Suddenly I gasped.

"What is it?" asked the ranger.

My heart lurched as I recognized the names of my sister Savannah's children, along with two more I hadn't even known about. Savannah had made up different first and last names for herself, but wisely used her children's real first names. To her, I was likely Satan incarnate, but seeing her name made me realize just how much I had missed her. I'd been strong this whole time, but this was too much, and for the first time I cried in front of the officers.

Quickly I gathered myself again, as we were on a serious deadline. Time was rapidly running on out on the search warrants—law enforcement had only a week from issue to be on the ranch. Locksmiths from San Antonio had been brought in to crack the safes in the temple and the annex building I was in. The priority was the temple annex vault, where we speculated the records still were since the temple was not yet dedicated. Brooks also brought in a jackhammer crew and started creating a hole in the eighteen-inch-thick cement. They were making more progress than the locksmiths. Both vaults had air vents built in, so there was wariness in opening either vault as to what, or who, might be inside. Brooks warned both crews that they were taking their lives into their hands, as explosives could have been set to go off in the safes. When they got close to breach, he had me escorted out for safety. I was later informed when a large enough hole had been cut with the jackhammer, and Ranger Jesse Valdez, the slightest of all the men, crawled through carefully, armed only with a flashlight. Brooks let me reenter the area in time to see Valdez emerge from the vault covered from head to toe in thick white dust.

"I found them!" he said, smiling. He'd discovered forty-four boxes of records and several additional safes inside.

Law enforcement felt other repercussions, as the FLDS had launched a full-fledged propaganda campaign, using the hungry media to spin their story. In a *Deseret News* interview, three mothers reported they were being denied access to their children and housed in the most primitive of circumstances. On CNN, Merrill's wife Kathleen sobbed, "I want you to understand that we've been put in a compound, Fort Concho, over there, with brick walls. One hundred feet by forty feet...one hundred and seventy women and children, two bathrooms...We are being treated like the Jews were when they were escorted to the German Nazi camps."

Law enforcement reminded the FLDS members and the media that the adult women had come voluntarily and were free to leave anytime, but the media was coming down hard on Brooks, who didn't have time to call an official press conference to refute the lies.

I met him out on the lawn by the temple annex building, where he was pacing back and forth, furious.

"I do not have time for this shit! You know, Becky, when they first came here, we *welcomed* them. All they had to do was leave the young girls alone. When we showed up, they lied. And now they're lying again! How dumb do they think we are?"

In the meantime, he'd heard from Flora that she'd received more calls from Sarah.

"Something's not right here," Brooks told me. "I smell a rat."

I continued my work in the temple annex, trying to locate Sarah, validate records, and answer questions. For lunch, I'd been relying on the cook shed or chuck wagon that a local businessman had donated to feed an enormous number of the rangers and the residents. Most of the FLDS men ate in their own homes, but some of the young men and very old emerged periodically, so we had to be watchful, and I was always accompanied.

As I approached the chuck wagon that day, Ranger Jason Kinerd motioned to me to quietly follow him across the way.

"What can you tell me about this kid?" he asked me, pointing at Warren's son Tobias, who looked terrified as he sat on the ground, rocking himself. I told him about Toby, who was autistic and obviously wanted to be with his mother. Since he was over eighteen, he wasn't allowed to leave the ranch.

What I saw next touched my heart. Several gruff-looking rangers sat down next to him, comforted him, and offered him lunch from the wagon. I overheard them reassure him that he was not in any danger, and they went to great lengths to make sure he knew that his mother was not, either. Toby loosened up and ate three desserts—probably a big treat, as most FLDS were raised to eschew sugary foods.

After lunch, as I made my way back to the temple annex building with Joe by my side, Jason approached me again.

"Yeah, I got the dirt on you!" he cried. "You were listening to devil music!"

"What?"

"I read a confession letter from your friend Samantha."

I looked at the ranger, and back at Joe (who had finally started to trust me), and started giggling. I knew what Jason must have found in the records!

When I was a student at Alta Academy, Warren taught us that devil music began in the '60s when the Beatles sold their souls to the devil—a black man who gave them a record contract.

"If you take delight in this type of music," he said, "you are going down an immoral path, and taking on that black man's devil-worshipping spirit." I tried hard to be good, listening to church hymns and classical music. But the world was so melodious, and I was often drawn to other forms, like ragtime. (I could only imagine what Warren would say about *that*!)

"One night," I told the ranger, "Samantha called. 'Come and get me right now!' Right after family class, I told Nephi I had a quick errand, and I took one of the property's vehicles to pick Samantha up. She popped in some music and we drove around the back roads, turning it up really loud, screaming our guts out!"

"What was it?" the ranger asked. He was expecting some heavy-metal band.

"It was a group called A-Teens, singing their rendition of ABBA's 'Super Trouper.'"

"Hunh?"

"That was it, I swear! It was *baaaad*, because it had drumbeats and worldly lyrics—I think there's even a reference to a kiss."

"Dear God, no!"

"Oh yeah, I'm sure that was why Samantha says I crossed into dark, dark waters." We had a good laugh before we got right back to work.

Back in the annex, I realized soberly that most of the letters of repentance officials had found in Warren's Escalade and in boxes of records revealed secrets much more serious than Samantha's ABBA confession. Warren had once again found a way to blackmail his greatest supporters: forcing them to give up their darkest skeletons in exchange for their salvation.

CHAPTER 28

Sex, Lies, and Videotape

Brooks had warned me that first day that I might have to testify about what I was seeing on the ranch. Although I had turned down every request since Warren's criminal trial in Utah, as I promised Lamont and Roger I would, what I was observing in Texas made me realize that *someone* had to speak for the voiceless. Brooks recognized he had some solid criminal cases. At the same time, though, CPS was fighting a losing battle in a no-win fourteen-day hearing schedule.

Working superlong hours like the rest of the crew, Elissa and I had been missing our kids like crazy, especially since we'd never been away from them for long. We called them at least a few times a day. It was hard to talk to Ben, as he'd been growing more hateful every day. His family constantly reminded him that I had done more than enough damage to their Prophet. They believed I was now persecuting the common people, in cahoots with the government. Lamont was also upset and, like Ben, did not appreciate having to care for two young ones alone. Our husbands asked constantly, "When are you coming home?"

All we could answer was "I don't know."

By that Friday, which I spent with Elissa at the CPS building, the rangers had mostly pulled off the YFZ, though the mothers and children were still at Fort Concho. Lawyers and foster homes were being found, but it was a complicated process. While we were grateful for what CPS was trying to do, Elissa and I remained vigilant about the rights of the women and children. We had to repeatedly remind hundreds of different investigators and workers to use the term "marital relations" instead of "sex," as well as explaining Warren's peculiar indoctrination so they could understand our people better, without judgment.

In the meantime, at Fort Concho, the cultural rifts were glaringly apparent. A CPS worker told me that the first night the young boys spent there, an overnight guardian had come upstairs to check on them at five a.m. and found all of them awake and sitting fully clothed on the edges of their neatly made beds. She presumed they were preparing to run away.

"We're ready to go to work," one of the boys said, and the others nodded. "What work are we supposed to do?" they asked.

CPS was under fire from the public, DPS, and the media. No matter what CPS did to create order so they could take the very best care of the children, the women were constantly undermining the workers. They switched wristbands, spoke snidely to workers and volunteers, refused to cooperate, and still lied about ages and family groups. I knew, because I held many files on my own lap in which women I was well acquainted with had written lie after lie—names, ages, parents, etc.

Still, there were things CPS could have been doing better, and they all knew it. That week, CPS workers had come in from all over the state to help out. As we were looking at Texas's normal regulations for the removal of children and placement into foster care, I told them that their usual operations would not work in this situation.

"Please hear me on this," I said. "You will *not* find the drug problems that are normally in abusive homes. You will *not* find physical, domestic violence to the point that you might see in some of these other circumstances. While it does happen, it's not common. The sexual abuse through spiritual teachings *is* common—but it's a different problem than you have encountered in most of your cases in Texas."

"Okay," said Elaine Leonard, a high-level CPS administrator. "What do you suggest?"

"Is there any way to remove the fathers and return the mothers and children?" I asked.

"If it were up to me," she said, "we could, but we have to deal with structures that are already in place. We can't undo what's been done in this time frame, and we have to be *extremely* careful about setting a precedent." We kept trying to dream up better solutions, but time was against us. At one point, I saw tears on Elaine's face.

Later, a CPS official from Austin came in as I was answering questions.

"Who is this?" he said, looking down his nose. "Why should we listen to *her?*"

I erupted in frustration. "Look, I don't have the education you have. I don't have the background and credentials you have. But what you normally do is not the solution."

I walked away and escaped down the hall, blinded by tears. Turning a corner, I ran straight into Brooks.

"What am I doing here?" I asked him desperately.

"Who said something to you?" he asked. He prodded me until I blurted it out. Brooks immediately marched into the CPS room.

"I don't care who you think you are," he said. "We are mighty damn grateful that Becky has come to help us. What you need to know is that things would be much worse without her. Out of all of the hundreds of people and cases out there, there's probably only a handful of people that she doesn't know or isn't related to. Can *you* identify any of those people? I didn't think so. You listen to her and treat her with respect."

To add to the turmoil, Ben called, angrier than ever. Two different flights I'd booked out had come and gone. Elissa was preparing to leave to engage in some big media on the book she had written, hoping to educate the public about the plight of all FLDS women. Ben couldn't understand why I wouldn't leave, too, but there were hearings and issues that urgently deserved resolution here in Texas.

"So what's it like down there with all your cowboy boyfriends?" he said accusingly. "How does it feel to be so important? You want everyone to think you're so cool?" I couldn't handle it any longer. I sat on a sofa away from the others and sobbed.

"Look," I told Ben, "I'm doing the best I can. I'm sorry. I thought I would be done."

"Well, it affects me, too, Beck. Get home. Get home *now.*" The line went dead.

At that moment I felt like such an idiot, working with people at CPS who couldn't care less, trying to help people who hated my guts. If that wasn't crazy making, I didn't know what was. Even worse, I missed my kids with a physical ache.

After a deep, private cry, I realized that deep down, part of me felt responsible for what was going on here. I had escaped it—and it ended up in the laps of little girls. If I had stayed, could I have made a difference? Could I have stopped any of this madness?

Doran's exceptionally kind wife, Lenette, knew I would be alone after Elissa's departure, and she invited me to their home for a Texas-style BBQ Sunday evening. Nothing had been going right. The day before, Dale Evans Barlow, accused husband of the elusive Sarah Barlow, met with Texas Rangers in St. George. They discovered he was definitely not their man. Women from Fort Concho were calling the *Deseret News* from their cell phones until a judge ordered the phones confiscated to prevent further false statements and staged pictures going out. That had turned the public tide against law enforcement and in favor of the FLDS once again. Doran was the most discouraged I'd ever seen him.

Nonetheless, the Dorans offered me a warm welcome. Doran's brother cooked steaks, and I ate okra for the first time. The sheriff had beautiful grandchildren, one of whom was very close in age to Natalia. It made me miss my children even more. I tried to be sociable, but I was homesick and was still really torn up about not being able to connect with Ally and Sherrie.

"Hey, Becky," said the sheriff, "I know you're exhausted, but you're not your usual chipper self. Is there anything we can do?" I was about to say no and thank him for his kindness when a thought occurred to me.

"Do you have a violin handy?" He looked at me in surprise, then made a few calls and found one almost immediately from a church member. I lovingly shouldered the instrument, tuned it, and began to play by the fire. The music spun its magic, and I felt my spirits lift.

Shortly thereafter, Randy and Kathy Mankin came by. I'd not yet met them but was impressed immediately. Yes, they had been the first to break the news in that little town, but they had integrity about what they reported—and when they reported it. Whereas other newscasters had almost compromised the case for ratings, the *Eldorado Success* was diligent about facts and sources. I was also delighted to discover that Randy played the guitar. He strummed for us and sang Marty Robbins

ballads. Together we played around the chimney campfire that evening, and it provided a wonderful respite from the pain of the work
we'd been doing.

What we didn't know that night was that Willie Jessop, Warren's
henchman, had been driving around Eldorado, staking out the sheriff's
home. The next day, Willie confronted Randy Mankin at his office.

"I *saw* you with Becky Musser!" he snarled, insinuating some sort of
conspiracy between me, Randy, and the sheriff's office. Randy laughed
and explained the situation, but Willie didn't believe it. The self-
appointed spokesman for the FLDS since the beginning of this investigation, he had taken every opportunity in front of a camera to stretch
a tiny bit of truth halfway across the state of Texas. The Texas Rangers
had their eyes on him, having been warned by Utah authorities that he
was known for violence, possessing both legal and illegal weapons, the
use of explosives, and verbal threats and various other forms of intimidation. All I knew was that wherever Willie was, Warren's edicts were
not far behind.

I woke up early Monday morning feeling more rested than I had for
days. I met the sheriff and Elaine on the lawn outside Fort Concho.
Another call had come in from Sarah, wherein she gave precise details
about the playgrounds and the women's schedules. Worse, she also
sounded like she might be slightly drugged again.

I wore a baseball cap, sunglasses, and a floppy jacket so as not to be
recognized, since the women at Fort Concho didn't yet know that I
was there. It was best to keep it that way. As we scoured the playground
areas and tried to figure which room was Sarah's, it was eerie to see the
curtains move in the windows and see girls and women stare out at us.

Come on, Sarah. Where are you? Something just didn't feel right.

CPS was going to announce later that day that they were moving the
women and children to the Foster Communications Coliseum in San
Angelo, which was much bigger and had locker rooms with showers, so
it would have been the perfect time for law enforcement to slip Sarah
out of there safely. Frustratingly, we couldn't find her.

That Tuesday, I was at the sheriff's office when one of the officers
suddenly turned up the volume on the big-screen television. Larry King
was interviewing three FLDS women—unmistakable in their pastel

prairie dresses—with a larger group of women behind them. I knew each woman—Esther, Marilyn, and Sally—quite well. They'd given their real first names, but when King asked them about their children, the lying began. We were used to it.

But then came the clincher, when he asked about relationships between older men and teenage girls and younger:

LK: Did you see others at the ranch getting married younger?
Sally: Not that I'm aware of...
LK: Marilyn, had you?
Marilyn: Not that I have ever seen.
LK: Esther, had you?
Esther: Not that I have ever seen.
LK: So all of these stories are false, or just you haven't seen them?
Esther: I believe they are false.
Marilyn: I believe they are false.
Sally: Me, also.
LK: So you're saying there were no young girls at that ranch, ever, ever married to, say, men in their twenties or thirties?
[All three women shake their heads no.]
Esther: Not to our knowledge.

"Oh my God, what bullshit!" I jumped up from behind the desk, a small mountain of files still in my hands. *"What a bunch of freaking bullshit!"*

Two of the rangers just stared at me as I slammed back into my seat. They knew it was garbage—they had heard more lies from the FLDS than the truth—but they didn't understand the significance of what I was saying.

"I have these women's files right on my lap, right now!" I shouted. "I've got a file of a fifteen-year-old, Janet, who married Raymond Merrill Jessop and had his child at age sixteen."

I looked up and pointed furiously at the third woman on the right. "Sally is her *mother*! And the *grandmother* to the baby. She was the attending *midwife* at the baby's birth! And that's Sally's full daughter, right there in the middle! She is Janet's full sister. I cannot believe they're lying like this!"

The rangers' eyes grew wide at the revelation and my outburst. The reality hit home again that these were children having babies—*those women's* grandbabies and great-grandbabies!

A stark realization came over me and I realized why the fire was so strong inside of me. It wasn't just because of the lies, but because literally no one was telling the truth! Not one FLDS person was standing up for these girls the way their own mothers and grandmothers *should* have. In my heart, I was still Grandmother Becky, and fierce protectiveness washed over me. No matter what had happened in the last week—the comments of ignorant CPS workers, the digs into my reputation, the repercussions on my tenuous marriage...I had to keep fighting for those girls.

CHAPTER 29

Balm of Gilead

The next day, CPS hearings began in the Fifty-First District Court, with Judge Barbara Walther ruling in an overflowing courthouse. But I wasn't there—instead I was making my way through a sea of people, including my sister-wives and their babies, at the coliseum where they were now staying. Behind my sunglasses and baseball cap, I went unrecognized by those I had loved for so long. Still, the hollow looks in their eyes haunted me.

Rebecca Baxter, my CPS contact that day, had worked with one young woman who she felt would be amenable to speaking honestly with me. She escorted the girl into the interview room where I sat without my disguise, and introduced me as her friend.

I looked directly at the young girl.

"Heather," I said gently. "Do you remember me?" She shook her head. "I'm Mother Becky, and I was married to Uncle Rulon."

Heather's eyes grew large as recognition dawned on her. Suddenly she reached out and hugged me hard. We both began to cry.

"Look at you—you're all grown up!" I exclaimed. "And you're so beautiful!"

She beamed for a moment, before her sweet face turned somber. "It broke my heart when you left."

"Oh, sweetheart...Don't you think it broke mine to leave?" I told her why it was the most painful decision I had ever made—and the best. I also explained to her that the state had been forced to investigate allegations of abuse, but they'd had no intention of searching every home or removing anyone except Sarah and her immediate family, declaring that Merrill could have avoided all of this.

"Heather," I asked tentatively, "what can you tell me about Sherrie and Ally?"

"Oh, let's see...They're both here."

My heart skipped a beat.

"And I think they're both married." She thought for a moment. "Oh yes, they are, both Sherrie and Ally. And Sherrie has a baby."

My little Sherrie, a mother? And my little Ally, married? She would have been just fifteen that year. It took all my power to hold it together. I almost missed what Heather said next.

"Wait! You said Uncle Merrill Jessop is married to Ally?" I cried.

"Yes."

"Wow," I said, dumbfounded. "Is she happy?"

Heather smiled, but it was hollow. "I think so..."

According to Heather, Ally had wed our uncle by marriage when he was in his seventies. No wonder he'd called on Valentine's Day to have the missing person reports cleaned up! He didn't want their union to have legal ramifications. I hoped beyond hope that Merrill would have respected my sister in a sexual way, yet I knew that he had given his own twelve-year-old daughter, Merrianne, to Warren, who had gone on to molest her in the temple in front of others.

Just before it was time to leave, Heather leaned over and whispered conspiratorially to me, "They snuck Ally out yesterday!" My heart stopped for a moment. What? How? And how many others had been taken? I quickly realized how much Heather had compromised by telling me, and I would not throw her under the FLDS bus, but my mind was racing.

I hugged Heather tightly to say good-bye. When she and Rebecca left the room, I lost all composure, crying for her, and for Sherrie and for Ally.

Several minutes later, Rebecca returned. "I went to find Sherrie for you, but she's gone to the park," she said. "Is there anyone else you would like to talk to?"

I was scared, but I knew it would be my last chance, so I asked to talk to Savannah.

Quickly I pulled myself together and put my sunglasses back on. Rebecca led Doran and me to another part of the coliseum. We passed LeRoy Jeffs's daughter, who was standing with a couple of Warren's daughters. I looked at them, the young girls I remembered teaching in musicals and PE and loved so dearly. Evidently, word had spread quickly, as they regarded me with silent but cold malice.

The moment Savannah stepped into the interview room, holding her little girl, Generous, who was Kyle's age, I wanted to tell her how much I loved her. But her eyes were wide and wary, like she was walking into a den of snakes. Savannah was shaking and didn't say a word. I closed the door and removed my sunglasses and hat. My older sister stared at me, hard.

"Why are *you* here?" she spat. "Haven't you done enough? How could you be a part of all of this? They came to our doors and forced us out by gunpoint. They put guns to our sons' heads! It was just like in '44 and '53! How *could* you?"

I was floored. Savannah honestly believed her own words about the rangers forcing people out at gunpoint! Had I not seen the footage, and known firsthand how the rangers treated those women and children, I might have believed her. I realized that this story had become so ingrained in her, it had become her truth. Not just Savannah but her peers sincerely believed that all of their rights had been taken, that the government had been pillaging their homes and touching their children inappropriately.

I wanted to share truth and light, but I tried to put myself in her shoes first.

"Please, just give me five minutes of your time." Happily, five minutes turned into two hours as we caught up, and I finally got to tell her what had happened those final weeks with Warren, including Warren's words that I would never forget.

Her lips tightened. "I don't believe that."

Despite this, it was a tender time for us. I was able to express my love and tell her how our siblings were doing. But I saw in her something I'd seen in the others: Savannah seemed hollow, and her responses seemed canned, in her high-pitched, sickly-sweet voice. "We're so blessed... We're just so blessed."

But I rejoiced the few times I saw the real Savannah underneath.

She laughed when I told her I was still mad at Seth for leaving her in the garden to have her baby while he bounded off to play in St. George with some of Rulon's wives.

"I was so mad at him then, but when I went through my first labor with Kyle, I could have killed him for both of us!" Her eyes filled with mirth as she asked about Kyle and Natalia. I delightedly showed her pictures on my phone and described their vibrant personalities. Seeing the compassion and concern that Savannah had for Natalia's health was healing for me. We hugged before she left, and I waited a bit before I left the room, incognito once again.

On my way back I encountered Rebecca, who told me they had brought a group of women and children back from the park, but they still couldn't find Sherrie. From the beginning we'd been unable to find my mother. Now both Sherrie and Ally were nowhere to be found.

Once again, it seemed, my sisters had slipped through my fingers.

Finally, I had to resign myself to allowing Mom, Sherrie, and Ally their path. It was probably one of the hardest decisions I'd ever had to make. All the suffering, all the unanswered prayers…I didn't have the stamina for much more, and I knew then I had to honor their choices, once and for all.

The next day, I headed to another building adjacent to the coliseum, where many of the adolescent girls were residing. Not bothering with a disguise, I dressed in a professional skirt, soft blue blouse, black heels, and curled hair. They all knew I was there, and part of me wanted the women and girls to know that I was fighting *for* them. As I entered the building, I saw Uncle Roy's granddaughter staring at me. I sat down, leaned over to the CPS worker next to me, and murmured, "Watch the news spread." It was like a tidal wave crashing from girl to girl.

The first girl took out her notebook and flipped to a clean page before she waltzed up to me, the rest of the girls behind her.

"Who are you?"

"You know who I am," I said easily.

"Oh, do I?"

"Yes, you do." I stopped for a moment. "Look at you young girls! You have all grown up to be such beautiful young women. I was Mother Becky, married to Uncle Rulon. Do you remember me?"

She ignored my question. "Why are you here?"

"I am here to help."

"You're not helping."

"You know what might really help," I said, "is if you would stop switching around your names and wristbands."

The girls looked like they'd been caught with their hands in the cookie jar. But all I felt was love and compassion, especially for the girls on the bottom of the totem pole. I wished they could know they were valuable and exquisite, just for being who they were.

That afternoon, the sheriff took me to a place close to his heart, Our Lady of Grace Carmelite Monastery, just outside of Christoval. As we drove up through the desert to the beautiful Spanish Mission–style stone buildings, I did my best to reserve judgment, but my childhood indoctrination that Catholicism was the "great and abominable church" still lingered.

When I entered and saw the pictures of Pope Benedict XVI on the wall, I was reminded of how Warren's photo was in every room of his followers' homes on the YFZ. I was sickened by what had happened in the FLDS temple. Surely *this* was the same.

Then I met Sister Mary Grace. The moment she walked out to greet us, something within my soul shifted.

"Oh, my dear," she said, her voice breaking in compassion. "We have been praying for you. We have been praying for the highest outcome for everyone involved on the ranch." I stared into her gentle eyes in disbelief. She and her sisters had not only prayed for law enforcement; they were praying *for* my people—not against them.

After our talk, I wandered outside alone, looking up at the tall stone walls and feeling the warmth of the sun on my skin. Taking a breath, I entered the chapel alone. Awe-inspiring and yet intimate, it was intensely still. Too still.

I hadn't experienced any quiet since I had come to Texas. Finally no longer able to control my thoughts or emotions, I burst into tears of frustration and shame, anger and pain. My heart cried out to the God that I had begun to love but still did not fully understand. How could I have come from a people able to commit atrocities against children in his name? How could he allow it? I cried until all my emotions were spent.

Then something surprising developed out of my new stillness—a peace so profound that it covered my soul like a soft blanket. I could almost feel loving arms around me. And then I had the urge to embrace the love I felt right back.

I stepped reverently from that chapel with a startling realization. Man was fallible. No one, not the Dalai Lama nor any Prophet, pope, or minister, was beyond reproach. To follow blindly was to shut down our sacred voice of reason and deny the God that lived in each of us. I had to realize that everyone, even I, had the capacity to be a tyrant. And every one of us had the capacity to embody charity, love, and mercy. Nobody was all bad, and nobody was all good. We were human.

CHAPTER 30

The Marijuana House

Shortly after five o'clock that Friday morning, I was awakened by a disturbing call from the police telling me to gather my things immediately. Trying not to be terrified, I questioned the officer, who informed me that that morning an article had been published in Utah's *Deseret News* with the headline "Ex-FLDS Woman Cause of Raid," with the subtitle:

> Testimony offered by a Texas child protection supervisor revealed Thursday that a woman at the center of the Warren Jeffs trial was instrumental in persuading law enforcement to raid the YFZ Ranch.

Both the headline and article were wildly misleading; the article also mentioned my involvement in Warren's Utah trial, saying that my testimony helped convict him. While the *News* was requested to change the article and title for accuracy, papers had already been delivered, and law enforcement took no chances. For the next two days, I stayed at a duplex at the remote Our Lady of Grace. It was hoped no one would think to look for me there.

That day, Doran revealed that a woman named Rozita Swinton in Colorado Springs had been linked to the phone calls and that "Sarah Barlow" might have been a hoax! When I asked how she could possibly have that much working knowledge of FLDS lingo, Doran voiced Texas's suspicions: Rozita may have gathered information from a former FLDS member who was residing at the same rehab facility as she was.

While I was relieved that there was no young lady named Sarah being held against her will and beaten on that ranch, these calls had caused tremendous damage to many people's lives. And from this, the media was calling into question the entire investigation, raid, and removal of children and evidence.

When I talked to Brooks about it, he shook his head.

"Becky, I'll tell you one thing. I've been here more than once. We'll either be labeled as Texas's greatest heroes, or shit on a stick. What people think of us can't matter. We have to do our jobs—we must protect the people." He took off his hat and looked right at me. "Let's say I get a call about a marijuana house, and I get a search warrant to search for marijuana. Only thing is, I go in that house and I don't find a speck of marijuana... but I *do* find cocaine and methamphetamines and speed and LSD. I'm not going to turn around and leave just because I haven't found any marijuana. I'm going to do my job, seize evidence of crimes, and arrest the individuals committing those crimes."

I didn't know much about the law, but that made perfect sense to me. In reports that would become public a few days later, Texas authorities would disclose that 25 mothers on the YFZ ranch were under eighteen years old. Of the 53 girls aged fourteen to seventeen, 31 of them had birthed a child or were pregnant at the time of the raid.

Judge Walther heard twenty-one hours of testimony before ordering all children to remain in protective custody. She ordered children and adults to undergo DNA testing to prove family relationships. She then ordered that children be given individual hearings to determine their return home or placement in foster care. Officials tried to keep siblings together and to respect the beliefs of the FLDS, although that was hard with the number of siblings some families had. I felt the judge was acting fairly in trying to do what was best for the children.

Wrapping up the last of my CPS reports that night, I sighed. There was still so much to be done, but I had bills, a family, and a home to get back to.

I boarded a flight to Idaho, eager to see my children and anxious to see Ben, too. I hoped that somehow we could mend our rapidly deteriorating relationship.

*   *   *

One afternoon back in Idaho I rushed home, kids in tow, cell phone pinned to my ear. I'd had more than fifteen calls from Texas that day, beginning at six a.m., and I was still on one last call as I walked into the house. Ranger Nick Hanna called me often to verify information and photos. From the entire range of people, there would be only three I could not identify, and he was always grateful to me for my time and insight, telling me, "We couldn't do this without you." But I was determined to shut off the phone at night and be present for my family.

I set Natalia down inside and went back out to get the mail. When I opened my cell phone bill, I literally dropped to the ground.

"You okay, Mommy?" asked Kyle from the doorway, his blue eyes full of concern. I couldn't answer. How was I going to tell Ben that the bill for the previous month was over $700? Surely this alone was grounds for divorce! I quickly sent e-mails or texts to most of my Texas contacts, requesting that unless it was a dire emergency, they restrict our correspondence to e-mails.

That night after dinner when the kids were busy playing, I hesitantly showed Ben the bill. He hit the roof.

"Enough is enough!" he thundered. "They get paid for this shit and you don't! You are to cut off all calls and communication with *anyone* having *anything* to do with Texas!"

I was about to nod as usual, but something stopped me.

"No. I cannot, Ben. I know you don't understand, but this is serious, and I won't abandon any of them—our people…or Texas." As I held my ground for the first time in our relationship, I watched his eyes grow bigger in disbelief. He sat stunned for several moments, before turning red with anger.

"What did they do to you? Did you sleep with some cowboy down there or something? You're messed up in the head."

But I wasn't messed up at all. I'd been living in a canyon all my life, until I experienced freedom and equality that was as open and beautiful as the Texas sky.

Every night I watched the news as the fighting in the courts continued to intensify, and 111 children were relocated to foster homes. The FLDS were still unwilling to cooperate with government on any level. It hurt me to see mothers crying on-screen, yet hundreds of parents openly showed contempt of court by not appearing upon the judge's orders to be swabbed for painless, oral DNA tests. They were hurting themselves the worst. Willie Jessop continued his campaign of lies, asking Utah's governor to intervene, attempting to deliver a letter to President Bush while he was visiting his home state, and purportedly asserting huge pressure on the guardians ad litem of particular families.

State attorneys brought out scandalous evidence seized in the raid, the most damning a photo of Warren kissing Merrianne Jessop when she was so small that he had to cradle her in his arms. It was not a fatherly kiss. Fifty-year-old Warren was giving his twelve-year-old bride the romantic, intimate kiss of a husband. A version of the photo with Merrianne's face blurred was flashed on news screens throughout the world and caused a huge public uproar.

Despite this, the District Court ordered the return of all the children to their parents on June 2, having determined that CPS had not met the burden of proof required for their removal. Two days later, every child was back on the ranch, except two kept in foster care due to strong evidence of abuse in their home. As soon as the families regained custody, half of them absconded from the YFZ and relocated to other FLDS sites, most of them outside of Texas. Many others trickled out as time went on. Just as it had feared, CPS would no longer be able to protect these children.

The statistics were staggering to me. One hundred forty-six families were investigated by CPS. Out of 439 children, two of whom were born in protective custody, 275 were declared victims of sexual abuse as defined by the Texas penal code, and 262 had been subjected to neglect. CPS conservatively stated that more than one out of every four pubescent girls on the ranch was involved in an underage marriage, though I noticed the number was actually very close to half. One hundred twenty-four adults were designated "perpetrators" of abuse, meaning men who engaged in underage marriages, and parents who failed to prevent underage marriages while letting their other children see this cycle as normal.

Lawyers, politicians, and players all pointed fingers, but in my mind the focus needed to be on the future. While I still strongly believed in religious freedom, I wanted to know how a nation could protect those rights and still safeguard their most vulnerable citizens.

Something had to change.

CHAPTER 31

Destroying Ignorance, Not People

The YFZ raid sparked much controversy about the modern Mormon Church, whose members were understandably frustrated that people across the nation wrongly associated their beliefs with those of Warren Jeffs. After I came home, I did my own research to discover that there were no beds whatsoever in the modern temples of the Mormon Church. In fact, Mormon temple ceremonies had undergone a series of changes within the past century, each time more deeply honoring an individual's privacy. It was Warren who had taken something sacred and twisted it for his own pleasure.

Feeling like the stress of the raid and its aftermath was eating me alive, I decided to try yoga. As it became a daily practice, I began to feel a peace come from within. Yoga helped me to prepare for Natalia's first surgery. We had applied and qualified for a special program at Shriners Hospitals in Salt Lake City, and by some miracle, Dr. Siddiqi was to be the main surgeon for the series she needed! He actually donated two surgery days a month to Shriners. Recognizing a divine hand in the process, I was able to take a deep breath and let go of Natalia's tiny hand as she was wheeled away for the first surgery.

Though Natalia recovered without incident, Ben and I still fought regularly. Whenever he thought I was getting a call from out of state, he would grow icily cold. We both knew it was time to get away or our marriage would not survive. We scheduled a vacation with a friend and her family for a few days on the California coast.

Diana was stunningly beautiful. She had escaped the FLDS with the young man she chose to marry. Had they not left on their own, he would have likely joined thousands of lost boys, and she would have been given to an older, elite member.

Early one morning, Diana and I went for a walk down the beach while everyone else was still sleeping.

"How do you feel about all of the men being indicted in Texas?" she asked.

I bowed my head, unable to look at her. A month before, with no support from Ben, I'd flown to Texas to testify in front of a grand jury, which would determine whether any criminal indictments would be issued against FLDS members. For my safety, law enforcement didn't want anyone besides Ben knowing I was there.

"It's very upsetting to me," I said, my voice cracking. "Men that I loved for so many years—some of them all of my life. Men that I respected, and looked up to..."

"And now?" she asked cautiously.

Unsure about what I could legally share, I told her only what had been made public. "After all the evidence I've seen, and more on the way...I'm so disgusted, so sad and angry! Every day more evidence comes to light. It's very sobering for all of our people."

Since the grand jury, I had been in a depression, and I hadn't sought out the names of men being indicted. But Ranger Nick Hanna had called me after the grand jury to let me know they were indicting twelve men. He'd been reading hundreds of "confession letters" that Warren had collected to manipulate his people.

"Becky," he had told me somberly, "there's some very sick, criminal behavior going on among these people. It may not be in every family, but it's rampant. We've gathered some pretty damning evidence that the governments of Canada, Utah, and Arizona would be mighty interested in."

Late that fall, I began to feel that something was drastically wrong with my body. The base of my spine was tight and I was experiencing enormously painful spasms. The ache became incessant, getting in the way of normal functioning with my kids and work. One day I felt a large growth at the base of my spine, and my doctor was unable to offer an explanation, which only added to the stress of the situation.

In December I was subpoenaed to meet with Matthew J. Smith, Mojave County special attorney, regarding the Arizona case against Warren. Despite the fact that I was in so much pain I could hardly move, I was deposed in Salt Lake City to answer questions from Warren's attorneys. He was expected to stand trial in Arizona early the following year. Smith warned me about defense attorney Mike Piccarreta, and I dreaded facing him. I had asked some friends at the holistic heath center to say a prayer for me. I was deeply touched by the prayer e-mailed to me:

> ...May they be strong and peaceful, may they destroy ignorance and not people, may they create not conflict but light, love, and understanding...May the judges and all involved have the clarity to hear Truth clearly...May the anger and pain in the room be removed. May you see each other as you are.

I hoped I could remember these words instead of the painful feelings I'd had during the early part of Warren's trial, my hands balled into fists as his lawyers questioned my integrity and my morals, and continually insinuated I had slept with Ben before I left the FLDS. I wrote "LOVE" on my hand as a visual reminder to keep me grounded, no matter what. Although Warren wouldn't be there, I still dressed in red. I may have been forced into the deposition, but I was a woman of free will.

Despite Smith's advice, I was unprepared for Piccarreta and the other defense attorney, Richard Wright, to act like spoiled children, throwing tantrums and not abiding by any modicum of polite behavior. It was appalling. I had to take an oath to "tell the whole truth and nothing but the truth, so help me God"—but the lawyers were bound by no such vow. With no judge or jury in the room, opposing counsel could apparently say almost anything they wanted to a witness.

As soon as Piccarreta asked a few preliminary personal questions, he jumped right into forbidden territory: "Now, have you had any contact with law enforcement in Texas in regards to the FLDS or the YFZ ranch?"

"I'm not at liberty to discuss any participation that I have had in any investigation going on in Texas."

"Why is that?" he probed.

"I'm not at liberty to say anything about that."

The assistant attorney general of Arizona backed me up, but Piccarreta wouldn't stop trying to get me to talk about Sheriff Doran, Brooks, CPS, money from Texas, and more. I stood my ground.

"Can you answer this—do you know Rozita Swinton?" I was mad. The woman who'd posed as Sarah Barlow had nothing to do with Arizona, only Texas.

"I do not."

"All right. Did you not have any communications with Rozita Swinton either before the search or after the search?"

"None whatsoever."

When Piccarreta finally began to focus on Warren's criminal trial in Arizona, I was open and very, very honest with him. I shared FLDS teachings about marriage, Rulon's health, Warren's power plays, Elissa's marital problems and abuse, as well as Warren's edicts for her to go home and obey her husband.

I could tell by the look on his partner Wright's face that he was not happy with my answers, which must have been fairly damning. Piccarreta asked me about my personal life up until 2002, when I left the FLDS.

"You didn't want to marry Warren?"

"Hell, no," I answered before I could stop myself. We covered some details about Elissa's life after my departure, and Piccarreta asked if I'd read Elissa's book.

"No."

"Have you read any of the books from—that people have written that have left other religions and have been critical of the religion they left?"

"I'm grateful for lessons I've learned. Warren has been one of the greatest teachers of my life..."

Wright's eyes widened, and he grabbed a notebook and pencil. The room went silent.

"I've learned some incredible lessons from that man, more so what *not* to be and how *not* to treat people."

I couldn't help but feel a sense of satisfaction when Wright hurled his pencil so hard onto the table that it bounced and clattered onto the floor.

CHAPTER 32

Power vs. Force

Not long afterward, Mike Piccarreta sought to have a judge compel me to answer questions about Texas. Texas's lead prosecutor, Eric Nichols, would have to come to stand up for Texas, as I had no lawyer of my own. In addition, I was in more physical pain than I could handle. Finally I was scheduled for surgery to remove the large and painful growth from my spine. Leading up to it, I slept poorly and was plagued by nightmares. Over and over I dreamed of being in a room where my sister-wives were gathered to pray for me—only they had gathered to pray for my death.

Patrice, a dear friend of mine who had also left Short Creek, did some Reiki, theta, and chakra balancing work on my body. It seemed to relieve much of the pain, although the growth was still there. After our session, she told me she had the strong impression the growth had been caused by negative energy being directed at me from the FLDS.

I looked at Patrice in astonishment. I hadn't told anyone about my dreams, or the fact that Nick had informed me that FLDS attorneys had just recently discovered I had gone into the temple. I remembered in 1999 when my sister-wives and I were directed to pray against Jason Williams, a former member who had the guts to sue the FLDS for custody of his own children. We were actually ordered to pray for his death.

Could negative feelings have that much power? Whatever the case, Patrice's work eased the pain until I went into surgery in March 2009. The procedure was easier than the doctor thought it would be, but he was clearly perplexed by the large, pus-filled growth he extracted.

That April, I received a warning from Brooks that on the one-year anniversary of the investigation, Willie Jessop had passed around a commercial bottle he had designed that looked like the most recognizable brand of ranch dressing. Only it was labeled, "Happy Valley, the Original Compound. YFZ Anniversary Edition."

The label on the back of the bottle read:

Special Cure-All for the following: Cyanide Poisoning, Broken Bones, Tempers, CPS Brutality, Texas Ranger BS, Underage Marriage, CASA Nausea, Bus Ride Sickness, Mean People, Grumpy Men. Use extra portions when dealing with the following: Doran, Long, Voss, Gutierrez & Malonis. Goes well with YFZ cheese and Grandma Gloria's Fresh Vegetables. TEXAS ATTORNEY GENERAL'S WARNING: Looks like Ranch, Tastes like Ranch, Smells Like Ranch, Feels like Ranch, but it's really "Compound." Happy Valley becomes toxic when mixed with the following: Diversity Foundation, Dan Fischer, Flora Jessop, Becky Musser, Sam Brower, Carolyn Jessop, Rozita Swinton, Randy & Kathy Mankin.

The last line was a little disconcerting:

If remedy fails, don't forget the "Cult 45" option.

It was sobering to receive word from some visitors to Short Creek sometime later that Willie Jessop had his ranch bottle proudly displayed on a shelf in his large conference room in Hildale, which he called "the War Room." And on the same shelf sat two large three-ring binders whose spines were labeled *REBECCA MUSSER*.

That spring, I found I could no longer stomach Ben's cruelty and constant, degrading comments. I recognized it was unhealthy for our children to be around, too, so the three of us separated from Ben and went to Salt Lake City, not knowing if we would ever return. While I was grateful for the hospitality of my siblings and friends, I felt vulnerable and afraid for my children and our future. We no longer had a home to call our own.

The next several months were an emotional roller coaster, as Ben begged us to come back. We returned to Idaho for a short while, but Ben and I couldn't make it work despite how badly we both wanted to stay married and how much we loved each other.

Things came to a head in July 2009, when we got a visitor from Texas: Eric Nichols, the special prosecutor for the FLDS cases, who'd asked to come all the way to our home to meet with Ben and me.

At first, Ben was resistant, saying, "Why don't you just tell him to go to hell?" Eventually he relented, even taking the kids for a drive so I could concentrate. Eric, full of energy and intellect, used our small kitchen table as a desk as he peppered me with questions and took careful notes. Then he laid out the reason for his visit. The prosecution team had collected sufficient evidence for all twelve indictments, but he said Texas sorely needed my help—again. Would I do it?

He pulled out a sheet of paper with names and trial dates and slid it across the table to me.

"Raymond Merrill Jessop, Allan Eugene Keate, Michael George Emack, Merrill Leroy Jessop..."

With each name, memories washed over me. These had been my Priesthood and community leaders, classmates, students. I knew every single one of these men personally.

"...Lehi Barlow Jeffs, Abram Harker Jeffs, Keith William Dutson Jr., LeRoy Johnson Steed..."

And I was related to most of them.

"...Frederick Merrill Jessop, Wendell Loy Nielsen, and Warren Steed Jeffs."

The time had come. I was being asked to testify not only against Warren but against several more of my own people.

Isn't there some other person who could do this? I thought of Ben and how we had barely survived my last trip. Maybe I could come to every other trial?

"Becky, it is critically important that we have you in the courtroom to authenticate evidence. Since Warren and their families will never allow the girls to testify against their own husbands, these will be 'paper cases.' They are much more tenuous. In order for this to stick, in order for the FLDS and others to get the message, in order for Warren to be stopped, we need you."

I knew the truth of his words . . . and I knew my answer. It was yes.

After Eric left, Ben confronted me. "Why would you do that, Beck? Is it the fame? It certainly isn't the fortune!"

"No," I said quietly.

Finally, my husband dropped his voice.

"Why then?" he asked, his voice full of anguish. "Why do this?"

"Ben," I said softly, "you have never been that young girl violated in the name of God."

The end of summer marked the very end of my marriage. I couldn't cry. I couldn't laugh, either. I was numb. On Kyle's and my birthday, Ben had left to go camping with friends, shouting, "I'm *done!*" and slamming the door. Early in September, while I was visiting a friend, he locked me out of my own house, moved all of the money from our bank accounts, and cut off our credit cards. Except for a tiny sliver of income I had coming in from real estate deals I had previously closed, I was penniless. He didn't prohibit the kids from seeing me, but he didn't make it easy, either.

Eric Nichols asked me to fly to Austin to help prepare evidence for the first trial. I told him that given the short notice they would need to cover the airfare in advance. I arrived in Austin, Texas, with less than $40 in my checking account. We worked long hours, so food was sometimes brought in for the whole team, but when others in my crew from DPS went out for lunch or dinner, I'd make an excuse to go to my hotel room and slip out to a 7-Eleven for crackers. Though I knew I would eventually be reimbursed by the state of Texas, I had no funds to pay in the first place.

I refused to let anyone know that my personal life was crumbling, motivated in part by pride, but also by reality. These officers and attorneys had enough to handle, and they had suffered from countless hours away from their spouses and children, too.

"I've spent so much time away from home, my little boy asked me how many wives I have in Eldorado!" chuckled Wes Hensley, the co–case agent from the attorney general's office. Wes's contagious sense of humor lightened my mood considerably.

It was especially fun to see Wes and Nick interact. Though from different state offices and different regions, the co–case agents connected like brothers.

"How is it you guys get along so well?" I asked.

"Even though Nick's the guy the lady reporters always want to talk to," Wes said, grinning, "when it comes to our work, it's a God-thang!" I giggled. Serendipitous happenings in Texas were always labeled a "God-thang." And while it was hard not to notice Nick Hanna's fan club, I witnessed both men's fierce devotion to their wives.

"I think it's because we're both daddies of little girls and boys," said Nick, "we feel the same sense of personal responsibility to these FLDS kids. I'm sure God orchestrated us being on the same team."

Security in the attorney general's office was tight. I had to be issued a badge before I was led to copies of evidence regarding the twelve men the press had dubbed "the Dirty Dozen." I would have been offended at the term, had I not already been privy to some pretty filthy evidence.

Wes brought me to greet Angela Goodwin, the other main prosecutor working with Eric Nichols, and together we went to the evidence room, where the copies of evidence from San Angelo were being stored. The team immediately began working on evidence for the first case, *Texas v. Raymond Merrill Jessop*. There was a laptop, FLDS texts, and a Book of Mormon. My job was to provide the critical continuity to their case and to present the information in lay terms the jury and judge could understand.

I left that night with a stack of copied CDs—audio that Warren had recorded from his revelations and activities. I was to flag anything that needed special attention. For security, Wes walked me to my hotel lobby and saw me into the elevator. It wasn't until I clicked the latch on the door of my room that I collapsed against it. The weight and reality of what I had to do was crushing, and there was no one to talk to about it.

I couldn't eat, so I pulled out a yellow legal pad and slipped the CD into the laptop. It was eerily familiar to be writing notes on Warren's sermons again. After I gulped back an intense wave of nausea, I started to transcribe. I went into a bit of a hypnotic or dissociated mode until something Warren said set off an alarm in my head. I looked down at my notes, in the FLDS shorthand of abbreviations only the FLDS would know so well, and became livid as I realized that this recording was another "teaching of the ladies." It had to do with being "comfort" wives.

Warren reported that he was suffering in the night with visions from God that would wrack his body with pain. His only solace was the "comfort" of his wives, often more than one of them at the same time. I was horrified. This was a definite aberration, not something that was ever deemed appropriate among the FLDS! He expanded further about a "man's needs," and how it was the duty of the wife to pleasure him, always, on demand and without question.

The paradox astounded me: first, he shamed women for desiring sexual relations. Yet, in the next breath, he shamed those who did *not* desire *him*, saying that by not being "close" to him, they were cutting themselves off from the presence of Heavenly Father. Those were not light words. They meant eternal death.

The next recording was from a time when Warren and Naomi were on the run but had secretly visited Short Creek to perform more weddings. Photos in evidence showed Naomi's hair cut and worldly in style. She had been wearing clothing and makeup like mainstream women to avoid bringing attention to Warren.

"Look what you have done to her!" Warren scolded his wives in Short Creek. There were gasps and cries of heartbreak. "You have not been faithful enough, not pure enough," he cried, "to stop the pursuit of law enforcement." He claimed it was their lack of faith that caused him and Naomi to suffer so greatly.

"You asshole!" I declared to the empty room. This was the same man who had reported in a revelation, "The Lord has told me I need to do some more suntanning today." His wives, who did not know better, were taking on all the guilt and shame that Warren was doling out.

All night my dreams were haunted by their suffering. I would sleep for an hour or two before I awoke sobbing, having dreamed I was in Short Creek among Warren's wives. I pulled myself together the next morning and met with the team. They could tell I'd had a bad night, but they didn't say anything. Brooks Long had joined us to go through more evidence. Our team was alone in the secure room when he and Nick mentioned a recording they had found in Warren's car. Warren had begun alluding to "quorums," but they sounded unlike any of the quorums or groups of anointed men talked about in the early days of the church—instead, they were all about women. But since Warren did not treat women with respect or grant them any authority, what were these quorums about?

"Becky, he talks about 'Heavenly sessions,' but it sounds an awful lot like S-E-X to me."

I took a deep breath. Everything that I'd been listening to either covertly or overtly pointed to exactly that—an obsession with sex.

That week I got to know Angela, the efficient attorney with beautiful, sharp eyes behind her glasses, and a dazzlingly organized mind. She was kind to me and conscious of my time away from my kids. I shared with her my anxiety about Natalia's next upcoming surgery, which was scheduled for right after I arrived back in Salt Lake City. It had to be timed perfectly so I could share her recovery period with her just after the first trial.

Toward the end of the second day, Angela said, "I need you to listen to something." Her eyes were serious. "We've got it down, but we would love you to have a stab at transcribing it because Warren's vowels are not always easily distinguishable. You know his voice better than anyone else here. I need to know if it says what we think it says..."

She handed me a headset and a copy of their attempt at a transcription. My hands trembled slightly, and I hoped she wouldn't notice. Then she handed me a box of tissues saying, "You might need this."

Oh, God.

I pulled out a new pad of paper from a stack and grabbed my pen. Angela put her own headphones on. My heart pounding, I turned on the recording.

Twenty minutes later, Angela gently touched me on the shoulder to indicate that the recording was through. I glanced down at my paper, which was completely wet with tears. At some point, I must have stopped recording notes, lost in the gruesome scene that I was hearing. I felt ashamed until I saw that she had tears streaming down her cheeks, too. I could hold it in no longer. Great, silent sobs shook from somewhere deep within me, while Angela put her arms around me and held me until it all came out.

The audio was a recording of Warren molesting his young wife Merrianne Jessop Jeffs, who had just turned twelve, in the YFZ temple, in front of witnesses. I would have been sickened at any recording of molestation, but I knew several of the people involved, and I was revolted at how Warren invoked the name of God to perpetuate this abuse. There were women I knew—had looked up to, learned from, and listened to— who were participating, and Naomi was front and center. I had to steel myself to listen to the recording a second time for content and accuracy.

The official transcript was heartbreakingly accurate:

"Always praise Him," Warren begins. *" 'That feels good'...now repeat the words from your mouth,"* he orders. *"How do you feel, Merrianne?"*

"Feels good?" the soft voice of a child responds.

There was rhythmic heavy breathing in the foreground. Warren instructs Merrianne on what to do while he orders the women around the bed to alternately come forward or back away. All the while, Warren's breathing is heavy and impassioned.

"Dear Sister Merrianne Jessop Jeffs, with the authority of the Holy Melchizedek Priesthood, by the keys and powers thereof in oneness with the Priesthood in the Heavens... placing hands upon your head, Thinking of the Lord. Please get on the other side of the bed...

"We seal the holy love of God in your mind and heart. Just loyal to you as a baby in peace from this time forth and even moment by moment, we bless you with the power of God. To now become Heavenly sensitive. We bless you through the power of God. Let the Heavenly comfort hear us, your childlike Heavenly comfort wife..."

Warren continues to instruct Merrianne and he asks for the "all-consuming fire from Heaven." Then he adds:

"Now prepare, dear sister, for the greater light, the revelations of God on your behalf... Move the ladies back away..."

The rhythmic heavy breathing gets faster, and goes on for three and a half minutes.

"What do you feel Merrianne?" Warren asks.

"I feel fine, thank you," comes the tiny voice again.

Several more agonizing minutes of heavy breathing went by, until Warren directed two wives, asking Naomi to "untie them," and asking Lori to "distract the child." More breathing took place until Warren ended with a prayer to God in Heaven, speaking about his "quorum" of three wives, and asking God to deliver them from all light-mindedness and selfish will. Warren also prayed about "advancing those who can advance" before ending the prayer and demanding that Merrianne come and give him a hug.

"I'm so sorry to do that to you," said Angela gently as I put my pen down, shaking.

"No, I needed to hear it," I said.

My face showed my intense shame. The level of depravity that had befallen the people was shocking in and of itself. But the fact that these grown women, leaders among their sister-wives, had allowed themselves to become abusers of a young child scarred my soul.

That week I struggled to look my team in the eye, or even myself in the mirror. This was my past, my training, my flesh and blood. Had I stayed, would I have fallen so far as to participate, too?

From the deepest levels of my heart, I wanted to cry out, *Hell no, I never would have!* How I wanted to believe that I would have left long before being forced to participate. But as I listened to Warren's orders and the women's responses, I knew with a deep shame that blind obedience was the very trap I had lived in for so long, the one that shackled each one of these women as boundaries were shattered again and again. I was not so different from them.

CHAPTER 33

The Rock of Genshai

When I arrived in Salt Lake City from Austin, I immediately turned on my cell. Ben was to bring Natalia down for her next scheduled surgery, and we'd planned to meet at the airport. I was excited to see my sweet toddler, and nervous for what lay ahead for her. The next moment my phone signaled a text from Ben.

"I can't bring Natalia down. Find your own ride home."

Two years of applications, appointments, tests, and travel to Salt Lake— all to lead to this appointment to measure balloon expanders for the implant surgery in just three weeks' time, including surgical volunteers at Shriners Hospitals that could complete the operation. *How could he?*

Without Natalia there, we were disqualified from the special programs at the hospital. I didn't know any other place where she could have the procedures done without $25,000 down and a 60 percent copay, which I did not have. Inconsolable, I sat with my face to the window as all the other people left the plane before me. I felt like I had nowhere to go.

The next few months I was virtually homeless, sometimes sleeping in my car, but mostly relying on the support of a few friends and family. The kids were often with me, sometimes having to spend nights in the car, too. I wasn't proud of it, but I was determined to create a better life for them. My good friend Kara took us in for several weeks while I searched for viable income. Still, I had to be honest: who would hire me? A woman with a crazy schedule of trials and surgeries, who desperately needed health insurance? I was going to have to do something flexible and yet profitable, but I didn't know how.

Patrice introduced me to a multilevel-marketing skin care company. Initially wary, I tried the products and realized that perhaps this was a way to care for my stressed body while providing income simultaneously. A powerful benefit was that the company initiated motivational training calls each Saturday from some of the best in the industry that we as distributors could access. One such call was from a guest named Kevin Hall who introduced an ancient, powerful concept from India called Genshai. It touched me deeply, and I wrote the word and its meaning in my cell phone, then went on with my busy life.

I attended a conference for the company with Patrice. Her boyfriend, Jamison, was the son of Michael George Emack, an FLDS leader charged with bigamy and sexually assaulting a child. Whenever she brought up the trials, I had always changed the subject.

That weekend, Patrice got right in my face.

"*You get him off!*" she shouted. "*Whatever it takes!*"

Patrice didn't understand that I did not have the power to get anyone out of his sentence. Second, she did not know that it broke my heart to have to sit on the stand as a witness for the prosecution of these men, particularly Mike Emack. Of all the men on the docket, he was one I truly respected. Only one thing kept me moving forward, and that was the photos of the young girls in evidence, and their rights and freedoms.

The first Texas trial scheduled was that of my cousin Raymond Merrill Jessop in Eldorado. I had not been close to Ray, but I had fond memories of cliff jumping with him and other cousins into the water of Lake Powell, all long sleeves and big smiles. However, Raymond was being charged with sexual assault of a child, a first-degree felony in the state of Texas. At age thirty-two, Ray had married Janet Jeffs, one day after she turned fifteen. Her mother was the same Sally Jeffs, who had denied the existence of underage unions on *Larry King*. Janet gave birth to Ray's child when she was sixteen. Through his lawyers, he denied paternity, even though DNA evidence marked him with a 99.9 percent likelihood of being the father.

I had been most disturbed with the evidence regarding Janet's labor. She had been prohibited from going to the hospital on orders from Warren to protect him, her husband, and the ranch from questions. Sally, the midwife, watched her daughter suffer immeasurably for three days. And now Raymond was not only denying her as his bride; he would not claim the child for whom Janet had nearly given her life.

Raymond's was the first paper case without a victim in the witness stand, and they had to fight for it with a solid foundation of evidence. It was taking a long time. By law, I could not be in the courtroom except when I was testifying (except for closing statements and jury sentencing), but I had loads of team members who kept me informed legally of almost every nuance of the trial. I was rarely in the dark, but it didn't assuage my loneliness while I waited on an isolated ranch where my security was strictly monitored. I was allowed off the ranch only for my time in court. To make matters worse, it was Eric's strategy to have me testify twice in each trial: first in the guilt-innocence phase, and again at the sentencing phase.

Each day I had to face the inner turmoil of testifying against my own cousin. Each day I had to be emotionally prepared—dressed, ready at a moment's notice with "LOVE" written on my hand. Each day I just sat there.

On Friday, October 30, I missed Kyle's Halloween party. The next day I missed both kids dressing up in the costumes I had helped Ben to put together before I left. Kyle was a fierce pirate and Natalia a darling dinosaur. I missed taking them trick-or-treating. In a vulnerable state of longing to connect with them, I asked Ben to send me pictures.

"Why?" he texted back. "So you can show all your cowboy friends what a great mother you are? Tell them the truth. You've abandoned your kids."

Nearly everyone from the attorney general's office had driven back to Austin for the weekend. Except for my guards and a few investigators, I was very alone—with only Ben's ugly texts, and calls from Patrice that I couldn't bring myself to answer. I played the violin for hours in an attempt to calm myself down, but my anxiety continued to build. I couldn't eat or sleep without nightmares. By the wee hours of Sunday morning, I was a wreck. I lay in that bed, thousands of miles from my kids, feeling totally useless.

Suddenly I was filled with anger. Hadn't I done enough? Hadn't I suffered plenty? Couldn't someone else do this? I threw the covers back and shoved on a pair of jeans, a hoodie, and sneakers. In the predawn darkness, I slipped away from my security detail, leaving the flat lawn and following the twisting path down the slope, far from my cabin. I finally came to a place where not a soul could see or hear me, and I fell onto a cold, flat rock, curling into a fetal position. In anguish I cried out to God, "*Why me?*"

I had already testified in Utah. I had already told the truth. There'd been hundreds of people on that ranch, hundreds of people who had left the FLDS...wasn't there at least one other person able to validate the records? My whole body shook with sobs as I cried like a child.

I continued crying until I was empty. I lay with my face pressed against the cold rock in total surrender.

In the burgeoning colors of dawn, the simmering Texas sun suddenly burst out of the thinning clouds. The rays seemed to caress my skin little by little with prickles of warmth and light, filling me like I had never been filled before. Then I was touched by a beautiful voice.

"Don't ask 'Why me?'" the familiar voice said. "Instead, ask 'Show me.'"

At first it didn't make sense to me, but I was too tired to fight. Long moments of silence later, I realized that asking *Why me?* kept me in victim mode: wallowing in self-pity, closed off to solutions. *Show me,* on the other hand, had totally different energy. Not only did someone believe that I had the strength to make it through; I would not be alone on this journey. I let the meaning sink deep within my bones as I lay there. *Okay. Show me, then.*

Suddenly the wake-up alarm on my phone sounded, and as I went to turn it off, I saw the definition I had written weeks before of the word *Genshai*:

Never treat another in a manner which would make them feel small; not anyone, not even yourself.

Recognition dawned inside me as strongly as the Texan sunrise. Since that day in the attorney general's office in Austin, I had been absolutely vicious to myself. It was a repeated pattern in my work, with my family, with Ben. In the trials I had allowed the brutal barbs of family, friends, and media to make me feel small, and guilt to make me feel worthless. But I didn't have to make that choice any longer.

It was okay for me to treat myself with respect. It was not wrong, egotistical, or selfish as I'd been taught. Just as it was the right of every one of those girls I testified for to live a life of dignity, it was my right, too. The ugly texts and calls would not stop, but I learned to take a deep breath, to treat myself with respect, and to say, "Show me." I did not have to wait long to be shown.

Other witnesses came to the ranch to await their time to testify as well. The next day I met Dr. Lawrence Beall, a psychologist from Utah. Dr. Beall's life work dealt with helping others to overcome trauma, abuse, and severe, unhealthy conditioning. He had worked with more than twenty former FLDS members, many of them women. He brought a powerful perspective to the courtroom, explaining to the jury what sexual assault does to the psyche of a young woman. Equally important, he established the difference between coercion and personal consent, and what conditions must be in place for one to really give consent—conditions rarely present in the FLDS culture.

In what started as a casual conversation, Dr. Beall and I talked about the struggles I'd faced in my relationships. Finally, I shared with him the intense shame I carried about the sexual, spiritual, and emotional abuse happening to my "children" and "grandchildren" in the FLDS community.

"You got out of the FLDS," Dr. Beall explained wisely, "now you've got to get the FLDS out of you." We discussed the belief paradigms among FLDS women, particularly the shattering of boundaries. I had one of the biggest breakthroughs of my entire life when Dr. Beall introduced me to a list of personal human rights written by Dr. Charles L. Whitfield in *Healing the Child Within*. To see my fundamental rights listed in black and white created a mammoth shift in the reasoning part of my brain, which had been forcibly blocked since my days as an Alta Academy student. I read out loud: "I have the right to say 'no' to anything when I feel I am not ready, it is unsafe, or violates my values." Just for breathing, I deserved the same fundamental human rights as everybody else—even men! For a woman from the FLDS, this was a huge awakening. This was Genshai.

Over the next several days, it felt like I was rebuilding the foundation of my life, stone by stone. Only this time, it was not built on the sand of unhealthy beliefs and nonexistent boundaries. I was able to walk into the courtroom on Wednesday, November 4, 2009, to testify with grace and strength. Now I wrote the words "LOVE" and "GENSHAI" on my hand. The repeated challenges of Mark Stevens, Raymond's defense attorney, could not move me. I was like that rock on the ranch.

The Schleicher County jury found Raymond Merrill Jessop guilty of sexual assault of a child. On November 10, 2009, the jury sentenced Raymond to ten years in state prison and an $8,000 fine. I sat in the courtroom as the sentence was read. Yet there was no triumph inside of me. The clinking sound of the handcuffs on my cousin's wrists startled me. I felt a visceral clinking in my soul. As they led Ray away, I felt a very real part of me went to prison with him.

CHAPTER 34

Truth and Consequences

Between the seesaw of the trial docket and Natalia's health, I was swamped with demands and looming deadlines that I *had* to be emotionally and physically prepared for. Even though I officially had no place to call home, I wouldn't let anything stop me from getting Natalia the care she needed this time.

Just before Thanksgiving, Natalia underwent her first major surgery at Primary Children's Medical Center in Salt Lake, which had accepted her into a special program. Dr. Siddiqi and his team expertly inserted balloon expanders in her forehead and behind her right ear. Natalia woke with a terrible headache and lay whimpering in my arms for days. As soon as she had healed enough to overcome the pain, she had to return to the hospital each week for painful new injections, for two months straight.

It was brutal to leave her and Kyle once again to go back to Texas for Allan Eugene Keate's trial in the first week of December 2009. Allan's wife Nora had been my eighth-grade teacher, and as I sat in the witness stand I was frankly disgusted as Allan allowed his lawyer to deny his marriages and his children. He had shamed his young victim—thirty-eight years his junior—before the Prophet when she was unwilling to submit to him sexually. In addition, Allan had proffered three of his own teenage daughters for marriage to other older FLDS Priesthood men of high rank. This included Veda, who had married Warren when she was only fourteen. The jury found Allan guilty of child sexual assault, sentencing him to thirty-three years in prison.

In early January 2010, Natalia underwent her biggest surgery yet, which cut most of the black congenital nevus away. Diana graciously put us up at her home in Salt Lake so I could spend as much recovery time with Natalia as possible. I was scheduled to fly out for Mike Emack's trial two weeks after the surgery, and the thought of leaving my baby in this tender condition tore at me. She clung to my neck as I carried her out to the car from Primary Children's Medical Center. All I wanted was to hold and comfort her. I had finally buckled my precious daughter in her car seat when Wes called.

"Becky, you're off the hook for this one. Mike Emack's trial won't be happening. He pled no contest to sexual assault of a child, and Judge Walther just found him guilty. He was sentenced to seven years in prison." Later Mike would also plead guilty to bigamy, sentenced to serve seven years concurrent to this one. The entire way to Diana's house, I could not hold back the tears of relief.

As Natalia healed, it was delightful to watch her look at herself in the mirror in great wonder. She still only had one eyebrow, which few people noticed, since she was so very blonde. One day my little diva noticed me using an eyebrow pencil. "Mommy," she asked, "you draw eyebrow me?" I took my brow liner and lightly sketched one in for her. She looked at herself severely from side to side. Abruptly she erupted into a torrent of giggles. She hugged me and ran from room to room, mirror to mirror. Giggles followed her—both hers and mine.

In early March, I returned to San Angelo, to testify against my cousin Merrill Leroy (Roy) Jessop, who faced charges of sexual assault of a child. At thirty-five, Roy was very close in age to me and was one of Warren's fiercest supporters. His arrogant treatment of FLDS women, including shaming young wives before the Prophet if they did not reach a certain level of submission—caused the jury to find him guilty and hand him a seventy-five-year sentence.

My father called, clearly upset. "Roy's sentence is proof that the government is persecuting the people and the church!" he cried. With all media banned in Short Creek, he and other members had been hand-fed these stories by their leaders.

"Dad, it's far different than what you're being told. Roy's letters to Warren were *sick*. Come and see the evidence for yourself."

That was the last I heard from my dad for several long months. He and so many others thought the evidence was planted to disparage the FLDS.

Patrice's brother Joe told me, "The government planted those things. They doctored pictures and documents."

"You all need to get over yourselves," I replied. "Do you really think they would spend millions of dollars just to trick a few thousand people?" Joe couldn't answer, nor could he accept what I had to say about it, either.

In April, Lehi Barlow Jeffs, my old schoolmate and Warren's nephew, pled no contest to sexual assault of a child and bigamy. Judge Walther sentenced him to eight years for each offense, to be served concurrently.

I'd barely had time to breathe during the past six months. Lehi's plea deals meant two glorious months of respite before Natalia's next surgery, which would be relatively minor in comparison. That was good, because I wasn't sure that Natalia, Kyle, or I could take much more. I decided to bring Kyle with me for the next trial so we could spend time together. I wished the worst of the trials was over, too, but it was the exact opposite.

In June I had to testify against Abram Harker Jeffs, Warren's brother and my "son," who was a few years my senior. Abe was convicted of sexual assault of a fifteen-year-old and bigamy. In his fervor to please the Prophet, he'd performed Warren's dirty work, such as pulling a barely weaned infant from an "unworthy" mother in Short Creek to bring the babe to a "worthier" woman at the YFZ. The jury sentenced him to seventeen years and a $10,000 fine for sexual assault of a child, which was much lighter than Roy's seventy-five-year sentence. His lawyer breathed an audible sigh of relief upon hearing the verdict.

Every single defense up to this point rested heavily on declaring evidence from the raid inadmissible. The search warrant was scrutinized every which way from Sunday, but Walther upheld it, as did other local judges.

Upon our return home, my sister Amelia offered up her house to my brother Jordan and me to rent. Finally, a place to call our own! For an entire year, I had felt like I was always in someone's way. Now, life felt like it was looking up.

In true fashion of the roller coaster called my life, I got a call at the end of July 2010 from a very upset Elissa. Warren's verdicts in Utah had been overturned due to faulty jury charges. It would have been so easy to get angry and give up! It seemed Warren could get away with everything. Loyal FLDS members would triumphantly proclaim that God had overcome the proud and wicked, that this was somehow a sign of Warren's innocence.

I reminded myself that my sisters and I had testified truthfully and we could walk away knowing that our contribution had been powerful, despite the eventual outcome. Warren wouldn't be let go—at least not immediately. Between charges in Arizona and those in Texas, he was sure to be behind bars for quite some time.

As if the trials and surgeries were not enough, at the end of August I was forced into a grueling deposition regarding Warren's legal issues in Arizona. They were fishing for more information about Texas, since Warren's and Uncle Wendell's trials were around the corner. I showed up in red, my power words on my hand. I was questioned by Jim Bradshaw, one of the most callous defense attorneys I had ever faced. Piccarreta had prepared me for this, and while Bradshaw didn't know it, his behavior prepared me to be a stronger, more confident witness in Texas courtrooms.

In the most miraculous development, Ben and I started getting along again. We had both realized that Kyle's and Natalia's well-being far outweighed any differences between us. I watched him step up in accountability and in his relationships with our children in ways he never had before. I think he saw positive changes in me, too. Although we moved forward with divorce proceedings, we were able to become great friends again and focused on being great partners in raising our children. Ben could never understand my commitment to the trials, but he began working with my schedule instead of against it, for which I am still grateful.

In October I prepared for Keith Dutson Jr.'s trial. It would be tough. I had adored him and his family, but it was obvious that like Abram, Keith had changed and let his desire to please the Prophet supersede his decency. He'd been twenty to his victim's fifteen, which wasn't as shocking as some of the older leaders' age differences. However, his domineering behavior reared its ugly head when his wives did not submit to him sexually.

The defense ridiculed me and questioned my morals at every trial, but Keith's lawyer, Stephanie Goodman, was particularly disparaging, insinuating that my greeting hugs to Deputy George Arispe and some Texas Rangers constituted adultery.

"Miss Musser, isn't it true that it was your inappropriate relationship with law enforcement that caused your divorce?" I had to breathe and deliberately look at the words on my hand before Eric sprang from his seat and objected rigorously to her smear tactic. The jury was instructed to ignore her comment.

In closing arguments, Eric boldly informed jurors that FLDS ways were simply too ingrained in Keith to ignore.

"We're not talking in the abstract about what someone believes," Eric said. "We're talking about what this man believes... It's not just that the seed was planted... *It sprouted.*"

The jury found Keith guilty of sexual assault of a child. He was sentenced to six years and a fine of $10,000 for sexual assault of a child. Eric's poignant statement rang true in my ears. The Keith I once knew no longer existed. He had changed in a culture that now worshipped and honored criminal behaviors modeled by their Prophet—behaviors Keith had aspired to. In fact, one could argue that given that culture, the only difference between a Keith Dutson Jr. and a Merrill Jessop or even a Warren Jeffs was... *time.*

Warren's appearance in Texas was fast approaching. In February 2011, Warren excommunicated unprecedented thousands of followers, including my father, who e-mailed me in the midst of his great sadness. Warren had even excommunicated his most vocal follower, Willie Jessop. Had the tables been turned on the man who used to harass and bully others in the name of the Prophet?

Warren's lawyers fought hard to avoid extradition, but he was forced to return to Texas accompanied by Nick and Wes. Warren knew he was in trouble: the bad acts prosecutors continued to amass against him were breathtaking.

Through their law enforcement connections, Wes and Nick had been keeping an eye on Warren. They told me he had been busy during his long incarceration. Besides his self-imposed fasts and suicidal tendencies, there was a long period where he masturbated deliberately in front of surveillance cameras as many as fifteen times a day. I speculated at that time he was going for an insanity plea. Lately, however, he had been busy writing harsh revelations from God. Having survived beyond his humble "I'm not the Prophet" stage, he had fully claimed the mantle of church leader again. As the FLDS Prophet, he sent a "Warning to the Nations" in a revelation for President Barack Obama, signed by several hundred followers, demanding his release. It was full of thinly veiled and outright threats. Warren was getting desperate to hide the extent of his depravity from the world—especially from his own people.

After all these years, Warren still seemed to have control over my schedule, and I was sick of it. Within six months, he fired seven lawyers to delay trial. As shrewd as Judge Walther was in allowing Warren his rights, she was growing tired of his antics, too. Despite a childhood disease that left her limping, her legs in braces, Walther was a force to be reckoned with, and he knew it. Warren sought to have her recused several times over. It didn't work. I found it quite fitting that Warren was facing a powerful woman who would not back down from him.

The days leading up to Warren's trial were like a three-ring circus. He retained two new high-powered attorneys, but after the jury was selected and seated, he pulled another desperate move and invoked the right to represent himself.

Walther was very careful to advise against it, but he wouldn't listen. The no-nonsense judge was far more accommodating than she would normally be, not giving Warren any viable excuse to have her recused or to file a successful appeal.

Eric Nichols called me after a few days of whipping through witness after witness, telling me to be prepared to get there quickly. The trial that had taken three years to happen was proceeding at lightning speed. I flew into San Angelo right away and was escorted to a very large but secluded game ranch. From all indications, by what I was hearing from the courthouse, first it seemed like I might testify immediately, since Warren was making no objections and no comments on his own behalf.

The prosecution was an hour into Friday's case before Warren stirred at all, when, I was told, he suddenly rose from his chair during the prosecution's announcements of his very young wives' and children's birthdates from the YFZ records.

For nearly an hour, Warren apparently preached on the background of polygamy and the Lord's sanctioning of it. He argued that the FLDS way of life should be protected under religious freedom, before ending with an "Amen." This type of diatribe was not normally allowed in Walther's orderly courtroom, but she let him ramble since he'd given no opening statement.

From that moment, the court watched Warren curiously. He apparently objected when he shouldn't have, and kept eerily silent when he should have spoken. By early Monday morning, the courtroom was packed when I arrived under guard. I still didn't know if I would testify that day or not, but before court began for the morning I stepped into the gallery briefly. Warren had less than a handful of supporters, including his brother Lyle, who was supplying him with supporting documents. Under order, Lyle and other loyalists left the courtroom anytime "sacred records" regarding the Priesthood or the temple were revealed. This time Willie Jessop remained with his arms folded across his burly chest and a look of disgust upon his face. Reporters, authors, and artists kept furious pens to paper. I saw many others who had come, feeling a personal stake in what was taking place with the YFZ, like Bitsy Stone, who had opened her home to social workers from outside the region during the raid and custody battle; and Carmen Dusek, who had helped put the children's legal team together and at one point had represented young Merrianne. Nick Hanna's wife and other law enforcement spouses came to see the man who had kept their loved ones from home for so long. Curious friends and neighbors whose churches had helped to feed and clothe the disenfranchised FLDS members during the raid joined trial fanatics who had traveled halfway across the country to be part of the next most exciting case since Casey Anthony's trial.

Hours into the day, my security informed me that Warren had attempted again to have the judge recused. That was not shocking, but I was appalled at what Warren had written in his motion. First, reminding everyone that he was the "holy and noble authority on earth," he demanded, "Let Barbara Walthers [sic] be of a humbling to know I have sent a crippling disease upon her which shall take her life soon." I was infuriated that he would use the judge's childhood disease as his own crutch! If any of his people were disobedient enough to watch the news, he was counting on them to glorify her leg braces as the crippling God was sending for not setting him free. Warren was not crazy—but rather diabolically brilliant and dangerous.

Another member of my security detail observed the courtroom for a while and reported to me that Judge Walther sounded like she was talking to a two-year-old. "Mr. Jeffs, please take your seat." "Please sit down, Mr. Jeffs." "Mr. Jeffs, you must confine your comments to the appropriate times." Warren had slowed the process down yet again, and I went back out to the ranch until the following Monday, when I'd finally be facing Warren Jeffs once again in the courtroom.

CHAPTER 35

Prosecution vs. Persecution: God Bless Texas

From a small cement patio on the secluded ranch, I looked out on the very hot, very vast Texas desert, which was experiencing its worst drought in a century. Though it was very early, the horizon was already wavy due to the extreme heat wave, yet it was stunningly serene. I forced myself to think of dinosaurs, astronauts, and women voting. I thought of horses, four-wheelers, and one clandestine kiss. That led to thoughts of my two beautiful children, to whom I would return when this was all over, and the freedoms they had that were denied the people under Warren. I rose from my chair with songs and stories and feathers, beliefs and lessons, ringing in my head.

I entered the courtroom on the afternoon of Monday, August 1, 2011, dressed in a bright red blouse and black pencil skirt, my words etched in pen upon my left palm. For the very first time since I left the FLDS, I would have to confront my old teacher, principal, "son," and one-time leader. To say I felt rocked to the core was a gross understatement. Since I had first learned that Warren was representing himself, I'd been secretly terrified. Despite my now-vast experience on the stand, I would have much rather confronted Warren's nastiest lawyer than face him in person.

My heart beating wildly, I walked up the aisle of the tightly packed courtroom toward the judge, the jury, the prosecution, and the accused.

I stepped up onto the witness stand and gave my oath, that I would tell the truth, the whole truth, and nothing but the truth, so help me God.

As I turned to sit, I looked over at the prosecution, the Texas Rangers and attorney general's officers, the security for the proceedings, and those attending Warren's trial. I gasped almost audibly. There before me was a veritable sea of red: red ties, red dresses, red flowers in red hair. Nearly everyone was wearing some type of red. I glanced at Wes and Nick, who both wore wide Texas grins and red ties.

Once I looked at Warren, my heart stopped pounding and my body ceased trembling. Fire filled me again as I thought of all of those little girls.

Eric questioned me for hours regarding church teachings and trainings, and especially church documents and their importance in the FLDS. I identified several types of records and a Book of Remembrance, which represented the Book of the Lamb of God in Heaven. During my testimony, Warren objected often, standing up when I talked about the Priesthood, about Celestial Marriage, and about what he himself had told me was my duty to my husband in the bedroom. But he never once met my eyes.

This was my chance to give his preteen and teenaged victims a voice. The prosecution had already established DNA evidence in both cases that showed with 99.9 percent certainty that Warren was the father of those underage girls' children, but now it was necessary to establish the girls as real people, with emotions, flesh, and blood, for the jury.

Eric asked me if I knew Veda Keate. I explained that I did, as I used to chat with her and her sister Patricia often. I identified Veda in several pictures, along with her father, Alan, and his wife Nora, Warren's younger sister.

"When was the last time you saw Veda?"

"At Rulon's funeral."

Eric showed more pictures, some of which I had seen once or twice. There was a picture of my sister-wife Ora next to Veda. They held a portrait photo of Warren Jeffs between them, indicating their shared husband. Then Eric showed two more photos, of Veda, very pregnant and holding a picture of Warren.

After establishing that information on Veda Keate, Eric moved on to the youngest documented victim of Warren Jeffs.

"Did you know Merrianne Jessop?" he asked me.

"Yes. She was my cousin and the sister of many of my sister-wives. She would come to our house to play."

"Would Warren interact with Veda and Merrianne?"

"Yes. Warren would walk through the center of our home. He would go out of his way to greet them, get down on their level. He was the principal of their school. He would always ask, 'Are you keeping sweet? Are you being obedient?'"

Eric showed the jury pictures of the little pixie Merrianne, who still looked like a young child even at twelve. In the next few photos, she wore a lavender dress and had rosy cheeks and braided red hair as Warren held her in his arms and kissed her.

I was done that day, but the trial was far from over. Eric continued to lay down evidence after evidence of Warren's motives, of his behaviors, and of his documented sexual assault. The next day, against another torrent of objections, Eric played an audio recording I had verified in which Warren was taking Veda on a car ride with other wives for training to be "a good wife." The next tape, almost an hour long, was of Warren going into vivid detail of training his youngest wives in a quorum of twelve. I sat upstairs, knowing what the jurors and galley were listening to, as Warren graphically told the girls how to shower, shave their pubic hair, and dress in white robes before they came to him. Then he said, "You have to know how to excite sexually and be excited. You have to be able to assist each other," as well as, "Each one who touches me and assists each other will have my holy gift."

On Wednesday morning, Eric played for the jury the recording of little Merrianne in the temple, the one that would haunt me forever. My security told me that jurors who previously had shown no emotion were visibly shaken. One woman held her hand over her face, and another let a tear slip down her cheek. In the gallery, men and women alike were silently crying.

If the importance of the trainings had been lost on anyone, Warren's journal entry in 2004 summed it up. "These young girls have been given to me to be taught and trained how to come into the presence of God and help redeem Zion from their youngest years before they go through teenage doubting and fears and boy troubles." The narcissistic Warren went on to write, "I will just be their boy trouble and guide them right, the Lord helping me."

For his defense, Warren tried to convince the jury that the FLDS deserved freedom from religious persecution, and even compared his struggle to the 1960s civil rights movement.

I was allowed back into the courtroom during closing arguments, where I witnessed Eric's inspiring and impassioned plea for justice for Veda and Merrianne. Finally, it was Warren's turn to give his closing statement. I watched closely as he stood silently, staring at the ground for nearly every minute of his thirty-minute allotment. The judge let the clock run as the whole room sat in hushed silence.

At the twenty-minute mark, Warren did something that made my blood turn cold. I watched as he looked up at the jurors, silently staring at each one of them in the eyes. It reminded me of the time he would look out at his father's wives or his congregation, and take inventory. I glanced at the jurors, relieved to see them take it in stride. I recognized a fire in them as they stared back, not lowering their eyes, not cowing to his manipulations.

"I am at peace," murmured Warren, and sat down, looking at the floor again.

The jurors deliberated for three hours and forty-five minutes, starting Thursday afternoon. They wanted to listen to the audio recordings again, and asked for the transcript of my testimony. Upon their return, the jury declared that they found Warren Jeffs guilty of sexual assault of a child for Veda Keate, and guilty of aggravated sexual assault for Merrianne Jessop.

Now that the guilt-innocence phase was over, it was time for the jury to decide Warren's sentence. During what is called the punishment phase of a trial in Texas, the prosecution did not hold back in order to weight his sentence sufficiently. I testified about my personal dealings with Warren, after which the jury also heard the traumatic sexual abuse experiences of Warren's nephew Brent and his niece Jerusha at his very hands. The jury showed emotion more openly at their agonizingly painful personal testimony.

When I went in for closing arguments, I was impressed that Eric Nichols and his team had stacked an eye-opening array of evidence against Warren, citing all of his "bad acts": Warren had married 24 child brides who ranged in age from twelve to seventeen, married a total of 78 women illegally, arranged 67 marriages between older men and child brides—many of them his own daughters; facilitated 500 bigamous marriages, and personally destroyed 300 families by reassigning wives and children. In addition to stealing, he had created refuges to hide women from law enforcement, evaded state and federal law enforcement, and participated in at least six additional acts of sexual misconduct.

I felt like the prosecution had brazenly scattered their feathers, and there was no need to gather them up. Only Texas had the guts to spread them out for everyone to see, and call it what it was. If there was any doubt that Warren was not only in his right mind, but knew full well what he had been doing, Eric quoted Warren from his own record of January 2004:

There is a girl...the Lord wants me to take. She is thirteen. Oh, I just want the Lord's will...If the world knew what I was doing they would hang me from the highest tree.

The jury went out for deliberation on August 9, 2011. It took only thirty minutes for them to return with Warren's sentence: life plus twenty years.

The courtroom went silent. I felt numb for a moment, lit only by a spark of hope that Warren would never get out to terrorize his people again.

There were not the expected cheers of jubilation or pats on the back. Reporters did rush out to report the verdict to the world, but it seemed to me that as I connected with the others involved, we did not search out one another's smiles, but instead our eyes and our very souls.

The men and women of Texas who had sacrificed so much to help FLDS children and bring Warren to justice hugged one another softly or shook hands. Most then simply stepped outside into the hall to call their spouses and families and to weep that it was finally over.

Wes had once told me, "If you've done it, it ain't braggin'." I noticed after Warren's trial was over, Wes didn't brag. No one did, not even Brooks, who certainly had the right to feel vindicated after the hell he went through with the media and with public outcry. He did repeatedly remind reporters that they had had most of these details since 2008. Still, I saw more tears than triumph.

Speaking publicly for the first time, I gave a statement to the press, while secretly praying my people would hear it, too. Clothed in a red dress, I spoke a little of my background, that I had been testifying against the atrocities of Warren Jeffs since 2006, and that I was deeply grateful to the men and women of Texas.

> ...What I have witnessed here...is not the persecution of a church, but...the prosecution of one man, Warren Steed Jeffs.... However, it does not bring back the victims' innocence or their childhood, nor does it assist the many who are still in bondage. Not everything that is faced can be changed, but nothing can be changed until it is faced.... this case is now public record, and the truth is in your hands....
>
> I stand before you wearing red, as a symbol of freedom in choice, and triumph over tyranny. My greatest desire is for every man, woman, and child to understand their God-given human right to own themselves, and to claim their power to choose...
>
> God bless Texas!

I meant it.

The New Millennium

After Warren's trial ended, the Texas prosecution turned its focus to the final three indicted FLDS leaders: LeRoy Steed, Uncle Merrill, and Uncle Wendell. On November 1, 2011, LeRoy Johnson Steed was sentenced to seven years in prison after pleading no contest to two counts of bigamy and one count of child sexual assault. LeRoy Steed's plea came during Uncle Merrill's trial. By this time, I had no qualms about testifying against my uncle, despite his age and health. Merrill had given eleven of his own daughters and two granddaughters to Warren, and participated in sixteen underage marriages in Texas alone. Frederick Merrill Jessop was convicted of conducting an unlawful marriage ceremony involving his twelve-year-old daughter and given the maximum sentence for conducting a ceremony prohibited by law: ten years plus a $10,000 fine.

While I was home preparing for Uncle Wendell's trial, Warren had begun sending out hundreds of bizarre revelations—large, multipage documents—to courthouses across the United States. Texas Rangers warned me that Warren had included me in his last set of revelations:

115. Let also all who are of prosecution way first examine lives of false witness who is adulterer way of living; also betrayed own eternal order of former living herself; Becky Wall; of evil

intent; open lying as her way, with aim to only destroy family way of Eternal Union Order; herself a full way immoral adultery way.

116. Let such never be trusted.

117. All such are called apostates.

118. Let such be of the way of fear. Amen.

The rangers and my family were very concerned, as Warren still had thousands of loyal followers, but I didn't have time or energy to dwell on it.

I found Uncle Wendell's upcoming trial more difficult, as no sexual assault was involved; rather, he was being tried for bigamy with his adult wives. I hadn't resolved all of my complicated feelings toward polygamy. As the product of polygamy, I struggled with the inherent inequality of the practice as well as the severe abuse that polygamy seemed to spawn across many different cultures, not just in the FLDS. Wendell Nielsen was found guilty on three counts of bigamy. He was to serve ten years for each concurrently and pay $30,000 in fines.

As soon as Wendell's trial came to a close, I felt a tremendous burden lift from my shoulders, as I knew that my time in courtrooms was over. Still, I felt a very real sadness as Wendell was led away in handcuffs, one I'd felt with every sentence handed down. While the FLDS might not claim me, they were still my roots, my people. I knew that my people saw any investigation as persecution, rather than holding men accountable for their crimes.

How had we fallen so far?

The FLDS inner circle had become, as Texas called it, "an organized crime unit in the name of God." It was an apt description of the violent downward spiral of our community, and the sobering lessons it held for all of humanity. What started with Rulon and the implementation of one-man rule became a dangerous catalyst for total corruption in the hands of his son. And Warren would not relinquish his suffocating grip on the blindly obedient.

From his cell, Warren continued to control every aspect of the lives of his people. With great precision, he kept their focus strictly on his release, using doomsday prophecies to lead them in their mass confusion and fear. In the months following his sentence, Warren first focused his people on building an enormous conference center on the YFZ. He explained through his leaders that this was where the saints would gather during the destructions. Like the temple, the huge building going up at such a dramatic pace sparked intense interest from the public, as well as speculation about a three-story statue crafted to go inside the conference center, a bronzed image of Warren standing tall with scriptures in one hand and his other resting gently on the shoulder of a very young FLDS girl.

Diana and I, along with hundreds of our friends and family who were now out of the church, became very concerned about the new, stringent orders for Warren's faithful. Piece by piece, we discovered that in order for them to be lifted up at the end of 2011—of course the real, true apocalypse this time, according to Warren—each one had to be strictly interviewed, declare their utter loyalty to him as their Prophet, and be rebaptized into Warren's church.

More than one young female who participated in interviews with Priesthood leaders never came home. Utah's attorney general, Mark Shurtleff, received calls from concerned ousted family members who recognized the deeply disturbing pattern of disappearances. Shurtleff announced he would look into it, yet not one arrest or public statement ever came of it. The girls have not resurfaced; they could be in houses of hiding still spread across the nation. Or they could be in Mancos, Colorado, or near Pringle, South Dakota, where Warren's faithful have built a smaller compound similar to that of the YFZ; the Texas property has been largely deserted.

Most of those ousted were hurt, confused, and lost, as they didn't know what they had done to be cast out. Utah's child and adult welfare services became overwhelmed with the numbers of uneducated youth ending up in their system, and nonprofits like Holding Out HELP found themselves trying to help unprecedented numbers of people. Vans of reputable volunteers roamed the streets at night, picking up children as young as five who had nowhere to go.

To make matters worse, that December, Warren disbanded all marriages among the FLDS. In a clandestine phone call where he preached to his people in the chapel in Short Creek, he forbade his people to have sex until the walls of the prison fell and he was freed to reseal their marriages. Husbands were to be "caretakers" only and were not to bed their wives. Any children conceived during this edict would be considered Sons of Perdition. On New Year's Eve, the faithful gathered in deep and fervent prayer throughout the United States and Canada. When they were not lifted up and gathered, and the walls of the prison still held him, Warren blamed the people for their unworthiness. Someone snuck a poster bearing the Prophet's photos and his insinuations circulating among the people to a reporter from the *Salt Lake Tribune*:

> Where is the faith to set me free? How much longer will it take to have a clean prepared people that will obey Father's command-ments? I have been in prison for ___ days. What are you doing about it?

That poster made me sick inside, but not as sick as when I learned what Warren now dictated. In May 2012, he reinstituted the ability to have sex and create children. However, his people were required to apply for *permission*, as the act itself was considered a Priesthood ordinance. What floored me was that Warren designated just fifteen "worthy" Priesthood holders from the whole community to sire *all* FLDS babies: any woman who wanted a child could go only to one of these fifteen men. As an added horror, husbands were supposed to participate in this "holy" Priesthood ordinance by being a *witness* to their wives being bedded by a worthier man. Diana and I and others speculated on this with the hope that this twisted edict would force people to reconsider their commitment to Warren. Somewhere around two hundred people did get up and walk out of church at that announcement, but the rest stayed, more frightened and obedient than ever.

As far as criminal prosecution, in November 2012 the Texas attorney general's office moved to seize the mostly deserted YFZ ranch. Accord-ing to the attorney general's website, sect leaders used laundered money to purchase the property "in a failed attempt to establish a remote out-post where they could insulate themselves from criminal prosecution for sexually assaulting children," making the property contraband.

In the meantime, Nick Hanna, Wes Hensley, and other officers served up a banquet of evidence involving sexual assault and organized crime that could have easily put dozens of leaders in prison and set a precedent of accountability to the law in at least two countries. The

Texas Rangers and the attorney general's office were severely disappointed to see that Utah, Arizona, and Canada primarily sat idle with the information, even as the statute of limitations was quickly running out. Not every state was willing to risk tens of millions of dollars or their reputations to bring justice.

It was thought that law enforcement might actually be taking a different tack. In June 2012, using evidence collected by local rancher Isaac Wyler and others, the Justice Department brought a civil rights lawsuit against the towns of Colorado City and Hildale in order to address the lawlessness running rampant in Short Creek, which still boasted a police force and local leadership fiercely dedicated to the jailed Prophet. Federal marshals were brought in to bring order and accountability to the community and to preserve the rights of those who had left the sect. This lent hope to Isaac and others that significant changes might finally take place.

As 2012 wound to a close, family and friends watching Short Creek were greatly concerned. Warren began prophesying doomsday again, this time to coincide with the Mayan calendar. Stores closed and the Prophet ordered that all males, young and old, be circumcised. He proscribed several dietary restrictions and instructed members to pack specific-colored backpacks and be ready to head out at a moment's notice—to where? No one seemed to know. Warren placed his brother Lyle back in power, though he'd been excommunicated and former members of the FLDS suspected him of taking money from the church for personal use. This showed how much power Warren still retained from behind bars—that he could pluck a deceitful leader out, replace him, and just as easily place him back in as the second-to-ultimate authority without the slightest hesitation.

When the world did not end that Sunday, December 23, Warren said it would be a few days more. Twenty thirteen came, and yet his followers remained steadfast. As of June 2013, it remained to be seen what Warren would do to keep his adherents under his supreme control.

Outsiders have repeatedly asked why the people stay loyal to Warren Jeffs. The only answer is that the indoctrination has been deceptively strong, and Warren remains exceptionally skilled at wielding the salvation stick. These are his core group of obedient souls, who have never drawn the line in the sand. Therefore, he can keep crossing no-longer-existent boundaries.

As I learned more about choice, and looked over the extensive evidence in all of the cases I had testified in, I realized that what was happening in the FLDS was human trafficking—both for labor and for sex. In mainstream society, money and lust are the currency. In the FLDS, salvation and position are the currency, but the forced acts of labor and sex are the same—the very definition of slavery. And whether greed or God is the currency, it is not right to own another's free agency.

The good news is that those who have been cast out have begun to discover that they can choose a life of happiness outside the FLDS. It takes great resiliency to leave, and then survive, and then thrive, like many of my siblings have shown. What people may not realize is that it involves a long and tedious journey requiring compassion and forgiveness and openness—beginning with the self. Still, it is possible. And there is great joy on the other side of freedom.

As for those who are still in, we have received disparate reports about their well-being and their whereabouts. I've had to accept that wherever Mom, Christine, Savannah, Brittany, Sherrie, and Ally are, whatever their married status or standing in the community, they, indeed, might be exactly where they want to be—and I have had to find it within me to honor that.

In the process of writing this book, my coauthor and I interviewed my father, Donald Wall, and discovered that his version of certain events doesn't match my own. He feels that he conveyed to me that I had the right to say no to marrying the Prophet, and he was surprised by my memories of the beatings he, Irene, and Maggie delivered to me and my siblings. My father said he didn't recall the severity of his beating of Zach, nor of Irene's thrashing that put Cole in the hospital. In fact he said that he hadn't been around enough to know if we were beaten by his first and third wives. Though his remembrance of events differs greatly from mine, I still respect his great intellect and I hope that he will find enlightenment and happiness in his own life.

Whatever the case, the FLDS world is shifting, albeit slowly. But change is change, and it is our hope that the scales can be tipped in favor of happiness—away from guilt, shame, and slavery.

Epilogue

Several months after Warren's trial, I was asked to give a motivational speech. As I stood on a stage in Coronado, California, dressed in red, I spoke with the same passion, compassion, and fire that I had used in the courtroom. Trembling, I had written the words "LOVE" and "GENSHAI" across my palm again. It was not easy.

I had become a passionate advocate for the rights and dignity of victims of human trafficking and sexual slavery, and I had been asked to speak on that topic. Human trafficking continues to be the second-largest crime in the entire world, next only to drug trafficking. It is rarely talked about because of the shame surrounding it. I knew that shame, because I was once owned, too.

"Slavery is no longer legal anywhere in the world," I told the audience, "and yet it is more prevalent today than at any other time in human history! An estimated twelve to twenty-seven million people in the world today are slaves, and more than half of those are being sexually trafficked. It's not just overseas; it's in our backyards. Ninety U.S. cities are documented as actively engaging in sexual slavery. Law alone will not abolish slavery. I have testified over twenty times to save women and children from the same fate that I suffered, and yet girls are being violated this very minute where I come from. . . . Individually, we must not accept slavery into one little section of any part of our hearts, our minds, or our community..."

As I finished, I reminded them that I was just one person.

"I am asking you, as one more person...to do what you can do." I wanted them to realize their very real opportunity and ability to change the world.

When it was over, a beautiful older woman approached me timidly, but with urgency in her eyes.

"My husband has something for you," she said. Her voice made a shiver run through me. "I asked him three times, are you sure you want to give this to her?" she said, shaking her head. "He has *never* even thought of giving it to someone else. He's carried it with him every day for years..."

Full of curiosity, I let her lead me out of earshot of the others to an older gentleman. He was a little taller than me, with gentleness and great wisdom etched upon his face.

It was his eyes that caught me, however. They were compelling and filled with tears as he grasped my hand and pressed something cool and weighty into my palm. In awe, I glanced down to see a large silver coin with wings on one side and writing on the other. It was a 10th Special Forces Group coin inscribed with his name and his many years in service. It read: *De Oppresso Liber*—Free the Oppressed.

The man, whose name was Jack Lawson, could hardly speak for the emotion welling up inside him. "As I sat and listened to your speech, I told my wife, I know I have carried it all those years for her." I gasped at the enormity of what he was saying to me. "I've gone behind enemy lines around the world," he continued. "So many fathers came to me in the fields of Vietnam, eastern bloc countries, and Africa, where they would bring me their daughters and beg me, 'Take my daughter! Take my daughter!' as they believed I could somehow give her a better life than what she was destined for in their fields and their cities and their brothels.

"In all the work that I have done," he said, his voice breaking, "I realized that I carried this coin for twenty-five years to give it this day to you."

Words cannot describe how I felt as he wrapped my fingers around the coin and hugged me. I remain very humbled to have received that kind of acknowledgment. I'm not different from any other person on earth, and with the greatest of reverence, I honor the journey of each person, and their purpose. Like Jack and so many others, I happened to have experienced enough fire and then had the opportunity to step into a moment of truth. I think we each have many of those moments in life. It's what we choose to do with them that counts.

In both the pages of my past and those of my people, horrendous atrocities have occurred. It is a reality. Yet most of us dared not stand against it. We became enslaved to our denial, and the sickness of our secrecy became a breeding ground for supreme societal control.

Like the others, I strictly adhered to the belief that one man's way was the only way: first my father, then the Prophet, and then Warren. One man could—and in our belief system *should*—have literally dictated every aspect of my life, especially as a woman. We all suffered, men, women, and children, believing this one man was beyond reproach simply because of his title. "The Prophet *always* does right" was the extreme brainwashing. It robbed us of our ability to determine healthy or unhealthy decisions regarding our very own lives. Like Dorothy in *The Wizard of Oz*, we were not supposed to see what was behind the curtain, but I finally discovered how critical it was to take away names and titles and look honestly at patterns of *behavior*. I had to analyze Warren's behavior with absolute honesty. But I also had to take gut-wrenching, personal inventory to own up to my own accountability. It was only in that moment of brutal honesty that I was able to gather the strength and courage to flee from what I had finally and clearly defined as oppression.

Interestingly enough, later in Texas when I was introduced by Dr. Beall to the personal bill of rights, I was stunned and almost speechless. I felt a surge of deep, honest recognition, as if my soul knew these rights and had wondered up to that moment why God didn't allow women to have them. In my society, and even during the trials in Texas, I hated it when men and defense lawyers would say, "You had every right to _____" —whatever their argument was. But I was quick to clarify that women did *not* have every right. With few exceptions, results show that men's and women's rights are vastly different in the FLDS, because women are treated as chattel, to be yoked and chained and traded like mere possessions and property. Those who say that women have the same rights within the FLDS culture are either misinformed or not telling the truth.

Perhaps one of my biggest lessons was learning the healthy difference between *passive, aggressive,* and *assertive* characteristics of behavior. I think this is one of the great balances necessary for healthy individuals and cultures, and I have considered it carefully. To be passive means you don't stand up for your own rights. To be aggressive means that you stand up for your rights while not honoring the rights of others. Both of these patterns of unhealthy behavior were dominant in our society, with men and women in substantial measure and in all of their relationships. What was missing was assertiveness, as it was predominantly programmed right out of us. Assertiveness means that you stand up for your rights while honoring the rights of others. It is difficult to be manipulated or to manipulate others when you are genuinely assertive, so that was why it was a danger in a culture built on manipulation.

I have watched some of my siblings on the outside develop this healthy, powerful quality of assertiveness, as well as other members who have left. In regard to my siblings and parents, we are each still on our own unique journey. My mother, two youngest sisters, plus three older sisters are still deeply entrenched within the FLDS, at least for now. My family members who have left or been kicked out often struggle to bond together. We learned how to shield one another in battle but are still learning how to love fully. I readily admit some mistakes I've made in alternately opening my heart and shutting it off again when it has felt threatened. But the beauty I see lies in the possibilities. Since I am not the same person I was ten or even five years ago, I choose not to hold another person hostage to anything except their magnificence. I certainly will not label what others are or are not capable of because of my choices, fears, and humanness.

I have seen miracles happen. I have tasted the deliciousness of life in their midst! And I will forever believe in miracles and in people. We are not alone in our struggles and our triumphs in the outside world. This is why I believe transformation is possible. It is the true spirit of Genshai—the delicate balance needed for transformative change to occur: transformation of a person, of a community, of a nation, and of a world.

I know it is possible, one person at a time.

Acknowledgments

From Rebecca Musser:

I have been touched and blessed by literally hundreds who directly and indirectly supported us in the writing and creation of this book. What I wouldn't give to mention you all! Please know that the spirit of your contribution resides within these pages.

For my new life outside the FLDS, I express my love and gratitude for so many people who have become family, believing in me when others believed I was evil incarnate. I will be forever grateful for those who helped me sort myself out in Coos Bay: Michelle Inskeep; Martha, Leah, and Mary Houghton; Dr. Bob and Kim Richards; Vinnie and Alison Cavarra; Martin and Sequoia Abts; Jona Artz, Carol Jackson, and my Opry family at the Little Theater on the Bay. In Idaho and Utah, my special love and thanks to my children's adopted "grandparents" and very special friends, Wayne and Pat Stutzman. I am forever grateful for your example of charity and love for me and my extended family. I would like to acknowledge my brother Todd, and his daughter Lexi, who have come through insurmountable odds to create a new life, and whose acceptance and love have continued to inspire me; and to Megan Galligar, whose love has helped to deeply heal in unexplainable ways. I express appreciation and great love as well to Kara Currey, Kim Bruce, Robin Hollis, Craig and Kristin Van Engelen, Tiffany Mills, Zanny Young, Sarah Dutson, Dianne Hawkins, Leslie Ward, John and Jane Close, Ben Musser, Jill Reiher, Brian and Sandy Kendall, Jim and Tijon Moore, the Gardner family, the Dan Fischer family, and Bonnie Jackson. Special thanks to those who were so patient in the writing of this story and who came to be a part of it: BreeAnna, McKenzie, and Brent Cook; along with Doug Burch and his daughter Baily; and Eric and Val Gibbons.

It is impossible for me to name every Texan who deserves acknowledgment for his or her incredible service in the quest for truth and the protection of FLDS children. I especially wish to acknowledge the families of every person who put forth the grueling efforts behind the FLDS investigation. Your sacrifice has not gone unnoticed. With special thanks to Texas Attorney General Greg Abbott; all attorney general officers and staff not limited to but including the incredible Angela Goodwin, Eric Nichols, and Wes Hensley; all legal assistants in and out of the courts; all investigators on behalf of the state of Texas; all attorneys and guardians ad litem who volunteered their time on behalf of the FLDS children; the Texas Fugitive Units, who provided security for every trial; the Texas Department of Public Safety's officers and staff; every Texas Ranger, most particularly Brooks Long and Nick Hanna; and Fifty-First District Court judge Barbara Walther.

In addition, I must acknowledge all those in their untiring efforts to bring compassion and continued justice: the county clerks and office staff of Schleicher and Tom Green counties; court reporter Debbie Harris; the Schleicher County sheriff's office and staff, with special thanks to David and Lenette Doran and George Arispe; the Christoval Carmelite Monastery; the presiding judges of Tom Green and surrounding counties; all the jury members for your untiring efforts to hand out fair and even justice; and finally, the Texas CPS investigators and the numerous staff who spent countless hours in their attempts to protect women and children. May you all be blessed a thousandfold for your momentous efforts in a case that was supposed to be minuscule and turned out to be larger than Enron in terms of manpower, dollars, and evidence. I also must thank the families of each of these people. I know firsthand the many sacrifices you made while your loved ones served on this enormous case. Special thanks to Bitsy Stone, Sam Brower, and Kathy and Randy Mankin as well as others who followed the story through the years, seeing beyond the propaganda to the human drama unfolding before their eyes—and helped wherever you could to bring truth and compassion.

I would not be the advocate I am today without the professional support and coaching of powerful, inspiring mentors who helped me to heal myself before reaching out to serve others: my special Idaho counselors—you know who you are; Dr. Larry Beall; Dave Blanchard, Og Mandino Group; Mike Johnstone; Michael Ken; Tiffany Berg; Carrie Purser; Kevin and Sherry Hall; Pat and Jack Lawson; Greg and Melodie Neel; Matt Spencer Photography and Sam Marvin Photography; and Sam Silverstein and Mike Domitz. Also, I would like to acknowledge several powerful organizations: SHEROESUnited.org; Positively Positive; Nuskin; my friends in both the Idaho real estate community and in the Genshai community.

Bridget and I are so honored to work with an amazing team in bringing this book together. First, special thanks to Margret McBride and Faye Atchison from the McBride Agency, for seeing the possibilities of this story and supporting us through the process of finding a fantastic publisher! And so to that wonderful publisher, beginning with the visionary mind of Jamie Raab, who saw that this was more than a story and could be an entire movement, and to the extraordinarily talented Emily Griffin from Hachette, who has patiently assisted us in whittling away at the voluminous manuscript to make it intrinsically valuable to the readers while preserving the essence of Rebecca flowing within its pages. Thanks also to Mark Steven Long for copyediting. And thanks to Eric Rayman for his advice and assistance. And to publicist Linda Duggins, working so graciously and effectively with media.

You wouldn't be holding this particular book in your hands if it weren't for my coauthor, Bridget Cook, who shared her gifts on this project. Testifying more than twenty times on meticulous details about my life, never had anyone asked me, "How did you feel when...?" I had no idea I had so much intense, unexpressed emotion inside. Bridget had the courage to walk beside me as I shared the darkest points of my life and even my unresolved pain. Yet she did it without planting seeds of hatred or vindication. Instead, she supported me in bringing light and healing to the most painful memories and joyously welcoming the future. She has cried with me, celebrated with me, laughed with me, and most of all, she has loved me and my children. In Natalia's words, "My friend Bridget is one of my favorites!" I wholeheartedly agree, and

I am forever grateful our paths have crossed. From the depth of my soul, I thank you, Bridget.

Last, but not least, I am honored to give special acknowledgment to a coach and mentor who made me seek bigger and fly higher than I ever thought possible: Kim Flynn at KimFlynn.com.

And finally, I joyfully honor all of the angels along the way who have been beacons of light, have touched our lives, and breathed hope into the writing of this book. You know who you are, and so do we. Namaste.

From Bridget Cook:

Before any other acknowledgments, I first salute the courage and strength it took for Rebecca Musser to share intricate and often painful memories in the desire to serve her people and others. With her nearly eidetic memory, it's obvious why her ability has continually impressed members of law enforcement and baffled defense attorneys. From her interviews alone, I gathered enough material for well more than three volumes of her remarkable journey. She brought that willingness to be truthful and authentic in the courtroom directly into this book. Thank you, Rebecca, for your profound legacy.

I am exceptionally grateful for the literally hundreds of hours of interviews among those Rebecca listed in Utah, Idaho, and Oregon, and especially the men and women of Texas, who considerately took the time to make sure the events and facts of a very complex situation were accurate, namely, Eric Nichols, Brooks Long, Wes Hensley, Nick Hanna, and David Doran. Special thanks to Carmen Dusek, Randol Stout, and others who strove diligently to represent the children and bring fairness and compassion. And to Bitsy and Sara, for your gracious hospitality.

I would like to thank Ezra Draper, Zanny Young, Brent Jeffs, and many others for providing additional insight into having been raised within the FLDS. May you continue to discover your rich, innate value as you discover a new world. To those still in polygamy because they believe in it, thank you for honestly sharing your views.

Rebecca and I both express deep gratitude to the following: Holly Hansen, Cindy Iman, Steve and Maureen Burch, Emily Cox, Jessica Parry, Emily Christopolus, Pat Werling, and Jeanne Doyle. Your multiple perspectives from within the mainstream LDS culture and from outside of it, your honesty in editing and your willingness to assist helped to create a more balanced and informed view and, frankly, a much better book. History leaves tremendous clues in the study of a particular people. Special thanks to two of the foremost scholars on the subject of polygamy, Newell Bringhurst and Craig Foster, who have provided an overview of polygamy from the early beginnings with Joseph Smith down to the present day of the FLDS with refreshing objectivity. Their essay can be found on a website existing at the time of publication: www.TheWitnessWoreRed.com/appendix.

To my cohort, Eric Gibbons; his beautiful wife, Val; and to Leland Gibbons, who I trust will see their contribution to this project ripple out into the world, just as you do every day in business and in life. May God bless you a thousandfold for your graciousness. And to Tom O'Connor, for seeing that long-term vision and utilizing your vast skills to creating continuing miracles. Special thanks to Bianca Atilano, Darci Patterson, Cortney Lui, Wes Hainsworth, Josh Watterson, and the rest of our amazing team, who prove to the world that people can bring both ethics and joy to this world! Know that you are all a priceless treasure. To Dan Follett and Tom Christopolus, who believed in Rebecca and me enough to open beautiful new doors. To Stedman Graham, who assisted me in recognizing my value as a speaker and messenger. And to Faye Helm and Paula Fellingham, two shining examples as to the contribution entrepreneurial women can make in the world.

To all my SHEROESUnited sisters and adopted sisters: Celeste Gleave, Julie Harman, Micaela Choo, René Johnson, Sandra Hudson, Rebecca Musser, Pamela Okumura, Becky Swanson, Debi Aguirre, Jacqui Voland, Elise Peterson, Ale Cox, Mandy Aguirre, and Gina Monibi; and to Mary Ellen Shivers—who first taught me what a SHERO was. And to my WIN sisters for reminding me of the enlightenment women already are bringing to the world in the most profound ways! To Cindy Iman, my beautiful butterfly, who teaches me to spread my own wings while fanning them during my busiest and most essential times—always. To Bonnie Jackson, my sweet sister who worked tirelessly by my side for years as a loving support and without whom this book would have never happened. And to Sarah Gillen, who has been a sounding board, friend, mentor, my girl Friday, and the bringer of laughter, sanity, and stability. And finally to my family, who has never given up on me and who loves me in all of my humanness. That means more to me than you will ever know.

About the Authors

Rebecca Musser is a highly sought-after motivational speaker and agent for social revolution. She empowers women around the world to escape from bondage in all its forms, because as she has said, "I was once owned, too." Born into the FLDS, an extreme, isolated, polygamist sect of the Mormon faith, as a teenager she was married to the eighty-five-year-old Prophet Rulon Jeffs, destined to be his nineteenth wife of sixty-five. After enduring years of violation, upon her husband's death she escaped from his son, Warren Jeffs, when he tired to force her to remarry. On behalf of her little sisters and other voiceless young girls trapped within that culture, Rebecca testified over twenty times against cult leaders to bring evidence to light and freedom to her people. Today, Rebecca is the founder of ClaimRed.org, a nonprofit organization dedicated to bringing dignity, hope, and healing to victims of human trafficking.

M. Bridget Cook is a national best-selling author well-known for penning riveting tales of transformation. Her gift is her courage to bring light into the darkest places of humanity, and illuminating paths that awaken readers to their own magnificent journey. Her powerful work has been showcased on *Oprah*, *CNN*, and *Good Morning America*, and in *People,* among others. She is coauthor of the best-selling *Shattered Silence: The Untold Story of a Serial Killer's Daughter* with Melissa G. Moore, and *Skinhead Confessions: From Hate to Hope* with former neo-Nazi T.J. Leyden, and her stories continue to rock readers around the world. In writing as in life, she loves to refute stereotypes. Bridget runs two trucking companies while enjoying her four amazing children and more pets than her beloved husband can handle. An internationally sought-after speaker and activist, Bridget wows audiences on the subjects of tranformation, conscious business, and how to leave the footprints of an inspired legacy.